❧ THE ❧
DOCTRINE
AND PRACTICE
of
HOLINESS

THE
DOCTRINE
AND PRACTICE
of
HOLINESS

ERROLL HULSE

EP BOOKS
Faverdale North, Darlington, DL3 0PH, England

web: http://www.epbooks.org

e-mail: sales@epbooks.org

EP BOOKS USA
P. O. Box 614, Carlisle, PA 17013, USA

www.epbooks.us

e-mail: usasales@epbooks.org

First published 2011

British Library Cataloguing in Publication Data available

ISBN 13: 978-085234-739-3
ISBN: 0-85234-739-1

Printed and bound by J F Print Ltd., Sparkford, Somerset.

To my beloved wife Lyn, who has
always exemplified Proverbs 31

Contents

List of Windows

Bibliography

Relevant books have been recommended at the end of some of the chapters and sometimes in footnotes. For instance the helpful writings of Professor John Murray are referred to in chapter six and the light that streams from Jonathan Edwards' classic *The Religious Affections* is present in chapter ten. The lasting value of treatises by Thomas Watson, Wilhemhus á Brakel and E F Kevan are described in the windows. Chapter 24 describes principal authors who have had a major influence on the subject of sanctification such as John Owen, J C Ryle, B B Warfield and J I Packer. Derek Tidball's *The Message of Holiness* (338 pages) was published in 2010 by IVP. Its value lies in its clear exposition of many passages of Scripture and in its Study Guide. Dr Tidball declares that his work is not in the style of Systematic Theology but is written in a biblical theological style in which the texts speak for themselves. He confesses that his book is eclectic in character. It does not grapple with controversial issues such as perfectionism and Romans seven.

This book is systematic in character. It is not eclectic. It follows the Reformed and Puritan legacy which is that the Bible does not teach different ways of sanctification, leaving us to take our choice, but consistently lays before us at all points an entirely consistent framework for holy living and provides all the equipment that we need for that battle.

For 25 years Jerry Bridges' 118 page *The Pursuit of Holiness* has been popular and deservedly so as it is doctrinally firmly grounded in the Reformed tradition and is extremely practical.

Preface

This book began life as a series of sermons at Belvidere Road Church, Liverpool, and then developed into articles which have been published in *Reformation Today*. About half the book is newly written in order to embrace and comprehend what is the most practical of all subjects and the full-time business of all Christians.

I thank Stuart de Boer and Brian Beevers for retrieving sermonic materials and turning them into electronic working order and Robert Lytton for paginating the whole, John Noble for the indices and the EP Books staff for their skills in the overall production.

The Windows

The windows are designed to add interest and carry the reader forward keeping the whole subject in perspective. Each window is not necessarily wedded in substance to the chapter next to which it appears.

Justification	Sanctification
Is righteousness imputed.	Is righteousness imparted.
Is by the declaration of God the Father.	Is by the internal working of the Holy Spirit.
Is God's external work outside us and for us, like clothing.	Is God's internal work inside us.
Is the work of a Judge which is legal.	Is the work of a surgeon who gets inside to accomplish his work.
Is God reckoning sinners to be righteous.	Is God's working in us to make us holy in heart and behaviour.
Concerns guilt.	Concerns pollution.
Is legal or forensic which takes account of Christ's righteousness on our behalf.	Is the spiritual work enabling believers both to will and to do God's good pleasure.
Is complete and perfect and knows of no degrees.	Is never complete or perfect in this life.
Is the foundation of our acceptance before God.	Is a purifying work God does within us because he has accepted us.
Is a once-for-all act never to be repeated.	Is a work which prepares us for heaven.
Our good works have nothing whatsoever to do with it.	Good works are the evidence of saving faith.

Justification and Sanctification

E veryone knows that the foundations of a high-rise building must be rock solid. Architects and engineers make sure that foundations are secure. This brief introduction is the foundation to the chapters which follow.

Rock solid foundations are needed in theology. In a recent e mail a missionary in Latvia lamented that there were no books in Latvian on Systematic Theology, no commentaries, nothing about justification or any other major Christian doctrine.

'For any Latvian Christian who wants to read serious Christian literature, or study the Bible in their native language, there is literally almost nothing available for them. This has huge implications for the churches in this country, and we see some of those being worked out on a daily basis – theological confusion, leaving people wide open to all kinds of dubious teaching; theological inconsistency, which results in Christians being unclear about even the basics of doctrine; the Christian life being largely focused on *me and my problems/progress* instead of on God, his attributes and wonderful deeds on behalf of his people.'

This lack in Latvia is sadly true of many other countries. We need doctrinal books which have solid theological foundations.

Foundational to the subject of holiness is the relationship of Justification to Sanctification. The apostle Paul sets this matter out clearly in his letter to the Romans.

With righteousness as the theme the Romans letter can be divided as follows.

1. Introduction (1:1-15).
2. Theme: Righteousness from God (1:16,17).
3. The Unrighteousness of All Mankind (1:18-3:20).
4. Righteousness Imputed: Justification (3:21-5:21).
5. Righteousness Imparted: Sanctification (chs 6-8).
6. God's Righteousness Vindicated (chs 9-11).
7. Righteousness Practised (12:1-15:13).
8. Conclusion and Greetings (ch 16).

In 1:16,17 the apostle proceeds straight to the subject of righteousness: 'I am not ashamed of the gospel, because it is the power of God for the salvation of everyone who believes: first for the Jew, then for the Gentile. For in the gospel a righteousness from God is revealed, a righteousness that is by faith from first to last, just as it is written: "The righteous will live by faith."'

We can see why Paul was not ashamed of the gospel:

1. It is good news which is the meaning of the word gospel.
2. It is the power of God – he is actively at work revealing his righteousness.
3. It is salvation which is what we so desperately need.
4. It is about our God who cares passionately about justice.
5. It is for everyone, Jews and Greeks. None are excluded. There is no discrimination. All sinners are invited.
6. It is a salvation that comes by faith. I do not have to earn it. It is a free gift.
7. It is salvation which leads to a life of faith. God is with me as I live by faith, as the text says, 'The righteous will live by faith.'

That is all good news.

God the Father loves his Son perfectly and delights in his righteousness. When we preach the gospel the Father reveals a righteousness that saves. The verb in the Greek text is *apokaluptetai* which is a frequentative passive present verb. God's wrath is being revealed. But so is his righteousness. God is with us when we preach the gospel. His power is present with us. He is revealing the righteousness which saves.

God enables the sinner to see in Christ this righteousness he needs and to come to him by faith. The Father then imputes that righteousness to the believing sinner. Then he declares that sinner to be righteous in his sight.

This is illustrated in the experience of Martin Luther who in the 16th century was used to recover the saving gospel of Christ and initiate the great Reformation which changed the religious landscape of Europe.

Luther is famous as a theologian, seminary professor, prolific author, Bible translator, hymn writer and reformer. 'Luther's preaching ministry was remarkable, his productivity prodigious – almost miraculous.'[1]

As a monk in an Augustinian monastery Luther tried to find salvation by observing all the rituals of the Church. He used every measure especially the confession of his sins. These efforts proved futile. He was of course seeking salvation by human good works. Luther was tormented by deep theological matters such as inner blasphemy against God. 'He was not troubled by the problems which seemed to exercise a St Benedict, who would roll his naked body in thorns to quell lust, or of St Cuthbert who stood all night up to his neck in that ghastly cold North Sea off the coast of Northumberland to subjugate the flesh. Luther cheerfully remarked once, "Women never bothered me. I was always concerned with the really knotty problems."'[2]

When he was appointed to teach theology in the University of Wittenberg he discovered the word 'righteousness' in Psalm 31:1.[3] 'Deliver me in your righteousness.' What does righteousness mean here? The Hebrew is *tsedqah.* Then Luther turned to Romans 1:17. The Greek word for righteousness is *dikaiosune.* It dawned on Luther that this righteousness is a free gift from God which is put upon or placed over the sinner. He testified that when he saw and believed this he was instantly liberated and felt that he entered the gates of heaven.[4] A vital change took place in Luther's mind at that time which was through coming to grips with Psalm 22.[5] *Anfechtungen* is a German word that has no equivalent in English. It means unendurable desolation of soul, dreadful anxiety and horror. Luther saw that our Lord became the victim of *anfechtungen.* By his active and passive obedience Christ became our righteousness. 'God made him who had no sin to be sin for us, so that in him we might become the righteousness of God' (2 Cor 5:21).

This experience of the Reformer represented a recovery of the gospel. Augustine the early Church Father wrote in Latin. He had conveyed the idea that to justify is to make righteous rather than declare righteous. Imparted righteousness as the basis of justification is the teaching of the Roman Catholic Church. Imputed righteousness as the basis of justification is the teaching of holy Scripture.

Abraham is the Old Testament prototype of justification by faith. 'Abraham believed the Lord, and he credited it to him as righteousness' (Gen 15:6; Rom 4:3). That became clear to Luther who believed in the same way to receive imputed righteousness.

You will remember that at the city of Worms Luther was made to give an account of his books and to renounce those books in the presence of Emperor Charles V. In the course of his trial Luther was chided, 'How can you, a simple monk, be right and all the bishops and popes of a 1000 years be wrong?' Well, they were wrong because they did not exegete the Scriptures correctly.

Salvation is never attained by works of righteousness that we perform. Salvation is the free gift of God and is received by faith alone. The basis of God's justification of the sinner is the imputed righteousness of Christ.

The righteousness that comes from God can be called an alien righteousness. That is, it comes from the outside. It comes from outside us. Say I received a garment made in China and I put it around me. It would be alien in that it comes from the outside. It is from another world. It is not of my making.

Here are some facts about this alien righteousness which makes us acceptable before God and gives us a right to be in his family as sons and daughters.

(i) This righteousness comes from God the Father. It is a gift.

(ii) This righteousness is reckoned to us by God the Father. It is an act not a process. It is a once-for-all act never to be repeated. We believe and we receive and come into union with Christ by faith.

(iii) This righteousness consists of the complete and perfect life of Christ. It is the sum total of his obedience (Rom 3:21-26). He has rendered obedience and kept the law perfectly. Jeremiah 23:6 sums the matter up, 'This is the name by which he will be called The LORD Our Righteousness.'

(iv) This righteousness is given because of Christ's propitiation. He is the burnt offering which satisfies the justice of God. This propitiation satisfies the wrath of God.

(v) The imputation of this righteousness precedes justification. Note the order. Righteousness is imputed. Then justification follows as an act of the Father.

(vi) There is absolutely no merit in receiving this righteousness. I receive it not because I am obedient. I receive it through faith as an instrument and not through faith as a merit.

(vii) This righteousness is a human righteousness. We are human. Our sins emanate from our fallen sinful humanity. We are born with Adam's first sin imputed to us. We are born moreover with Adam's sinful nature. The righteousness which is the basis of our justification is the human obedience and human perfection of Christ.

(viii) This imputed righteousness leads us to a life of righteousness. We are justified out of faith (*ek pisteōs*) and led to live a life of faith (*eis pistin*) (Rom 1:17) as it is written, 'He who through faith is righteous shall live' [RSV].

(ix) The righteousness imputed to us is never the same as the righteous life we live. And the righteous life we live is never the basis of our justification. Christ's perfect righteousness imputed to us is always and only the sole basis of our justification.

(x) The righteousness which the Father imputes to us is external. It is legal. It has to do with justice. The righteous life implanted into believers by the Holy Spirit is an internal thing, is progressive and is never perfect in this life.

---

1   Roland Bainton takes his readers into the time and culture of 16th-century Germany so well that it is not surprising that his biography of Luther with the title *Here I Stand* is the most popular. The Lion Paperback 412 pages edition was published in 1983. A note says that over one million copies had been sold. My favourite biography is by the German, E G Schwiebert, *Luther and his Times*, Concordia, 1950. Much valued is the excellent study by James Atkinson, *Martin Luther and the birth of Protestantism*, M M and S, 352 pages, 1968. Commended is Bernard Lohse, *Martin Luther; An Introduction to his Life and Work*, T and T Clark, 1987, and James M Kittelson, *Luther the Reformer*. Augsburg, 1986. Those who read German will value Gerhard Ebeling, *Lutherstudien*, 5 vols, Tübingen. A nine page select bibliography including a page of website locations is found in *Essays on Martin Luther* edited by Donald K McKim, Cambridge University Press, 2003.

2   James Atkinson, *Martin Luther and the birth of* Protestantism, M M and S, 1968, page 102.

3   *Ibid*, page 76.

4   Luther's own account of what came to be known as the great *Turmerlebnis*, the Tower Discovery, was published in 1545.A detailed description of Luther's experience and the relevant part of Luther's written testimony is found in E G Schwiebert's *Luther and hisTimes*, Concordia, 1950, page 282ff. James Atkinson in his treatise *Martin Luther and the birth of Protestantism* informs us that many distinguished Luther scholars (Boehmer, Vogelsang, Scheel, Wendorf, Stracke, Hermelink, Bauer – the list is long) have sought with great learning to pinpoint the moment of Luther's break-through while others have criticised such pinpointing. page 101.

5   Roland Bainton, *Here I Stand*, page 62.

Thomas Watson on progressive sanctification

1. Sanctification is a supernatural thing; it is divinely infused. We are naturally polluted. To cleanse us, God takes the prerogative. 'For I the LORD, which sanctify you, am holy' (Lev 21:8). Weeds grow themselves. Flowers are planted. Sanctification is a flower of the Spirit's planting; therefore it is called 'the sanctification of the Spirit' (1 Peter 1:2).
2. Sanctification is an intrinsic thing; it lies chiefly in the heart. It is called 'the adorning ...the hidden man of the heart' (1 Peter 3:3,4). The dew wets the leaf, the sap is hid in the root; so the religion of some consists only in externals, but sanctification is deeply rooted in the soul.
3. Sanctification is an extensive thing: it spreads into the whole man. 'The God of peace sanctify you wholly' (1 Thess 5:23). As original corruption has depraved all the faculties: 'the whole head is sick, the whole heart faint,' no part sound, so sanctification goes over the whole soul.
4. Sanctification is an intense and ardent thing. Its properties burn within the believer. 'Fervent in spirit' (Rom 12:11).
5. Sanctification is a beautiful thing. It makes God and angels fall in love with us. 'The beauties of holiness' (Ps 110: 3). As the sun is to the world, so is sanctification to the soul, beautifying and bespangling it in God's eyes.
6. Sanctification is an abiding thing. 'His seed remaineth in him' (1 John 3:9). He who is truly sanctified cannot fall from that state.
7. Sanctification is a progressive thing. It is growing; it is compared to seed which grows: first the blade springs up, then the ear, then the ripe corn in the ear; such as are already sanctified may be more sanctified (2 Cor 7:1).

(*Gleaned from Thomas Watson's Body of Divinity*).

Holiness Is Full-time

As we will see, holiness in the Bible is both apartness and beauty. To be holy is to be happy. That is the very life of the triune God, who is perfect in holiness and perfect in love. Because he is perfect in holiness and love he is perfectly blessed or happy.

Writing in his great classic work on the attributes of God Stephen Charnock affirms of holiness that it is the glory of all the attributes.

'Holiness is the glory of every perfection in the Godhead. As his power is the strength of them, so his holiness is the beauty of them. As all would be weak without omnipotence to back them, so all would be uncomely without holiness to adorn them. Should this be sullied, all the rest would lose their honour.' He continues: 'His name which signifies all his attributes in conjunction is holy (Ps 103:1)' and, 'If every attribute of the Deity were a distinct member, purity would be the form, the soul, the spirit to animate them. Without it, his patience would be an indulgence to sin, his mercy a fondness, his wrath a madness, his power a tyranny, his wisdom an unworthy subtlety. Holiness gives decorum to them all.'[1]

The purpose of this book is to provide the doctrinal structures for holiness, structures which are basic and urgently needed as we advance into the 21ˢᵗ century. Western Europe, once the home of the Reformation and many powerful revivals, is now dominated by secularism and postmodernism. The ingredients of postmodernism are deconstructionism (which rewrites history and includes twisting and revising or even deleting biblical narratives), moral relativism in which God's holy commandments are nullified, pluralism in which no one body of truth is allowed to claim to be the only truth, existentialism in which emotionalism supplants the intellect, and evolutionary humanism which is the deception of thinking that all the vast complexities of creation happened by chance, which robs our Creator of his glory (Rom 1:18-25). Television is the medium of postmodernism and viewers are unlikely ever to hear the word 'sin' or the word 'holy' in a biblical context.

The effect of all this on the up and coming generation of believers is profound because it lessens the seriousness of sin as something which is an affront to a holy God. The word 'sin' is replaced by the word 'mistake'.

The chapters which follow are trinitarian in structure. We begin with the work of God the Father who organises our sanctification so that in the end every redeemed soul will be perfect in holiness. Two expressive Greek words describe this in Revelation 21:2, words which describe the holy city. The holy city will be inhabited by those who over a period of time have been subject to preparation and have now been perfected. Moreover the inhabitants of the holy city have been made beautiful.[2] All three Persons of the Trinity are active in our sanctification. Union with Christ is how this is achieved. Then there is the comprehensive work of the Holy Spirit which is why beginning with the new birth four chapters are devoted to what he does in us and for us.

Satan is implacably opposed to holiness and he will oppose us all the way. Conflict is inevitable. Satan is the enemy but the full armour of God is provided for the fight. Why does the apostle deem himself wretched? I have devoted a chapter to that. The occasion when holy is repeated three times occurs in the calling of Isaiah but the holiness of God is also at the heart of the song of the angels (Rev 4:8-11). I will not here refer to all the chapters of this book but return to the fact that the triune God is active in the work of sanctification at all times. Our attention should be engaged full-time in the work of holiness. I will conclude this introduction with an illustration from my early experience.

During six years at university I followed a simple régime to keep fit. The rigours of the architectural course are very demanding on time. Reluctantly I gave up my dreams to do well at my favourite sport of cricket and concentrated rather on athletics. I played in the first rugby team at school but at university the standard was so high that it did not take long for me to decide to abandon that sport. So from Monday to Thursday on my way home in the afternoon I stopped at an athletics track and trained hard for one hour. Friday I rested and then competed in athletic competitions on Saturdays. After resting on Sunday I resumed training on Monday.

In those days sport was for amateurs even at the highest level of competition. I trained and competed alongside a fellow student who was the best half-miler in South Africa. His time of one minute 52 seconds was excellent during that era of amateurs. (On track it is now the 800 metres which is about the same distance as a half-mile). Now athletics at the higher level is professional. Today one minute 52 seconds for 800 metres falls well short of what professional athletes can attain. At top levels the athletic scene, as with most sports, is dominated by professionals who devote themselves full-time to the disciplines they have chosen. Their diet, time-keeping and personal habits are under constant scrutiny. It is very much a full-time business.

I use this experience to illustrate that in Christianity there is no such thing as being an amateur. Every believer is a professional. Holiness in the life of a Christian is not part-time but full-time. As a Christian it would be ludicrous to say that I practise holiness for an hour a day. It is equally absurd to suggest that I practise holiness on Sundays but not the rest of the week. Also it is ridiculous to suggest: Yes, I do practise holiness all the time but then I have an annual holiday when for two or three weeks I ignore the demands of holiness as I go off on a non-holiness vacation.

In terms of holiness every Christian is a professional. The whole of life is dedicated to the practice of holiness. No time and no area of life is omitted. The Holy Spirit does not live in us for some of the time, say Mondays, Wednesdays and Sundays and then absent himself on the other days. He is a constant, abiding, indwelling Spirit. The Holy Spirit who indwells us never takes days off or goes on holiday cruises.

The apostle Paul expresses it this way, 'Therefore, I urge you, brothers, in view of God's mercy, to offer your bodies as living sacrifices, holy and pleasing to God – this is your spiritual act of worship. Do not conform any longer to the pattern of this world, but be transformed by the renewing of your mind. Then you will be able to test and approve what God's will is – his good, pleasing and perfect will' (Rom 12:1,2).

There is totality of commitment, body, mind and soul. 'You are not your own; you were bought at a price' (1 Cor 6:19,20). 'Since we have these promises, dear friends, let us purify ourselves from everything that contaminates body and spirit, perfecting holiness out of reverence for God' (2 Cor 7:1). The professional athlete disciplines his mind and body as he has a prize in view, a prize which is only fleeting. But we strive for a crown which is eternal as Paul tells us: 'Do you not know that in a race all the runners run, but only one gets the prize? Run in such a way as to get the prize. Everyone who competes in the games goes into strict training. They do it to get a crown that will not last; but we do it to get a crown that will last for ever. Therefore I do not run like a man running aimlessly; I do not fight like a man beating the air. No, I beat my body and make it my slave so that after I have preached to others, I myself will not be disqualified for the prize' (1 Cor 9:24-27).

In his writings Francis Schaeffer used the term 'super-saints'. He suggested that we should reject the idea that there were special Christians who were special because they claimed to have a powerful post-conversion experience. We should not be prejudiced against power experiences. After all Pentecost represented a power-imparting experience. It is possible to find many testimonies which show that leaders have been empowered for service. What we reject is any idea that there are two kinds of Christians, one group living on a higher deck and all the others on a lower deck. All believers run on the same level and all run on the same track when it comes to holy living.

---

1   Stephen Charnock, *Works in nine volumes*, vol 2, London, 1815, page 496.
2   *hētoimasmenēn* and *kekosmēmenēn* , perfect passive participles.

The meaning of 'holy'

The word 'holy' occurs about 650 times in the Bible. The first time the word is used is in Genesis 2:3, 'God blessed the seventh day and made it holy,' that is, he set it apart from the other days. When Moses was confronted by the Lord in the burning bush he was told to take off his sandals from his feet because the ground upon which he was standing was holy ground (Ex 3:5). Israel was to be a holy nation, that is a nation set apart for God (Ex 19:6). When the children of Israel came out of Egypt a tabernacle was established in a place central to the camps of the twelve tribes. At the end of the tabernacle, separated by a curtain, was 'the holiest of all' which was where the ark of God was kept. This inner court where the ark was kept was called the Most Holy Place (Ex 26:33).

Holiness meant separation for the service of the Lord. Hence the furniture in the tabernacle was holy as was the altar of burnt sacrifices in the outer court. The sacrifices were designated holy. The priests were set apart to serve God and were holy. The high priest was to wear holy garments for his exclusive use. On his forehead he wore a golden plate inscribed with the words 'Holiness to the LORD'. All the sacrifices were holy but some were described as 'most holy' (Lev 2:3 and 10).

The Hebrew word *qadōsh* means separate or set apart. However it also conveys the meaning of brightness. God is light; in him is no darkness at all (1 John 1:5). Also conveyed is the meaning of glory or beauty. 'Who is like unto you – majestic in holiness, awesome in glory?' (Ex 15:11 *cf.* Ps 27:4).

In the New Testament there is one word for holy (*hagios*) which carries the same basic meaning as the Old Testament word *Qadōsh*. In English we use two nouns, namely, holiness and sanctification. Holiness and sanctification are synonymous.

Chapter 1

What Is Holiness?

ollowing the death of the leading priests Nadab and Abihu the LORD said to Aaron, 'You and your sons are not to drink wine or other fermented drink whenever you go into the Tent of Meeting, or you will die. This is a lasting ordinance for the generations to come. You must distinguish between the holy and the common, between the unclean and the clean' (Lev 10:9-10).

The background to this exhortation, 'to distinguish between the holy and the common' is the disobedience of Nadab and Abihu. Different suggestions have been made as to why the sentence of death was so severe. What did Nadab and Abihu do to deserve so terrible a punishment? One suggestion is that they were drunk when attending to the duties of their holy office. This idea is based on the stipulation made above for the sons of Aaron to refrain from alcoholic drink. As John Currid observes in his excellent commentary on Leviticus[1] there is nothing to suggest in Leviticus 10:1-7 that Nadab and Abihu entered the tabernacle in a state of drunkenness. Their sin was that they scorned the command of God and substituted their own wisdom in place of God's command and thereby were deliberately disobedient. They imposed their own will on the service of Yahweh. For this they paid the supreme penalty. The same fire that 'came out from the presence of the LORD and consumed the burnt offering and the fat portions on the altar' (Lev 9:24) consumed Nadab and Abihu.

This severity is not confined to the Old Testament. At the time of the birth of the Christian Church a couple called Ananias and Sapphira thought that they could deceive the apostles by pretending to give the whole value of some property they sold to the Lord's work, when in fact they conspired together to keep part of it back for themselves (Acts 5:1-10). For this deceit they were both struck dead. Holiness is comprehensive. It applies to every part of human behaviour.

At the dawn of human history our first parents Adam and Eve sinned and drew death not only on themselves but their entire progeny (Rom 5:12). Noah survived the flood but soon after that fell into the sin of drunkenness. A further shock comes very soon after the emergence of Israel as a nation. When Moses was long absent in the mountain of Sinai the people dragooned Aaron into making a golden calf which they then worshipped. 'So priestly trespass emerges immediately upon priestly ordination.'[2]

The saga of the dramatic death of Nadab and Abihu is part of distinguishing between the holy and the profane or common. Israel was set apart as a nation to serve Yahweh. They were a holy nation. In their service of the tabernacle with sacrifices and a priesthood they were set apart and made different from all other nations. 'Whoever belongs to God must have the essential character which accompanies such a relationship.'[3]

The words that are used for holiness

Qadōsh in the Hebrew clearly means 'set apart, distinct from or unique'. The holiness of the Triune God is entirely unique. Another way of expressing this is that he is 'wholly other'. 'God is supramundane, exalted, incorruptible, absolutely unique.'[4] The supreme faultless purity of God demands from mankind a corresponding purity. The question is, Does *qadōsh* in the Hebrew suggest the idea of purity? In Arabic and Persian the root is *kada* (Farsi/Persian holiness is *Taghados*) which means pure. Assyrian *kuddushu* means clear or brilliant.[5]

The word 'holy' occurs about 650 times in the Bible. The first time the word is used is in Genesis 2:3. 'God blessed the seventh day and made it holy.' He set that day apart from the other days. When Moses was confronted by the LORD in the burning bush he was told to take off his sandals from his feet because the ground upon which he was standing was holy ground (Ex 3:5). Israel was to be a holy nation, that is, set apart for God (Ex 19:6). When the children of Israel came out of Egypt a tabernacle was established in the centre of the camps of the twelve tribes. At the end of the tabernacle, separated by a curtain, was 'the holiest of all' which was where the ark of God was kept (Ex 26:33-34). Holiness meant separation for the service of the Lord.

The usage of the word in the different biblical settings provides material to build up the idea of God's holiness as something which is brilliant, glorious and beautiful. The fact that all God's attributes are holy is irrefutable. Also God is immutably (unchangeably) holy. He is incomparably holy. He is exclusively holy. He is transcendent in his holiness. There is nothing relative about God's holiness. It cannot be improved or added to. The extraordinary acts of redemption which display Yahweh's power and holiness evoke our worship. 'Who among the gods is like you, O LORD? Who is like you – majestic in holiness, awesome in glory, working wonders?' (Ex 15:11).

This song of Miriam arose out of profound gratitude. No one was like Yahweh who glorified himself by showing that he was holy. He revealed his holiness in the punishment of sin on the one hand and in the redemption of his people on the other. The phrase 'majestic in holiness' literally translated means holiness glorified (*qadōsh adar*). 'God had glorified himself in holiness through the redemption of his people and the destruction of his enemies.'[6] The psalmist comments on this extraordinary event in biblical history: 'Your ways, O God, are holy. What god is so great as our God? You are the God who performs miracles; you display your power among the peoples. With your mighty arm you redeemed your people, the descendants of Jacob and Joseph' (Ps 77:13-15). This comment demonstrates that we are to learn about God's holiness by his redemptive acts in history.

Psalm 29:2 reads: 'Ascribe to the LORD the glory due to his name; worship the LORD in the splendour of his holiness.' At first sight this looks like a description of God's holiness, that is, that he is glorious in holiness. However it is uncertain whether the splendour is a reference to God himself or to the splendour of the vestments in which the priests were to be dressed. An almost identical phrase is used in Psalm 110:3 translated 'arrayed in holy majesty'. This gives support to worship in the splendour of the vestments as the correct translation in Psalm 29:2. (see also 2 Chronicles 20:21).

The popular hymn expresses admirably the sentiment of worshipping the LORD in the beauty of his holiness.

> O worship the Lord in the beauty of holiness;,
> Bow down before Him, His glory proclaim;
> With gold of obedience and incense of lowliness,
> *Kneel and adore Him; the Lord is His Name.*[7]
> (J S B Monsell)

The New Testament

As stated above 'Whoever belongs to God must have the essential character which accompanies such a relationship.' To that end the purpose of the three Persons in the Trinity is to transform the people of God into a holy people. This not only makes them consistent with the faith they profess but prepares them for their ultimate end of perfection for the eternal kingdom that is being planned for them (John 14:3; Rev 21:2).

In the New Testament there is one word for holy (*hagios*)[8] which carries the same basic meaning as the Old Testament word *qadōsh*. In English we use two nouns, namely, holiness and sanctification. We can see the need for this when we examine the expression 'to holify'. That would not be right. 'To sanctify' is correct.

Whenever we speak of sanctification we think of it as a process by which believers are gradually transformed in heart, mind, will and conduct. Many texts express clearly this gradual progressive work. For instance Paul exhorts us to purify ourselves from everything that contaminates body and spirit, perfecting holiness out of reverence for God (2 Cor 7:1), and prays, 'May God himself, the God of peace, sanctify you through and through. May your whole spirit, soul and body be kept blameless at the coming of our Lord Jesus Christ' (1 Thess 5:23).

There are about twenty-five references to 'saints' in the Old Testament. An example is Psalm 116:15, 'Precious in the sight of the LORD is the death of his saints.'[9] About eighty references to saints occur in the New Testament. These are explicit references to those who have experienced definitive sanctification, a single event that has taken place. For instance the believers at Corinth are addressed as 'those sanctified in Christ Jesus and called to be holy' (1 Cor 1:2). Later in the same letter Paul reminds the Corinthians that they were washed, sanctified and justified (1 Cor 6:11). This demonstrates that conversion is a stupendous event. Regeneration, definitive sanctification and justification take place in one act. When Paul refers to believers in Acts 20:32 and 26:18 he describes them as those 'having been sanctified'.[10]

The primary passage describing definitive sanctification in the New Testament is Romans 6:1 to 7:6. Having expounded the doctrine of justification by faith, the apostle Paul turns to the subject of sanctification. In so doing he demonstrates that union with Christ simultaneously effects both justification and sanctification. The righteousness of Christ is imputed to the believer on account of union. That same union achieves new life. Positionally the believer has been placed into spiritual union with Christ. That is a definitive act. The ongoing result is a vital living union whereby the Christian possesses spiritual life and holiness. That is why it is utterly incongruous to suggest that a Christian should entertain the idea of sinning. We know that these great realities of justification and adoption are simultaneous; nevertheless if we are to think of a logical sequence then positional sanctification precedes justification and adoption because it would not be possible for the Father to justify the sinner unless he were first joined to Christ.

1   John Currid, *Study Commentary on Leviticus*, Evangelical Press, 2004, page 125.
2   *Ibid*, page 123.
3   Schaff-Hertzog Encyclopaedia of Religious Knowledge, vol 5, page 316.
4   *Ibid*, page 318.
5   The Gesenius Hebrew Lexicon gives the general meaning of the word *qadōsh* to be holy and says it is the same in all cognate (descended from a common ancestor) languages. The ancient language used in Ethiopia is Amharic and the words used for Holy Bible are *Metshaf Q'dus*.
6   Keil and Delitzsch, vol 2, page 53.
7   *PRAISE!* 194.
8   *hagiazō* to make holy, *hagiasmos* holiness, *hagiasthētō to onoma sou* hallowed be thy name.
9   The Hebrew word often used and translated saints is *chasid* meaning devoted, pious or faithful.
10 These verbs are perfect passive participles.

The Transcendent Holiness of God

Stephen Charnock wrote,

'God only is *absolutely* holy. *There is none holy as the* LORD (1 Sam 2:2). It is the peculiar glory of his nature. As there is none good but God, so none holy but God. No creature can be essentially holy, because mutable; holiness is the substance of God, but a quality and accident in a creature. God is infinitely holy, creatures finitely holy. He is holy from himself, creatures are holy by derivation from him.

'He is not only holy, but holiness; holiness in the highest degree is his sole prerogative. As the highest heaven is called the *heaven of heavens*, because it embraces in its circle all the heavens, and contains the magnitude of them, and has a greater vastness above all that it incloses; so is God the *Holy of holies*; he contains the holiness of all creatures put together, and infinitely more. As all the wisdom, excellency, and power of the creatures, if compared with the wisdom, excellency and power of God, is but folly, vileness, and weakness; so the highest created purity, if set in parallel with God, is but impurity and uncleanness; *thou only art holy* (Rev 15:4), it is like the light of a glow-worm to that of the sun; *the heavens are not pure in his sight, and his angels he charges with folly*, (Job 15:15 and 4:18).'

'Though God has crowned the angels with an unspotted sanctity, and placed them in a habitation of glory; yet as illustrious as they are, they have an unworthiness in their own nature to appear before the throne of so holy a God; their holiness grows dim and pale in his presence. It is but a weak shadow of that divine purity, whose light is so glorious, that it makes them *cover their faces* out of weakness to behold it, and cover their feet out of shame in themselves. They are not *pure in his sight*, because though they love God, which is a principle of holiness, as much as they can, yet not so much as he deserves: they love him with the intensest degree, according to their power; but not with the intensest degree, according to his own amiableness: for they cannot infinitely love God, unless they were infinite as God, and had an understanding of his perfections equal with himself, and as immense as his own knowledge.'

(Stephen Charnock, *Works*, Parsons edition, vol 2, page 500, the italics are Charnock's).

Chapter 2

The Holiness and Happiness of God

Of all concepts that we can contemplate not one can equal the holiness of God. Here we are confronted with transcendence, purity, profundity, mystery, beauty and blessedness. There are pressing reasons why this subject is of prime importance and relevance.

Firstly, how we conceive of God lies at the foundation of all our religious thought and practice.

For instance, the holiness of God can be viewed in an unbalanced way so that the soul is overwhelmed, even devastated. God's holiness taken only from the perspective of transcendent purity and wrath against sin will lead to despair. That was Luther's pre-conversion experience.

Wrote Luther:

> 'Do you not know that God dwells in light inaccessible? We weak and ignorant creatures want to probe and understand the incomprehensible majesty of the unfathomable light of the wonder of God. We approach; we prepare ourselves to approach. What wonder then that his majesty overpowers and shatters us!'[1]

Nothing seemed to help Luther in his distress. He confessed that he could not love a God who is a consuming fire. Love God? Luther confessed that he hated him! 'Who, then, can love a God angry, judging, and damning? Who can love a Christ sitting on a rainbow, consigning the damned souls to the flames of hell?'

The mere sight of a crucifix was like a stroke of lightning to Luther. He would flee then from the angry Son to the merciful Mother.

How do you think of the holiness of God? Do you think of purity only?

Secondly, the subject of the holiness of God is important because it provides the main explanation for judgment , whether judgments in the history of mankind such as the Flood, or that which came on Sodom and Gomorrah, or upon apostate Judah at the time of their captivity in Babylon, or whether it is the final judgment of eternal punishment. The urgency of the gospel is seriously undermined by the teaching of annihilationism. The holiness of God is directly related to this subject because it is impossible for God to lie. He is a holy God. His nature as holy is the best explanation we have of eternal punishment.

Thirdly, this truth is essential for salvation. The vast majority deceive themselves into thinking that God is not holy. He will not punish sin severely. They think of him as a God of love who will not act in wrath. The essence of revival or true religious awakening is a felt sense of the awesome holiness of God. It is the absence of this element that explains the lifeless condition of so many churches, even churches that are orthodox in believing the Bible.

Fourthly, and related to the above, our view of the holiness of God has a radical effect on our worship. How we pray, how we sing, and how the Word is preached in public will reflect what we believe about the nature of God, especially his holy character. This is something which is an inherent part of us. Artificiality is repugnant. Any conscious act to impress others should be avoided at all costs. It is futile to try and act as though we fear the holiness of God. If we truly love God as holy and have had developed within our spiritual lifestyle a filial relationship with the Father as holy, and union with Christ as Shepherd, and the indwelling of the Spirit as our Guide and Teacher, holiness will be reflected without our ever having to think of it by way of external expression.

As a grim and miserable demeanour indicates a distorted view of God as holy, so does flippancy in worship. It is common today for a jovial and jolly kind of spirit to be worked up as though worship were just another great fun spree. That is self-deception. I am not advocating that humanity should be extracted out of our worship. No purpose is served in our being paralysed. We are united to a Saviour who is both divine and human. There must be freedom to worship God but we must avoid generating a false euphoria. True worship is a blend of godly fear and trembling together with joy that we are accepted in the Beloved.

Fifthly, the truth of the holiness of God is essential for holy living. The Lord says, 'Be holy, because I am holy' (1 Peter 1:16). This exhortation is challenging because again we are confronted with the question, How do we conceive of the holiness of God as the model for our holy living?

Sixthly, we must hold on to the holiness of God as expressed particularly in the moral law, because fallen men most wish to argue with God about his holy character. They insist on having their own rules and standards. When God says that homosexuality is sinful there are those who say it is natural. When God says that adultery is evil multitudes will insist that it is normal and enjoyable. God hates divorce (Mal 2:16) but men say it is convenient. We can go on and on. The argument is always against the holy character of God. There is an inveterate unwillingness to acknowledge that he is holy, that his law is holy, and that the great final judgment will proceed along the lines of holiness.

How should this subject be approached in order to have a truly biblical view of God as holy? We will follow this outline.

1. We will consider some of God's actions in history, actions which confirm that he is essentially holy.
2. We will see that the holiness of God is related to the whole of his nature and best describes his being.
3. We will extend our view of the holiness of God by viewing holiness as the work of the three Persons of the Trinity in our redemption.
4. We will contemplate the happiness of God.

1. God's holiness is declared by his actions

The holy character of God is declared by his love of righteousness and his hatred of wickedness (Heb 1:9). All his actions without exception endorse that.

Whenever judgments fall on wicked men their crimes are first laid bare. Pharaoh long contended against Yahweh until he provoked him by going out to destroy Yahweh's own people. God's holiness is seen both in the deliverance of his people and in the destruction of Pharaoh and his army.

The people of Noah's time were prodigious in wickedness and unrestrained in violence. God bore long with them and strove with them but eventually the judgment that came upon them was cataclysmic just as it was upon the depraved people of Sodom. Simultaneously with judgment the work of salvation goes forward and makes progress because God in his holiness delights in righteousness which he imputes to believers, then working holiness within them.

Impressive measures were taken to confirm the fact that the law of God as expressed in the Ten Commandments is holy. Apartness was stressed. The mountain became a visible throne. The people had to keep their distance. The law was written by the Lord himself on stone tablets. There was the sound of trumpets. The law was uttered audibly. That same law is written in our consciences. That moral law, the decalogue, is holy and just as God himself is holy.

The holiness of God is declared by the Cross of Calvary. How could it be that the Lamb could suffer so intensely and so completely? In his agonies he tells us the reason. 'Yet you are enthroned as the Holy One' (Ps 22:3). Justice needed to be upheld. If justice were not satisfied then the holiness of God would be destroyed. When a crime is committed against an innocent victim then the cry goes up to heaven for justice to be done. Where is justice? It has not been neglected and never will be. Justice will always be met in full because God is holy. '"It is mine to avenge; I will repay," says the Lord' (Rom 12:19). Vengeance for our sins has not come upon us but has fallen upon the head of the one to whom we are united. Christ died in our place. Justice has been satisfied. God's holiness is upheld.

2. The holiness of God is related to the whole of his nature

The first consideration with regard to the nature of God is that God is indivisibly one. He is unique. There is no other. Hence the preface to God's holy law which outlines the substance of all he requires of us is, 'Hear, O Israel; the Lord our God, the Lord is one. Love the Lord your God with all your heart' (Deut 6:4). As we think of the unity of his being it is at the same time important to conceive of him as Spirit, infinitely so, eternally so, omnipotently so. In his essence as Spirit he is everywhere present, all-knowing and all-wise. He is to be distinguished from every other thing and especially so from all created matter. In that sense in the whole of his being he is holy, that is, apart. In all his attributes he is essentially one. He cannot be divided. It is only that we might advance in our knowledge of him that we consider his perfections one by one.

God himself singles out holiness as an excellency by which he is able to pledge his promises and judgments as certain and sure. 'Once for all I have sworn by my holiness – and I will not lie to David – that his line will continue forever' (Ps 89:35). 'The Sovereign Lord has sworn by his holiness: 'The time will surely come when you will be taken away with hooks, the last of you with fishhooks' (Amos 4:2). There is no greater certainty in all the universe than the immutable (unchangeable) holiness of God.

This is demonstrated in Isaiah's vision in the temple. He heard the antiphonal singing of the seraphim. And they were calling to one another and saying,

"Holy, holy, holy is the Lord Almighty;
The whole earth is full of his glory" (Isa 6:3).

Reference can be made to the transcendent attributes of God: self-existence, self-sufficiency, eternity, infinitude, omniscience, wisdom, omnipotence and immutability. Then there are the personal or moral attributes. They are God's goodness, justice, love, grace, mercy, faithfulness, truthfulness, wrath, patience and blessedness.

Can we say that holiness characterises every one of the above-named attributes? The answer is very much in the affirmative. Holiness characterises God in the entirety of his being, but also characterises each attribute in particular. His love is holy and never merely sentimental. His justice is holy and on that account will be demonstrably perfect for all eternity. God's wrath is a holy wrath. Every attribute complements the others and all are vital. But essentially they are inseparable from each other as God is ever and always one.

In Scripture the names ascribed to God are chosen especially to reveal the nature of his being. The first great name is Yahweh (Jehovah) meaning I AM (Ex 3:14). That name points to his transcendence, uniqueness and pre-eminence. When Isaiah says God's name is HOLY (Isa 57:15), that name points to the overall nature and character of God (Ps 103:1).

3. The holiness of the three Persons of the Trinity is expressed in the work of redemption

Sin was the supreme challenge to the holiness of God and to the divine order in the universe. God's response to this was twofold. The first response is one of judgment and retribution upon all persisting in rebellion and sin. The second is the work of redemption. In the first God shows his justice and abhorrence of sin. In the second he demonstrates his delight in holiness and love.

The Father's delight in holiness is evidenced in the provision of redemption in his Son, in the application of that redemption to his people, and in the consummation of that redemption. The consummation is the Marriage Supper of the Lamb, the gathering of his people into the new earth where holiness and love will reign forever.

First then we see the Father's delight in holiness in providing the Son of his love to live a life of perfect holiness for his people and then to die in their place that their sins might be atoned for and blotted out. Through union with Christ it is the Father's purpose that all his elect people should derive holiness of character from Christ and be conformed to him in holiness. It is the Father's wisdom and delight that Christ should be made to all his people righteousness (imputed), holiness (intrinsic holiness of character born in them by the new birth and progressive sanctification), and final redemption, when they will be redeemed from the presence and power of sin once and for all.

The Father's pleasure in holiness is seen in his affirmation of joy in Christ's life and work on our behalf, 'This is my Son, whom I love; with him I am well pleased' (Matt 3:17). The Father's complacent love is expressed for his children as they love and obey him. Complacent love is a love of delight for the worth and character of the objects loved. If we obey Christ's teaching the Father will love us, come to us, and make his home with us (John 14:21 and 23). This is an evidence of his pleasure in holiness.

Such is his love for holiness that he will unite himself to us. We enjoy a mystical spiritual unity with the Father and with the Son (John 17:21-23). However this is only achieved by the propitiation made by Christ. In that way God can 'be just and the one who justifies the man who has faith in Jesus' (Rom 3:26).

Over-simplification of the way of salvation is an affront to the holiness of God. The moral attributes of God spring from holiness and are determined by holiness. God's holiness and justice require that the law be upheld and sin be atoned for. None but the Son of God could render satisfaction to the law or vindicate the requirements of the holy character of God.

The Father's love for holiness is seen in the complete Church when she reaches perfection. Then she will have been made beautiful in holiness (Rev 21:2). Not only will the bride of Christ be beautiful in holiness but her habitat, the New Jerusalem and the new earth, will be beautiful and shining in holiness. 'On that day HOLY TO THE LORD will be inscribed on the bells of the horses ... Every pot in Jerusalem will be holy to the LORD Almighty' (Zech 14:20,21).

The holiness of God in practice is exhibited in the life, ministry and teaching of Christ. In contemporary terms we may say that by possessing four Gospels we have cameras focused on him from every angle. In addition we have the prophetic descriptions of his ministry and sufferings as recorded in Isaiah and the Psalms and many other places. We tend to think of sinlessness in terms of avoiding actual sin but omission is sin. Love is the fulfilling of the law. The marvel of Christ's life was twofold; not only was he holy, blameless, pure, set apart from sinners (Heb 7:26), but he actually fulfilled the law of love by positive works of love and compassion.

To the Holy Spirit is ascribed the work of regeneration and progressive sanctification. There is so much work to be done in the battle against remaining corruption yet such is the Spirit's expertise, wisdom and power that he transforms God's people. With all patience and thoroughness he advances progressively the work of holiness in the believer (2 Cor 3:18).

4. The happiness of God

Blessedness as an attribute of God is referred to in 1 Timothy 1:11 where Paul warns against what is contrary to sound doctrine that conforms to the glorious gospel of the blessed God. Further in this letter the apostle enlarges his description: 'God, the blessed and only Ruler, the King of kings and Lord of lords, who alone is immortal and who lives in unapproachable light, whom no-one has seen or can see. To him be honour and might for ever, Amen' (1

Tim 6:15,16). It is profitable for us to meditate on the holiness and happiness of God and at the same time reflect on him as containing all happiness in himself and the reality that he has demonstrated and continues to demonstrate that it his pleasure to bestow happiness on his people.

At least three reasons can be suggested for the unique happiness of God.

The first is that he is holy in the transcendent sense. He is complete and self-sufficient, unchanging in all his glorious attributes. In his nature he is perfect in holiness as we saw earlier both in the purity and the excellence of his being. Hence he is the ever-blessed God.

The second reason for God's happiness is the nature of the Trinity. The inexpressible beauty of holiness in the transcendent sense characterises each Person of the Trinity. However, we must remember the moral attributes as well.

There is love in the Trinity. To love you need another. Other-person centredness characterises the three Persons. The Holy Spirit searches all things, even the deep things of God (1 Cor 2:10). Likewise the Son knows the Father in all the immensity of his being and in his love and wisdom. There is perfect blessedness and complacent love in the three Persons. There is equality because each Person of the Trinity possesses all the attributes of deity. Yet there is diversity of character in each for each performs a different work in our redemption.

The third reason why God is blessed or happy in himself is through the joy of redemption. 'He will take great delight in you, he will quiet you with his love, he will rejoice over you with singing' (Zeph 3:17). The love of Christ for his redeemed people is beyond description. It surpasses knowledge (Eph 3:19). Many waters could not quench it. It burns like a mighty flame. His love is stronger than death. Rivers cannot wash it away. He will comfort his own. Then the Father himself will be with them and be their God and they will be his people.

The attribute of joy is part of the blessedness of God triune. He imparts joy to his people. 'The joy of the LORD is your strength' (Neh 8:10). Joy emanates from him. 'Great is the LORD, and most worthy of praise, in the city of our God, his holy mountain. It is beautiful in its loftiness, the joy of the whole earth (Ps 48:1-2).

Says Peter, 'But just as he who called you is holy, so be holy in all you do' (1 Peter 1:15). There must be a likeness between the caller and the called. But how can we be holy as our Father is holy? Not in his transcendent holiness, for he is unique, but in the holiness of his moral attributes in which he delights in truth and righteousness and hates iniquity; in that way we can be holy. Moreover, we can be holy by doing good as he does good and by loving others as he loves them, especially the household of believers.

As his perfect bliss and blessedness are instrinsic to his holiness so our happiness depends on our being holy. Today people are obsessed with finding happiness. It eludes them for they seek happiness without holiness. Sin has always brought a harvest of misery with it. Instead of being holy and happy our first parents through their rebellion and sin became wretched and miserable. By living selfishly people live unhappily. In their self-centredness they become resentful and hard-hearted. They have lost the meaning of being created in the image of the triune God who is other-person centred by nature.

In conclusion we should regard the holiness of God as the ultimate guarantee of our eternal happiness. Holiness is what ensures the blessedness of God and holiness in all its beauty and glory is our happiness.

---

1   Roland Bainton, *Here I Stand – A Life of Martin Luther*, A Lion Paperback, 1978, page 57.

The Beauty of God as an Attribute

Should we regard beauty as an attribute of God? All God's attributes are integral to his being and cannot be separated except in our minds for meditation and reflection. As an attribute the beauty of God is closely allied to the holiness of God. We 'worship the LORD in the splendour of his holiness' (Ps 96:9 cf. 2 Chron 20:21).

In his classic work *The Religious Affections* Jonathan Edwards writes, 'A true love to God must begin with a delight in his holiness, and not with a delight in any other attribute; for no other attribute is truly lovely without this.' Edwards maintains that the other attributes derive their loveliness from God's holiness.[1] Edwards suggests, 'He that sees the beauty of holiness, or true moral good, sees the greatest and most important thing in the world.'[2]

'When the true beauty and amiableness of the holiness, or true moral good, that is in divine things is discovered to the soul, it, as it were, opens a new world to its view. This shows the glory of all the perfections of God and of everything appertaining to the divine Being. For, as was observed before, the beauty of all arises from God's moral perfection. This shows the glory of all God's works, both of creation and providence. For it is the special glory of them, that God's holiness, righteousness, faithfulness, and goodness are so maintained in them; and without these moral perfections there would be no glory in that power and skill with which they are wrought. The gloryifying of God's moral perfections is the special end of all the works of God's hands.'[3]

Referring to his conversion Edwards writes, 'The appearance of everything was altered: there seemed to be, as it were, a calm, sweet cast, or appearance of divine glory, in almost everything. God's excellency, his wisdom, purity and love seemed to appear in everything; in the sun, moon and stars; in the clouds and blue sky, in the grass, flowers, trees; in the water and all nature; which used greatly to fix my mind.'[4]

---

[1] Jonathan Edwards, *The Religious Affections*, Banner of Truth edition, vol 3, page 183.
[2] *Ibid*, page 200.
[3] *Ibid,* page 199.
[4] Jonathan Edwards, *Encounters with God, An Approach to the Theology of Jonathan Edwards* (New York/Oxford University Press, 1998) pages 34-35. Cited in *Jonathan Edwards, the Holy Spirit in Revival*, Michael Haykin, appendix 2, *Beauty as a Divine Attribute: the Western Tradition and Jonathan Edwards*, EP, 2005, page 165.

❧ Chapter 3 ❧

The Necessity of Holiness

M any jokes have been told and cartoons drawn of a man who arrives at the gate of heaven to meet Saint Peter sitting on a cloud with his harp. Peter asks the man for a reason why he should be allowed into heaven. No subject is more serious than where you spend eternity: eternal heaven (which in fact is the new earth) or eternal hell.

I sidestep humour and proceed straight to the uncompromising text of the Bible which says, 'Without holiness no-one will see the Lord' (Heb 12:14). Heaven is a place of holiness where the God of holiness reigns and we can be sure that nothing that is unholy will ever enter there.

This being so we need to be crystal clear about what this holiness means. Can I have this holiness? It is something to be possessed not just to be talked about.

Before proceeding it is worth noting that exclusion from heaven is expressed in other ways. For instance Jesus said, 'Unless a man is born again he cannot see the kingdom of heaven' (John 3:3). That is clear enough. Unless he is born again he will not see the kingdom let alone enter it. Another way in which exclusion from heaven is expressed is Romans 3:20, 'For by the works of the law no human being will be justified in his sight' (Rom 3:20, ESV). It is shocking to think that the great majority of human beings put their trust in their own goodness to get them through the pearly gates into paradise. Such 'self-made righteousness' is unacceptable. The prophet Isaiah expresses it, 'All our righteousnesses are as filthy rags' (Isa 64:6 KSV). Muslims hold the idea of balances. In one balance are sinful deeds and in the other balance are good deeds. The hope is that the good deeds will outweigh the bad. There is nothing certain about this. It is only a hope. But it is a disastrous hope, 'because by observing the law no one will be justified' (Gal 2:16).

Many think that holiness is completely out of reach so put it out of mind. They think of holiness as something that is for monks and nuns who give themselves full-time to it. Roman Catholicism and Greek Orthodoxy have perpetuated the notion of saints in the sense that sainthood is the exclusive business of exceptional people like Saint Teresa. However when Paul wrote his letters to the churches he addressed all believers without exception as saints (2 Cor 1:1; Eph 1:1; Phil 1:1). The reality is that imputed righteousness, holiness and final and certain redemption of the soul and body are a free gift possessed by every person united to Christ by faith. That number includes boys and girls, people of education and many with no formal education, rich people and very many who are poor, in fact people of every imaginable status in this world. This gift of a complete salvation is beautifully expressed as God's wisdom. When human wisdom failed to produce anything acceptable, God's wisdom provided the free gift of a perfect righteousness, an acceptable holiness and a final redemption of the soul and the body and that for all eternity. 'It is because of him that you are in Christ Jesus, who has become for us wisdom from God – that is, our righteousness, holiness and redemption' (1 Cor 1:30).[1]

'Make every effort to live in peace with all men and to be holy; without holiness no-one will see the Lord' (Heb 12:14). This exhortation comes toward the end of the letter to the Hebrews. 'Make every effort' is an excellent translation of the single Greek word, *diōkete* which is a present, active, imperative verb. It literally means to pursue with energy or to run after. As suggested in the introductory chapter the practice of holiness is the full-time business of every Christian. John Bunyan expresses this in his hymn 'He who would valiant be'. Pilgrim will not fear what men say. He'll 'labour night and day to be a pilgrim'.

There is a definite article in the Greek text as follows: 'without *the* holiness no-one will see the Lord.' There is the danger of a religious false holiness like that of the Pharisees. Philip Hughes comments: 'That it is possible, and indeed all too common, for men to pursue a spurious kind of "holiness" is plain from Christ's condemnation of the "holiness" of those religious hypocrites whose sanctimonious piety is a public display of self-esteem, manifested in the calculated ostentation of their devotional exercises and almsgiving, that they may be praised by men. True holiness, however, is inward and private, between a man and his God, and the good deeds which are its fruit are performed as secretly as possible as an expression of loving concern and with an aversion for all fanfare and publicity' (Matt 6:1-18).[2]

What does it mean to 'see the Lord'? The text says, 'Without holiness no-one will see the Lord.' The believer looks forward to the Second Coming of Christ when he will see the Lord and be like him. 'Dear friends, now we are children of God, and what we will be has not yet been made known. But we know that when he appears, we shall be like him, for we shall see him as he is. Everyone who has this hope in him purifies himself, just as he is pure' (1 John 3:2,3). Seeing the Lord refers to the time of glorification when we will be changed and be given our resurrection bodies. These will be derived from Christ who is the firstfruits from the dead.

Not to have true holiness and therefore not to see the Lord is total disaster for anyone. There can be no greater calamity for a soul than to be rejected and cast into hell forever. The context in which our text is found is a warning against contempt for God. Neglect of him however polite is to be destitute of that holiness which is absolutely essential.

Since this holiness without which no man will see the Lord is a necessity we must make sure that we possess it. Two factors are involved. First we must understand the doctrine involved. In other words, exactly how do we come to possess this holiness? Second we must grasp that this holiness is practical. It has to be woven into daily living.

The doctrine of holiness

Holiness comes to us by way of faith union with Christ. When we are united to Christ by faith his righteousness is imputed to us. Positionally we are in him. This is what the apostle Paul means when he says we are 'in Christ'. A chapter is devoted to this crucial matter. At the same time we are given the gift of the Holy Spirit and he initiates and carries forward the work of progressive sanctification. It is vital that we do not confuse justification with progressive sanctification.

Justification of a believer is a declarative act by the Father and is based upon the fact that he imputes Christ's righteousness to that believer. Apart from that righteousness there is absolutely no other basis or ground of justification. It is not a matter of Christ's righteousness plus my obedience or my good works. The differences between justification and sanctification are shown in the window.

Sanctification involves the three Persons of the Trinity.

1. The Father has predestined that his people should be conformed to the likeness of his Son (Rom 8:29). The chapter *The Organisation of our Sanctification* expounds the means employed to achieve his purpose. The Authorised Version aptly translates 1 Thessalonians 4:3: 'For this is the will of God, even your sanctification, that you should abstain from fornication.'

2. Believers are sanctified in Christ Jesus (1 Cor 1:2). The chapter *Union with Christ* expounds the reality of our unity with the Son of God. It is from him that we derive our holiness in the ongoing process of progressive sanctification.

3. Believers are sanctified through the work of the Holy Spirit (1 Peter 1:2; Rom 8:1-27). Chapters 7 to 10 are devoted to this subject.

Holiness is practical

The holiness without which no-one will see the Lord is a way of life. The apostle Peter expresses it this way, 'Be holy in all you do' (1 Peter 1:15). Of course this includes abstention from evil or pollution, but holy living is a way of life which reflects the beauty of Christ's character and the sterling qualities exhibited in his life.

The holy way of life is set out before us in the Sermon on the Mount (Matt 5-7), and in the letters of the New Testament.

In the Sermon on the Mount Jesus shows that the moral law as expressed in the Old Covenant is not abrogated. In the administration of the New Covenant the moral law is applicable at a deep spiritual level. Two commandments illustrate this. To have hatred in one's heart is like murder. To look on a woman lustfully is to commit adultery with her in your heart (Matt 5:22,28). Holiness respects all the commandments from the heart, that is internally and not merely externally. A holy life is like salt in the earth and like light in the world (Matt 5:13-16).

Note Jesus' words, 'For I tell you that unless your righteousness surpasses that of the Pharisees and the teachers of the law, you will certainly not enter the kingdom of heaven' (Matt 5:20). This is the same as saying that our holy way of life will have to be better than that of the Pharisees if we are to enter the kingdom of heaven. The Pharisees sought to enforce many laws that are not in Scripture. They were legalistic and their form of holiness was self-righteous and made them conceited.

The main thrust of Jesus' teaching in the Sermon on the Mount is that holy living is living that always has our adoption as sons and daughters of our heavenly Father in view. As his children we seek in everything to please him.

Paul in his letter to the Ephesians confirms this teaching and shows that holiness is the renewing of the mind in which we abandon lying and speak only the truth (Eph 4:25). Holiness is honest work and caring for others (Eph 4:28). Holiness extends to all family relationships, husbands loving and caring for their wives and children being obedient to their parents (Eph 5:22- 6:4).

In his letter James stresses that faith without works is dead. Holy living includes care for the needy. James expresses this eloquently. 'Religion that God our Father accepts as pure and faultless is this: to look after orphans and widows in their distress and to keep oneself from being polluted by the world' (James 1:27).[3]

The Bible's stress on caring for orphans and widows is strong from beginning to end. Job protested that he had been very careful to meet the needs of these people in their distress (Job 29:12; 31:16-20). The words 'in their distress' describe the condition to which we must respond with compassion and practical care.

Keeping oneself pure and avoiding moral pollution is one essential part of holiness in the life of the Christian. That is an inward discipline. The outward active work of holy living is to visit orphans and widows in their distress. Psalm 68:5 stresses that it is out of the heart of our Triune God that compassion and mercy flow to the helpless and distressed, needy people who are unable to care for themselves or perhaps are not able to survive economically. In Brazil for instance young girls are driven into prostitution because of poverty. Orphans are left destitute. The Christian Church in places where this phenomenon is rife like Africa and Brazil seeks to provide homes for them. It is an immense task. Widows multiply in times of war. Who will care for them in their distress?

By way of conclusion we need to return to the text, '*Make every effort to live in peace with all men and to be holy; without holiness no-one will see the Lord*' (Heb 12:14). The imperative 'Make every effort' applies to living at peace with all men as well as to the pursuit of holiness.

Living at peace with all men is linked with holiness. The Greek text simply says 'all' which means everyone. When the word 'men' is used in translations this is not chauvinism (men vaunting their superiority over women). 'Men' is generic or inclusive. It would be pedantic to have to say men *and women* every time.

To live at peace with all people includes all those in the church fellowship. The context requires that because the writer immediately refers to the possibility of a root of bitterness springing up and many being defiled, meaning many in the church fellowship.

Ill feelings and divisions in churches are sadly common. Rifts occur which take a long time to heal. Holiness is very closely related to living at peace and in unity with fellow church members. This living at peace with them often requires making every effort. I know of a church which is completely orthodox in doctrine yet has broken into personal factions. This has done harm in the town and to the cause of Christ.

In our multicultural, pluralistic society of many religions it requires every effort to live at peace with our neighbours who may be Jews, Muslims, Hindus or Sikhs. In most cases it is more likely to be those who have no religion at all. Western Europe is increasingly secular. People no longer believe that God created this world. They are evolutionary humanists who disdain religion and make their own rules. The difficulty is that we must make every effort to live in peace with those with whom we have radical differences of outlook. We must never compromise or sacrifice our faith or morality in order to please our neighbours or fellow employees in the work-place. Peace is not maintained at the expense of holiness. We must be careful to avoid anything in our behaviour that causes offence. However, there is nothing we can do to avoid the offence of the Cross of Christ (1 Cor 1:23). The manner in which we contend for truth must be gracious and gentle. The gospel wins people's hearts not by the sword of violence but by persuasion and love.

We should note of Melchizedek that 'first, his name means "king of righteousness"; then also "king of Salem" means "king of peace" (Heb 7:2). Melchizedek was a real man who came to meet Abraham who was returning from war. Melchizedek is a type of Christ our great high priest who is King of Righteousness and King of Peace. The principle to be observed is that peace must not be procured at the expense of truth and righteousness. 'Men may be so determined to maintain peace that they compromise principle, sacrifice the truth, and ignore the claims of God. Peace must never be sought at the price of unfaithfulness to Christ.'[4] 'Buy the truth and do not sell it' (Prov 23:23), is ever binding upon the Christian.

The English Puritan William Gouge in his commentary on Hebrews directs us to Ephesians 4:2-4 where the apostle outlines the means to procure and preserve peace. The first is humility, or lowliness of mind, readiness to prefer others before ourselves. The second is meekness which is a quiet disposition of the soul, a mild temper to others. Longsuffering is the third which is a patient disposition to bear with wrongs and which restrains thoughts of revenge. Forbearance is the fourth which is respect for the failings and weaknesses of others. Fifth is love which highlights the qualities of others who are made in God's image and a desire to do them good.

---

1   The three Greek words used for righteousness, holiness and redemption are *dikaiosunē, hagiasmos* and *apolutrōsis*.
2   Philip Hughes, *Hebrews*, Eerdmans, 1977, page 536.
3   The Greek word translated in the AV to visit is *episkeptomai*. The meaning of this word is to look after, to give relief, or to care for. Gordon J Keddie, *The Practical Christian, Commentary on James*, Evangelical Press, 1989. The practice of pastors or elders visiting the flock is excellent and has many advantages. Often this visitation is not to relieve distress. Priority needs to be given to those who are in distress.
4   A W Pink, *Hebrews*, Baker Book House, 1954, vol 3, page 96.

Eventual Perfect Sancification

The apostle Paul makes it clear that progressive sanctification is a work of God which is totally comprehensive and which will be completed when Christ returns.

> 'May God himself, the God of peace, sanctify you through and through. May your whole spirit, soul and body be kept blameless at the coming of our Lord Jesus Christ. The one who calls you is faithful and he will do it' (1 Thess 5:23-24).

The structure suggested is as follows:

Progressive Sanctification

1. The author *The God of peace*
2. The work *sanctify you through and through*
3. The extent *may your whole spirit, soul and body be kept blameless*
4. The conclusion *at the coming of our Lord Jesus Christ*
5. The certainty *The one who calls you is faithful and he will do it*

The work of sanctification is 'through and through' meaning all-pervasive. It permeates the mind. 'We take captive every thought to make it obedient to Christ' (2 Cor 10:5). When Paul says 'your whole spirit, soul and body' he is suggesting that there is no part that is not embraced by progressive sanctification. A person cannot be spliced up into parts except for the purposes of analysis. To carry Paul's assurance forward, we can say that a believer's mind, heart (affections), will, conscience and body are all subject to holiness. That this work is not completed in this life is evident because the text says that perfection will only be reached when Christ returns. Sanctification can be a hard work but we are comforted to know that the end product is certain because our faithful God will bring this work to completion.

❧ *Chapter 4* ❧

The Organisation of Sanctification

T homas Watson expresses sanctification as a beautiful thing. 'It makes God and the angels fall in love with us. Sanctification is an extensive thing: it embraces a man in the whole of his being. Sanctification is a supernatural thing: it is divinely infused. It is a progressive thing: it advances and grows. It is a comprehensive thing: it involves our Christian experience from beginning to end.'[1] Who organises this amazing thing called sanctification?

The Father is the organiser; Christ the procurer; the Holy Spirit the executor. The Father originates it; Christ supplies it (every particle of holiness we will ever have comes from him); the Holy Spirit empowers it.

The names given to sanctification are:

Definitive Sanctification which is the beginning of it; Progressive Sanctification which is the middle of it; and, Glorification which is the end of it.

Definitive sanctification is the once-for-all setting apart of the believer in Christ. Definitive means final and decisive. Positionally we have been joined to Christ. We are 'in him'. In that sense we are perfectly sanctified. Over 160 times we have the term 'in Christ' in the NT and over 60 times we have the term 'saints' which means those who have been definitively sanctified, set apart in Christ. 'You were sanctified' (1 Cor 6:11). Note the past tense.

Progressive sanctification is well defined by John Sheffield: 'True holiness is that inward, thorough, and real change, wrought in the whole man of a formerly vile sinner by the Spirit of God, whereby his heart is purged from the love, and his life from the dominion and practice of his former sins, and whereby he is in heart and life carried out after every good.'[2]

The organisation of progressive sanctification

The Scriptures emphasise that it is the Father who organises our sanctification. We observe this in Paul's benediction: 'May God himself, the God of peace, sanctify you through and through. May your whole spirit, soul and body be kept blameless at the coming of our Lord Jesus Christ. The one who calls you is faithful and he will do it' (1 Thess 5:23-24). It is especially with sanctification in mind that our Father works in all things for the good of those who love him (Rom 8:28).

Just what goes into this work of sanctification which involves transformation, a metamorphosis (Rom 8:29; 12:2; 2 Cor 3:18)? What does the Father use to achieve his purpose to conform us to his Son? I suggest the following factors most of which will be opened up in more detail in the chapters which follow:

1. A personal relationship with the Trinity
2. Church membership
3. Mortification of sin
4. Conformity to Christ
5. Trials, afflictions and chastisement
6. The development of a disciplined lifestyle
7. Unusual providences and crisis experiences

1. A personal relationship with the Trinity

We are baptised into the name of the Father and the Son and the Holy Spirit. In Scripture the name of God is put for all that he is. The baptismal formula asserts in the clearest and most powerful way the union of the believer with each Person of the Trinity; not partial, but full union is expressed. By union with Christ we come into union with the Father and the Spirit. The Christian's relationship to the Father is adoption. In the Sermon on the Mount Jesus expounds what it is to live for the Father in everything. All providence is interpreted as coming from the Father. We respond to him personally and daily examine our lives as we relate to him as Father. In all our decision making we examine our motives before the Father. We seek to eradicate everything that is displeasing and at the same time labour to do everything that is pleasing. The effect of living in this way cannot be exaggerated.

The exhortation to be holy even as our Father is holy (1 Peter 1:15) is always with us, especially since we know that he will judge every one of us impartially. But how can we be holy as he is holy when his holiness is utterly unique? His holiness is transcendent in purity and brightness, in a way which we cannot even approach to, still less imitate. The purity of his nature is epitomised in the moral law of Sinai. The effects of this law, which is 'holy, just and good', are expressed by Paul in Romans 7. The moral law shows how we sin and fall short of the glory of God. Yet the law in itself does not give us power. That power comes from our union with Christ. In Christ we see the perfect holiness of God. In Christ we have the only man who has loved God perfectly. He is the only man of whom we can say he is as holy as the Father.

We relate to the Son by way of union. In him we have not only a full and final redemption but also a pattern to follow. We seek to walk as he walked (1 John 2:6). He is unrivalled for love and compassion, gentleness, meekness and humility. But he was not only perfect in these positive graces but also in the negative graces. Nobody hated sin more than he and nobody has rebuked false prophets and false shepherds as he. Read Matthew 23 again if you doubt that. Nobody has ever behaved so selflessly under torments and injustice as he. No one has ever borne unjust and complete rejection and spurning as he did. Here is holiness exemplified. He requires that we be like him. He insists that we forgive each other since we ourselves have been forgiven so much, see Matthew 18:35. Our living union with Jesus has an immense daily effect on our progressive sanctification.

Likewise when we consider our relationship to the Holy Spirit we are acutely aware of the possibility of grieving him (Eph 4:30). The Holy Spirit monitors all our thought patterns. We relate to him as advocate. He represents us. It is only by his enabling that we can pray (Rom 8:26,27). He convinces us of our sins. He proposes correctives. He motivates and he directs. He interprets the Scriptures to us. He empowers us for service and worship. He is entirely intolerant of evil thoughts. In contrast to that his zeal for good works is immeasurable and he fills our minds and hearts with his presence. He directs us to good works so we can be fully involved in enterprises which please him. Again the implications of this relationship are enormous in terms of progressive sanctification.

2. Church membership

Throughout the history of redemption God has dealt with his people in a corporate way: Noah and his family, Abraham and his family, Israel as a nation, and now with his Church. To the three Persons of the Trinity the Church universal is essentially one (Eph 4:1-6). Every local church is a microcosm of the whole. All the churches should be to one another what believers are to one another. That is the ideal. The situation is enormously complex because of so many serious differences. Yet every believer is duty-bound to adjust as best he can to membership in a local church for 'each member belongs to all the others'. Every member derives his spiritual life from the same head and every member has been baptised by the Spirit into the same body and 'we were all given the one Spirit to drink' (1 Cor 12:13).

The closely interwoven life and interdependence of the members upon each other is vividly expressed in the text, 'From him the whole body, joined and held together by every supporting ligament, grows and builds itself up in love, as each part does its work' (Eph 4:16). Think of the influence of other Christians upon us in the sphere of sanctification. We are taught together through the preaching. We benefit together from the ordinances. We learn from one another in fellowship. We serve together. We run the race together. We rejoice together and we suffer together. We gain inspiration from leaders and outstanding members not only in real life but through literature. We are warned and corrected by cases of discipline. If we analyse the channels by which we are sustained and built up through fellow members, we would see that there is hardly anything of spiritual value that does not come through the body of the Church.

We can well understand why giving up meeting together is regarded as a disaster in Scripture. In effect that is the road that leads away from the life of God's people. It is the road of apostasy (Heb 10:25).

3. Mortification of sin

Mortification of sin in the Christian is not optional. It is essential. 'If you live according to the sinful nature, you will die' (Rom 8:13). Putting sin to death involves all the power of the will. Cutting the throat of sin is not done for us. I have to mortify the misdeeds of my body. True this is accomplished through the empowering of the Holy Spirit, but mortification is my work.

The two principal texts which command that everything impure be put to death are Romans 8:13 and Colossians 3:5. The latter reads, 'Put to death, therefore, whatever belongs to your earthly nature; sexual immorality, impurity, lust, evil desires and greed, which is idolatry.' The 'therefore' refers to the radical break with the world of sin, which has come about through union with Christ. In Christ's death we have died to that world of iniquity. Even though that is the case, that world is still our environment and there is remaining corruption in us. This corruption is in the mind but works through the body. In Galatians it is denominated flesh *(sarx)*. That is a stark word which needs no elaboration. Paul says that the flesh wars against the Spirit and the Spirit against the flesh (Gal 5:17). There is only one way of dealing with the problem and that is to get out a hammer and nails and crucify the flesh. Mortification is sometimes compared with the slaughterhouse. (The verbs used are expressive: *thanatoō* in Rom 8: 13 means to kill, and *nekroō* in Colossians 3:5 means to make impotent.) We must kill lusts because every sin is capable of very quick growth with a disastrous outcome. Lust can quickly become actual adultery; anger can soon erupt to become literal murder. Covetousness can soon turn into a criminal offence of fraud or theft. Rebellion toward God can turn into apostasy.

There can be no compromise with indwelling sin. It is like a deadly snake. A friend in Africa told me of an encounter he had with a full-grown mamba, one of Africa's most aggressive and deadly reptiles. Taking a large stick he knew that it was essential to kill the snake with the first blow. He prayed for the accuracy necessary. The Lord heard his prayer and that first blow circumvented the deadly retaliatory strike by the mamba. Would that we treated all sin in our hearts like deadly snakes are treated.

Mortification of sin is like clearing away the rubbish on a building site to make room for the new structure. It is impossible for the old rubbish to form part of the new building. This leads to the next major issue involved in progressive sanctification.

4. Conformity to Christ

God has predestined that we be conformed to the image of Christ. The Holy Spirit gradually and progressively affects this transformation to the likeness of Christ (2 Cor 3:18). The practical means employed is by the renewing of our minds *(metamorphousthe* is an imperative – you be transformed! Rom 12:2). In these places the word which is used is the equivalent of metamorphosis in English. It denotes a change which is inward, permeating and thorough. The only other place where the term is used is in Matthew 7:2 to describe the transfiguration of Christ.

Renewal is another word used to describe the idea of advance and progress. For instance we have 2 Corinthians 4:16, 'Therefore we do not lose heart. Though outwardly we are wasting away, yet inwardly we are being renewed day by day'; and Colossians 3:10, 'And have put on the new self' which is being renewed in knowledge in the image of its Creator.'

In what ways are we made like Christ? The answer surely is that we are conformed to him in the attributes of love, meekness, humility, patience, gentleness, a love of righteousness and a loathing of evil and so on. As Jonathan Edwards asserts in his treatise *The Religious Affections*, there is a beautiful symmetry in all the attributes of Christ-likeness. There is salt and light in the Christian as well as love, sweetness and compassion. This essential aspect of sanctification receives surprisingly scant treatment in books on the subject.

In practical terms progress in Christ-likeness can only take place as we study our actions in detail and compare them with the life and example of Christ and with the requirements of Scripture. That involves analysis and hence as suggested in Romans 12:2 the use of our minds.

5. Trials and chastisement

The promise is that if we suffer with Christ we will also reign with him. Because we are joined to Christ everything we suffer in soul or body is shared with him. All our trials, temptations, anxieties, pains and disappointments affect him and are shared with him. Everything that is adverse drives us closer in dependence upon God. For this reason it is often observed that a persecuted Church or a suffering Church is at the same time blessed in having a close walk with God.

The cardinal book in the Bible on this theme is Job. Job suffered extremely and in his trials made great progress in his spiritual experience. His friends were sure that Job was being punished for some sin or sins he had committed. They attempted to compel some confession of specific sin from him. However, we are informed at the beginning of the book that Job was a blameless and upright God-fearer. He was not being punished. His trials were not permitted in order to correct him in the sense that he needed a radical change in his lifestyle. Sometimes Christians are chastised in a severe manner, hence the word scourging (see the description of Proverbs 3 and Hebrews 12), because they need a radical correction or reformation in their lifestyle. However, as I will show later, chastisement can be understood as character training.

Job shows us that we need to distinguish clearly between trial and chastisement. Chastisement is corrective. King David was acutely conscious of the fact that some of his trials were chastisement (Ps 51).

In some ways all sufferings tend to humble the Christian and make him more gentle and sympathetic to others and hence more like Christ. The ingredient of correction may be small or great in our sufferings, but we can be sure that this factor in our lives plays a foremost role in progressive sanctification. As Paul says, 'We know that suffering produces perseverance.' James says that we should have a positive and not a negative attitude to trials because 'you know that the testing of your faith develops perseverance. Perseverance must finish its work so that you may be mature and complete, not lacking anything' (James 1:2,3). Grief has come, suggests Peter, 'so that your faith – of greater worth than gold, which perishes even though refined by fire – may be proved genuine and may result in praise, glory and honour when Jesus Christ is revealed' (1 Peter 1:6,7).

6. The development of a disciplined lifestyle

The Christian life is likened to that of the professional soldier who is always in training and always on the alert. In the spiritual life there is never a time when we can be off our guard. The Christian life is also likened to the disciplined lifestyle of an athlete (2 Tim 2:3-5; 1 Cor 9:24-27). Paul exhorts Timothy to train *(gumnazō)* himself to be godly. As there are set exercises in the gymnasium so there are disciplines and habits in the spiritual life which if neglected will result in a weak and flabby Christian. Time is to be redeemed and put to wise spiritual use (Eph 5:16; Col 4:5). The word used literally means to buy. That requires cost and effort. Wisdom is to be exercised in putting this bought back time to best use.

The establishment of a disciplined lifestyle will ensure that there will be daily private prayer and regular times of corporate prayer. We are to strive together *(sunathleō* denotes a striving together in an athletic contest) for the faith of the gospel (Phil 1:27). We are to strive *(sunagōnisasthai* – agonise together) with other Christians in prayer (Rom 15 :30). The mind is to be disciplined constantly (Rom 12:2) to include all thoughts. We take captive every thought (2 Cor 10:5). The paramount importance of self-examination and meditation can be appreciated when we think of what is involved in taking captive *every thought.*

In the context of the spiritual race and competing as an athlete the body too is to be disciplined and be made obedient. 'I beat my body and make it my slave' (1 Cor 9:27). By diligent use of these means, the channels by which our spiritual lives are nurtured are to be kept clean and flowing with the waters of eternal life. Paul so ordered his life that he could commend his lifestyle to others. To Timothy he could say, 'You have fully known my way of life', and could point to details such as patience, endurance and perseverance (2 Tim 3:10).

7. Unusual providences and crisis experiences

We have seen that there is no event so significant as conversion. In the effectual call of the Father the believer is regenerated, definitively sanctified, justified and adopted. We can well understand why no further major event is commanded in the New Testament or even suggested. All the means of grace, as I have endeavoured to show, are available for the ongoing work of progressive sanctification. While that is so it is noteworthy that crises are often used to advance a Christian's experience. There is the crisis of discovery. For many, coming to an understanding of the doctrines of grace and the sovereignty of God is not a mere intellectual stride but an overwhelming spiritual experience which has far-reaching effects. Some have made a great leap forward in the Christian life through an experience in which they have had to cast themselves by faith on God. Some, like the apostle Peter, have needed restoration. That was used in a powerful way.

The Wesleyan Methodists believed it possible to attain a state of 'perfect love'. It was muddled thinking. Yet in spite of the intellectual confusion many Christians showed tremendous love and zeal which could put many lukewarm Christians in our time to shame. I mention this not to commend in any way weak teaching but only to press home a point. That is we need to lay hold of the power of the truth. It is not enough to be clear about it. We need to be enthusiastic about it.

The importance of human responsibility in progressive sanctification

We have thought in terms of organisation of the use of means employed by our Father to achieve our sanctification. The place of our responsibility stressed in Scripture requires careful attention. It is appropriate to say we are partners with God in this vital work: 'Work out your salvation with fear and trembling, for it is God who works in you to will and to act according to his good purpose' (Phil 2:12,13). Innumerable imperatives stress accountability: 'Mortify!' – 'Be transformed!' – 'Pray continually!' We will be judged for what we do, in thought, word and deed. Christians will be judged in respect of everything done in the body (1Cor 3:10-15 and 5:10). The fear of the Lord sometimes dominates as a motive but at other times love for God with strong desires to reciprocate his love in faithful and sacrificial service dominates.

Have you analysed the influences and motives used in your own experience? Would you agree that adoption, union with Christ and the indwelling of the Spirit as a relationship must have the prime position?

---

1   Thomas Watson, *A Body of Divinity*, Banner of Truth, 1980 edition, page 242.
2   John Sheffield, *Cripplegate Morning Exercises*, vol 5, page 427.

Who Is Jesus?

Who is Jesus with whom we have union by faith?

The word Jesus means Yahweh is Salvation (Matt 1:21). He is 'the divine person who made the world, who upholds and governs all things that he has made. He is the Son of God, the second Person of the Holy Trinity. He is true and eternal God, the 'brightness of the Father's glory', of the same substance (or essence) as the Father, and equal with him. It is he who, at the appointed time took upon himself the nature of man, with all its essential characteristics and its common infirmities, sin excepted. He was conceived by the Holy Spirit in the womb of the Virgin Mary, a woman who belonged to the tribe of Judah, the Holy Spirit coming down on her and the power of God Most High overshadowing her. And so, as the Scripture tells us, he was made of a woman, a descendant of Abraham and David. In this way it came about that the two whole, perfect, and distinct natures, the divine and the human, were inseparably joined together in one person, without the conversion of the one nature into the other, and without the mixing, as it were, of one nature with the other; in other words, without confusion. Thus the Son of God is now both true God and true man, yet one Christ, the only mediator between God and man.' (Matt 1:22,23; Luke 1:27,31,35; John 1:14; Rom 8:3; 9:5; Gal 4:4; 1 Tim 2:5; Heb 2:14,16,17; 4:15).

The above is cited from *A Faith to Confess*, The Baptist Confession of Faith of 1689, rewritten in modern English and published by Carey Publications.

The four negatives, 'without confusion, without change, without division, without separation' were expressed at the Council of Chalcedon (451). They are 'like light-beacons which mark off navigable water in between and warn against the dangers which threaten to the left and to the right'. This illustration comes from G C Berkouwer's book *The Work of Christ*, Eerdmans, 1965, page 129.

✤ *Chapter 5* ✤

Union with Christ

There are three realities which for wonder exceed all others in the universe. The first is the truth of the Trinity, three Persons equal in deity, each different from the others, yet one. The second is the incarnation, that the eternal Son of God should unite in his one Person manhood and deity. The third is the spiritual union of the Church with Christ.

'By the Spirit our whole person is united to his whole person.'[1] That is an amazing reality which we should firmly grasp.

What the heart is to the body, union with Christ is to the soul. Union with Christ is the foundation of all our spiritual experience. It is central to sanctification. When the wisdom of the Graeco-Roman world, superior for its quality and breadth to any other civilisation, had failed to produce an answer to the problem of sin, our sovereign Creator demonstrated his wisdom in the provision of a perfect man, Christ Jesus. By joining lost sinners to Christ the Father provided a comprehensive remedy for sinners. Paul sums this up in a sentence: 'It is because of him that you are in Christ Jesus, who has become for us wisdom from God – that is our righteousness, holiness and redemption' (1 Cor 1:30). Our justification before God, progressive sanctification and the resurrection of our bodies are achieved through union with the Son of God.

How is this great theme presented in Scripture? We will examine four analogies which convey the truth of union with Christ. The first is that of marriage which has its roots in the Old Testament. The second is that of the vine and the branches as presented by our Lord himself. The third is baptism as explained by Paul in Romans 6. The fourth analogy often used by Paul is that of the human body. There are other figures such as building stones which rest for support on the chief corner stone (Eph 2:20,21; 1 Peter 2:6-8), but the above four will be adequate for our purpose.

Each of these analogies is set before us in the Scriptures with practical applications. We must not isolate the doctrine but note the biblical emphasis concerning the effect of that truth on our lives. The Puritan writers employed the term 'uses' and would elaborate these. I will use the word 'application' for each of the four likenesses.

Marriage

The prophets Isaiah, Jeremiah, Ezekiel and Hosea employ the analogy of marriage to describe Yahweh's union with his people. 'Your Maker is your husband' (Isa 54:5). The tie of husband and wife is sacred and indissoluble. Legally the two are one. The interests of the two are the same. However the picture employed is one of unfaithful Israel. '"But like a woman unfaithful to her husband, so you have been unfaithful to me, O house of Israel," declares the LORD' (Jer 3:20). Nowhere is this likeness of marriage more strikingly portrayed than in Ezekiel 16. Jerusalem came into being by adoption from a position of utter humiliation, a newborn babe in its birth-blood thrown out into a field. Taken up and saved, this discarded, helpless child is nurtured to become a beautiful woman. She is married to Yahweh. But as the story unfolds we find that she turns to evil living and becomes a prostitute. This of course leads to a total breakdown of the marriage. Amazingly however repentance is predicted followed by reconciliation. The main lesson is the faithfulness of Yahweh. Powerfully illustrated is the factor of union in marriage. Sovereign grace is depicted throughout. Here is great comfort for sinners who feel acutely their former shame and wonder how salvation is possible. But salvation is by union with a husband who is faithful.

'Then you will remember your ways and be ashamed' (Ez 16:61).

The analogy of marriage is the theme of Ephesians 5:22-33. As husband and wife become one flesh in marriage, so the Church and Christ are declared to be one. This picture of marriage is further portrayed in Revelation, the wedding of the Lamb and his bride (19:7,8), and the Holy City, the new Jerusalem prepared as a bride (21:2). The union of the Church with Christ is a spiritual one in which every interest is united. In the Ephesians 5 passage there is a stress on the fact that the power of holiness to cleanse and beautify the Church is derived from her Head who 'gave himself up for her to make her holy, cleansing her by the washing with water through the word' (5:25,26). Stressed too is the love of Christ which does not falter. He is the Saviour of his Church in every respect not only in the redemption of the soul and body of his bride the Church, but in her temporal interests here on earth.

It follows that if we are married to Christ then we are blessed with the joy of communion with him. Are you conscious of this priceless relationship which is yours to cherish and enjoy every day? In communion we enjoy the glory of Christ's person and work. We enjoy the unchanging character of Christ's love for us, for he loves us with an incomparable love, a love we reciprocate in communion. A spiritual union of this magnitude requires daily attention.

Of commentators who have written commentaries on the whole Bible the English Puritan Matthew Henry (1662 – 1714) is the best known. He preached three sermons on daily communion with God. These were so popular that he was persuaded to publish them as a short book which has often been reprinted under the title *Directions for Daily Communion with God*. The outline used by Henry is straightforward. We are urged to begin every day in prayer (Ps 5:3). Then we are exhorted to spend the day in communion with God; 'My hope is in you all day long' (Ps 25:5). Finally we are reminded that we should conclude the day in communion with the Lord (Ps 4:8). Of course communion all day with God does not mean we can be involved in concentrated prayer all day long, but rather that we can be conscious of the felt presence of Christ with us because we practise communion. Our union with him is a wonderful privilege, enjoyment and strength, of which we partake less than we should.

The ideal in marriage is that the husband should love his wife and care for her, encouraging her in every way. Sadly this quality of marriage is seldom stressed today and rarely achieved by husbands. But in Christ the Church possesses the perfect husband. He loves us perfectly and we can rely on his faithfulness. In our trials he will never leave us or forsake us (Matt 28:20; Heb 13:5,6). Our marriage to Christ is a spiritual reality. We must draw upon that and be comforted by it to the full. This can only be done as we practise daily meditation and communion.

The vine

The picture of the vine and the branches is our Lord's own illustration of union with himself (John 15:1-8). We might think of the great vine at Hampton Court Palace in London, purportedly the largest in the world. It is several hundred years old and extends to about forty metres. Pruned back every year, it produces an enormous harvest of grapes. The roots must be extensive and since the river Thames is near we imagine that there is no shortage of moisture. Each branch produces fruit as it derives its nourishment from the trunk.

As Jesus presents this simple picture of the vine his first application is that fruitfulness is an absolute necessity. Every branch that does not produce fruit will be taken away by the Father.

His second application is that every branch will be subject to pruning by the Father. What is this pruning? In terms of progressive sanctification we think immediately of Hebrews 12:4-12, God disciplines all his children who are subject to his correction. We are reminded by this that justification and holiness of life can never be separated. You cannot have the one without the other. Justification is implied by the words of Jesus in verse three, 'You are already clean because of the word I have spoken to you.' Justification is legally conferred. Holiness is spiritually conveyed just as sap runs through the trunk of the vine to the branches,

His third application is the stress laid upon our responsibility to maintain union. 'Remain in me!' That is an imperative. Union is to be sustained. It is not to be taken for granted. Attention and care are required. It is only by maintaining this union that fruitfulness is possible. Great fruitfulness, 'Love, joy, peace, patience, kindness, goodness, faithfulness, gentleness and self control' (Gal 5:22,23), is possible through constant attention to our union with the Son of God. Jesus reminds us of the primacy of prayer and of meditation in the words of Scripture when he says, 'If you remain in me and my words remain in you, ask whatever you wish and it will be given you. This is to my Father's glory, that you bear much fruit, showing yourselves to be my disciples' (John 15:7,8).

Baptism

Paul uses this as a principal analogy to provide the theological found-ation for union with Christ. We must be careful therefore to do it justice.

We begin by noting the nature of the likeness. To baptise means to dip or to dye, to plunge into, or to immerse. Note the action involved. In spiritual baptism the action is one of moving the believer from one orbit into another. He is taken from the orbit of the world and placed into or baptised into the orbit of Christ. The prepositions in the Greek are used consistently, *eis* into, and *en* in, denoting total identification attained by the action of placing into. We can readily understand why Paul's favourite theological expression is 'in Christ'. He uses this expression many times. To be spiritually baptised into Christ is at the same time to come into union with the Father and the Holy Spirit. Hence the baptismal formula commanded by our Lord, baptising them in (*eis* into) the name of the Father and of the Son and of the Holy Spirit (Matt 28:19).

There is one spiritual baptism (Eph 4:5), namely, the joining of believers to Christ: 'For all of you who were baptised into Christ have clothed yourselves with Christ' (Gal 3:27). Romans 6:1-11 spells out the fact that we are united in our humanity with the humanity of Jesus. We are one with him in his death, burial and resurrection. The believer is identified with Christ so completely that he can say, 'I died! When Christ died on the cross that was my death. It was a dreadful death in which my Saviour bore God's wrath toward my sins! It was a death in which he died and was buried. That was my burial. Three days later he rose from the dead in resurrection glory. That was my resurrection.'

Romans 6 reminds us of the necessity of the incarnation. The only way in which we could be redeemed was for God's Son to take flesh and blood and share fully in our humanity. Thus in his death he destroyed him who holds the power of death, that is, the devil (Heb 2:14). The union we have with Jesus is a union with him as a man. In the incarnation he took manhood to himself. He possessed all the faculties of manhood in the same proportion as we do; physique, intellect, affections, conscience, will and individual personality. At the same time he never ceased to be God. He had no sin. It is to that sinless man that we are joined by faith. It is the man Christ Jesus who has taken our place. And it is Christ who will raise us from the dead as he said: 'I am the resurrection and the life. He who believes in me will live, even though he dies; and whoever lives and believes in me will never die' (John 11:25).

When a baptism is enacted the focus is on the union of that believer with Christ and the washing away of his sins (Rom 6:1-4; Col 2:12; Acts 22:16). But the primary focus is on union with Christ in his death, burial and resurrection. The believer is united to Christ in those momentous events of 2,000 years ago. Nevertheless the Christ of those events now reigns in glory and we reign with him.

A parallel which illustrates this is seen in the people of Israel. They were baptised into Moses in the cloud and the sea (1 Cor 10:2). They were united to their leader and transposed through his leadership into a new realm. They died to Egypt and were made alive in a new relationship to God. When the people passed through the Red Sea they were united as a new community to live in a new environment.

By way of summary, what exactly does Paul mean by the term 'in Christ'? First, it means complete identification of the believer with

Christ in his death, burial, resurrection and ascension, as historical events, Second, it means a complete union with Christ now as he rules the Church. To enlarge a little on the second point, we who are 'in Christ' live and reign with him now (Rev 20:1-6). We have been translated spiritually out of the old realm, 'Therefore, if anyone is in Christ, he is a new creation; the old has gone, the new has come!' (2 Cor 5:17).

In Romans 6:11-25 the idea that we can compromise with sin is firmly repudiated on the basis that we are united to the holy Son of God. Sin in every shape and form is totally incompatible with that union. We are alive in him and must count ourselves dead to the realm of sin. We must give our bodily members to God as instruments of righteousness. We are now the possession of God.

In Romans 7 Paul deals with our relationship to the law. He illustrates from his own experience the tremendous tension that exists on account of the fact that we remain in a fallen world and still have to contend with remaining sin in our bodies (designated 'flesh' in the KJV or 'sinful nature' in the NIV, see Galatians 5:16-18). In the violence of the conflict we are to be comforted by Christ's victory on our behalf and we must never allow ourselves to be moved away from the foundation of justification. There is now no condemnation for those who are in Christ Jesus (Rom 8:1).

The application of union with Christ continues in Romans 8 where we are informed of our absolute responsibility to put sin to death (8:13). That obligation is set before us in the context of life in the Holy Spirit. He, the Holy Spirit, leads us (8:14), assures us of our sonship (8:15,16) and enables us to pray (8:26,27).

This emphasis on life in the Holy Spirit in Romans 8:1-27 is reinforced by other Pauline writings. By believing in Jesus we have received the Holy Spirit (Gal 3:2). The Holy Spirit maintains our spiritual union with Christ. He works in us to transform us to the likeness of Jesus with ever increasing glory. This glory comes from the Lord by the Holy Spirit (2 Cor 3:18). The text says, 'The Lord, who is the Spirit.' In 2 Corinthians 3 Paul contrasts the old covenant with the new. This is the age of the Holy Spirit. The Spirit proceeds from the Father and from Christ to work in us the work of redemption. Jesus declared that the Spirit would live in us. He, Jesus, will come to us and will be in us (John 14:17-20). In the Trinity there is always concurrence of will and action. When Paul says, 'Now the Lord is the Spirit' (2 Cor 3:17), he is not confusing Christ with the Spirit. Rather he is pressing home the reality of the fact that the Spirit is powerfully carrying forward the work of holiness in us all based on our union with Christ.

In the new covenant the Lord puts his laws in our minds and writes them on our hearts. As God's people we are not sustained by an external code but by the Holy Spirit who as the life-giving Spirit is transforming us.

The human body

This analogy is employed three times and used in an extended way of application. In Romans 12:3-8 the point made is that all believers derive their function and gifts from union with Christ. Because all the members derive the life from the same Head they all belong to each other. Every member therefore must work in unity with the others for the common good. The dependence of the members upon each other is the emphasis in 1 Corinthians 12:12-31. Every member has been baptised into the body of Christ. He is the Head and every member derives his ability, his gifts and his directions from him, and always with the good of the body in view. The body must function as a unity which reflects the nobility and majesty of the Head. Ephesians 4:15,16 tells of our vital union with the head from whom the whole body is united, every part contributing to the building up of the whole.

The main thrust of this analogy is that unity with the head should be reflected in the unity of all the members. It is disastrous when one member says to another, 'I don't need you!' It is also injurious to the body when one member says to another, 'I am better than you!' If one church or group of churches takes a superior posture, 'We are the only ones doing God's work rightly!' or, 'We are the only ones who worship correctly!' then division is bound to follow.

If one church commends the truth of the gospel by good works, by displaying love, by consistent holy living, that must in itself glorify Christ. But as soon as a competitive spirit of pride enters in then there is division, just as there was at Corinth, one party glorying in the oratory of Apollos, another in the Jewish ruggedness of Peter, and yet another in the academic superiority of Paul. As it is ludicrous in a human body for one member to despise another or lord it over another, so it is in the body of Christ.

Commenting on 1 Corinthians 12:27-30 Don Carson says, 'In the New Testament, characteristically each local church is not a part of the whole church, but simply the church – the outcropping of the church or the exemplar of the church in any particular place. So also with Paul's language about the body. Paul does not mean that each congregation is part of the body of Christ, or a body of Christ. Each congregation, each church, *is* the body of Christ. Each local church, if I may put it this way, *is* the exemplification of the church.'[2]

The unity of the members of the Church is likened by our Lord to the unity that exists between the three Persons of the Trinity (John 17:20,21). There could not be a unity more sublime and perfect than that of the Triune God. Yet the union into which we are brought in Christ and by him with the Father and the Holy Spirit is of that order. That is truth of a superlative kind. We are to reflect on the responsibility to seek to maintain a unity of that quality with all members of the family of God. This means that we must study to avoid the impediments to that unity and seek to bring reformation in cases where abuse of church power or any other malpractice has created divisions, even if they seem to be beyond repair.

Division comes not only by quarrels and hatreds but by expressions of superiority alrcady referred to. Erroneous teaching is also responsible for major divisions. To cite Don Carson again, 'If the charismatic movement would firmly renounce, on biblical grounds, not the gift of tongues but the idea that tongues constitute a special sign of a second blessing, a very substantial part of the wall between charismatics and non-charismatics would come crashing down. Does 1 Corinthians 12 demand anything less?'[3]

The way believers are united to Christ is described in different ways.

First, this union is 'a faith union'. How do we come into union with Christ? The answer always is by faith. About fifty times we read of believing 'into' Christ (John 1:12; 3:16; 3:36; 5:24; Rom 10:14; Gal 2:16). We believe in him with a faith of obedience (Rom 1:5; 15:18; 16:26; Acts 6:7). A faith which does not result in obedience is a spurious faith. By faith we come into union with Christ and it is by faith that we continue to live for him. We are justified by faith to live a life of faith, as it is written, 'The righteous will live by faith' (Rom 1:17).

Second, this union is a gracious union. 'For he chose us in him before the creation of the world to be holy and blameless in his sight' (Eph 1:4). We have by God's glorious grace been given redemption in the One whom he loves (Eph 1:6,7). We have been blessed in the heavenly realms with every spiritual blessing in Christ (Eph 1:3). "Because of his great love for us, God, who is rich in mercy, made us alive in Christ even when we were dead in transgressions – it is by grace you have been saved. And God raised us up with Christ and seated us with him in the heavenly realms in Christ Jesus, in order that in the coming ages he might show the incomparable riches of his grace, expressed in his kindness to us in Christ Jesus' (Eph 2:4-7).

Third, this union is a spiritual union. As we have seen, this is a union sustained by the Holy Spirit (1 John 3:24).

Fourth, this union is a living union. 'Christ lives in me. The life I live in the body, I live by faith in the Son of God' (Gal 2:20). The union is vital in a living sense.

Fifth, this union is a federal (racial) union. As Adam is the head of a fallen race so Christ is the head of a new race (Rom 5:12-21). 'Through the obedience of the one man the many will be made righteous' (Rom 5:19).

Sixth, this union is a human union. We are one with the man Christ Jesus, the only mediator between God and men (1 Tim 2:5). This has been strongly asserted. Unbelievers maintain that the accounts of Jesus are myths and stories. Not so! Our union is with a real man, the risen man, Christ Jesus.

Seventh, this union is an experiential union. We are united to a 'felt Christ'. We are sensitive to his presence with us personally and sensitive to his presence in the assembly of worship, praise and prayer. We reciprocate the incomparable love that he has for us. We dread a situation in which he could say of us as he said of the Ephesians, 'Yet I hold this against you; You have forsaken your first love' (Rev 2:4). The marriage union has been stressed. You cannot have a valid marriage union without at the same time an experiential union. A missionary from Papua New Guinea described to me the communion services celebrated in a church of converted cannibals. They weep when they come to partake of the bread and wine because they feel intensely the meaning of union with the Son who saved them from a life of unspeakable cruelty. That illustrates heart experience.

Eighth, this union is a mystical or wondrous union. The term 'mystical union' can be unhelpful since it tends to give the idea of something mysterious and intangible. The word 'mystery' is used in almost every case in the New Testament to point to that which was hidden but has now been clearly revealed (Eph 1:9; Col 1:26,27). What is now revealed is 'Christ in you the hope of glory'. That is a wonderful fact.

Ninth, this union is a comprehensive union. To be united to Christ is to be united to him extensively in all he has done for us. As we have been reminded by the analogy of marriage our every interest and our every concern and our every anxiety are embraced in this union.

Tenth, this union is an indissoluble union. 'No-one can snatch them out of my hand' (John 10:28); 'Who shall separate us from the love of Christ?' (Rom 8:35). 'And so we will be with the Lord for ever' (1 Thess 4:17).

---

1   George Smeaton, *The Doctrine of the Holy Spirit*, Banner of Truth, 1961, page 207.
2   Don Carson, *Showing the Spirit*, a theological exposition of 1 Corinthians 12-14, Baker Book House, 1987, page 47ff.
3   *Ibid*, page 50.

Professor John Murray (1898-1974)

The youngest of seven John Murray was born on a croft in Badbea (in Scotland a croft is a small farm), a place so remote that you will not find it on the usual maps. In the World War 1914-18 John served in France and was wounded by shrapnel by which wound he lost one eye. Two of his brothers were killed in action. Immediately after the war he began studies which equipped him for the Christian ministry. His talents were such that he was invited to teach in the famous Princeton Seminary in the USA. That was the time of severe stress over Liberalism. After one year John Murray left Princeton to join the newly formed Westminster Seminary along with E J Young, Paul Woolley, Cornelius van Til, Ned Stonehouse and R B Kuiper. Murray laboured for 37 years as seminary professor at Westminster. He then returned to the family farm at Badbea, married and had two children. He made a vital contribution to the early growth of the Banner of Truth publishing ministry. Those who heard him preach at the Leicester Conference for ministers organised by the Banner of Truth will never forget the power and clarity of his preaching.

The Collected Writings of John Murray are available in four handsome volumes and these include a 160 page biography by Iain Murray. This biography has been published separately by the Banner. *The Collected Writings* do not include books by Prof Murray, the most noteworthy of which is his commentary on Romans which is my favourite. Professor Murray's two short crystal clear expositions on definitive sanctification appear in volume two of *The Collected Writings*. These represent a major step forward in helping us understand the distinction in the New Testament teaching between positional and progressive sanctification.

✤ Chapter 6 ✤
Positional Sanctification

In this chapter I will first of all expound the doctrine of positional sanctification and then compare that with the Holiness teaching which began with John Wesley and developed with Charles Finney and then spread widely to include a number of 'Holiness' denominations.

Whenever we speak of sanctification we think of it as a process by which believers are gradually transformed in heart, mind, will and conduct. Many texts express clearly this gradual progressive work. For instance Paul exhorts us to purify ourselves from everything that contaminates body and spirit, perfecting holiness out of reverence for God (2 Cor 7:1), and prays, 'May God himself, the God of peace, sanctify you through and through. May your whole spirit, soul and body be kept blameless at the coming of our Lord Jesus Christ' (1 Thess 5:23). Progress is seen in the exhortation of Jude, 'But you, dear friends, build yourselves up in your most holy faith and pray in the Holy Spirit' (Jude 20).

In a most helpful exposition with the title 'Definitive Sanctification' Prof John Murray observes that the most characteristic terms that refer to sanctification are used, not of progress, but of a once-for-all-definitive act.[1] Calling into union with Christ, regeneration, justification and adoption are acts of God effected once for all. These acts based on our union with Christ cannot be repeated. The idea of definitiveness is one which allows of no increase or improvement. You cannot be fifty per cent justified or fifty per cent adopted. You cannot be fifty per cent in Christ. Either you are set apart in him or you are not in him.

As we have observed, 'to sanctify' means to set apart. A saint is one who has been set apart in Christ. There are about twenty references to 'saints' in the Old Testament and about eighty in the New.[2] These are explicit references to definitive sanctification, to a single event that has taken place. For instance the believers at Corinth are addressed as 'those sanctified in Christ Jesus, called *to be* saints' (1 Cor 1:2, NJKV). The *to be* is in italics. Literally translated the text reads 'to the ones having been sanctified in Christ Jesus, called saints'. Later in the same letter Paul reminds the Corinthians that they were washed, sanctified and justified (1 Cor 6:11). This demonstrates that conversion is a stupendous event. Regeneration, definitive justification and sanctification take place in one act. When Paul refers to believers in Acts 20:32 and 26:18 he describes them as those 'having been sanctified'. The perfect passive participle conveys the idea that something decisive has taken place which has ongoing effects.

The primary passage describing definitive sanctification in the New Testament is Romans 6:1 to 7:6. Having expounded the doctrine of justification by faith, the apostle Paul turns to the subject of sanctification. In so doing he demonstrates that union with Christ simultaneously effects both justification and sanctification. The righteousness of Christ is imputed to the believer on account of union. That same union achieves new life. Positionally the believer has been placed into spiritual union with Christ. That is a definitive act. The ongoing result is a vital living union whereby the Christian possesses spiritual life and holiness. That is why it is utterly incongruous to suggest that a Christian should entertain the idea of sinning. We know that these great realities of justification and adoption are simultaneous; nevertheless if we are to think of a logical sequence (*ordo salutis*) then positional sanctification precedes justification and adoption because it would not be possible for the Father to justify the sinner unless he were first joined to Christ.

Positional sanctification is portrayed vividly in Ephesians 2:4: 'God, who is rich in mercy, made us alive with Christ even when we were dead in transgressions.' He has 'raised us up with Christ and seated us with him in the heavenly realms in Christ Jesus' (Eph 2:6). The same reality is expressed in Colossians: 'Since, then, you have been raised with Christ, set your hearts on things above, where Christ is seated at the right hand of God... For you died, and your life is now hidden with Christ in God' (Col 3:1-3).

What is the difference between positional and definitive sanctification? Positional sanctification points to union with Christ whereas definitive sanctification points to the act of God the Father in the decisive act of placing the believer into union with Christ.

The expression positional sanctification is helpful because it stresses union with Christ in the present tense. In that sense the Christian is perfectly sanctified. A believer should always be alert by faith to the fact that he is seated with Christ in the heavenly realms (Eph 2:20; Col 3:1-3). My personal preference is to stick to the term positional sanctification because that refers to my present position which cannot be improved upon. Definitive sanctification points back to when this took place initially.[3]

The Christian is perfect positionally but with regard to progressive sanctification he is subject to growth. His position is perfect but his state spiritually is subject to progress.[4] Our sanctification in Christ is perfect. We cannot be more united to him. In the positional or definitive sense it may sound odd but we can claim to be perfectly sanctified. Of course in the progressive sense we are never perfectly sanctified in this life.

Practical implications of positional sanctification

Baptism is designed to portray the momentous implications of positional sanctification. First, baptism is a burial. It is a funeral. Second, it is a resurrection.

Positional sanctification points to the fact that the believer is placed into Christ, that is, into his death, burial and resurrection (Rom 6:1-4). When a person dies he is cut off from his former world. You will not receive a letter from him. He will not telephone or email you. There is absolutely no communication. The apostle is saying that we must count ourselves dead to sin but alive to God in Christ Jesus. This means we are to have no communication with the old sphere of sin – no letters, no telephone calls, and no! not even any thoughts about that past world of sin.

Death to the old sphere is like having a new owner. Slavery was widespread in apostolic times. Death to sin could be likened to a change of ownership. When a slave was bought on the market he left his former home and went to a different home to work for his new owner. We have been bought out of the slavery of our old master the devil and now we serve our new master who is Christ.

Every effort to draw us back to Satan the old master must be resisted.

Believer's baptism includes the idea of a funeral. The old unregenerate self is buried for ever. I can never be what I was before when I served the devil and the world. Baptism is not only illustrative of a funeral, it also depicts a resurrection. It represents my new life. By union with Christ I have been raised from spiritual death. This can be illustrated by an event in the time of Elisha reported in 2 Kings 13:20,21.

'Elisha died and was buried. Now Moabite raiders used to enter the country every spring. Once while some Israelites were burying a man, suddenly they saw a band of raiders; so they threw the man's body into Elisha's tomb. When the body touched Elisha's bones the man came to life and stood up on his feet.'

Having been raised from the dead that man stood up on his feet and then had to run for his life away from the Moabite raiders. They were coming fast. It was essential to escape from them. Imagine the amazement of those Israelites as they looked behind to see the man they had buried running after them!

Yet that is exactly what happens whenever a person is joined to Christ. God places him into union with Christ's death by which Christ's merit and righteousness are put to his account. He is raised spiritually. He is a new creature in Christ. Old things have passed away and all things have become new. He now has new legs to run away from sin and run to God's people where he belongs.

It is impossible to exaggerate the importance of coming to grips with what it means to be 'in Christ', that is, to be positionally sanctified. We should note the following:

1. There can be no greater absurdity or contradiction than for one who lives in sin to claim to be a Christian.[5] To accept a person who lives in sin as though he were a Christian is like propping up a corpse and declaring it to be alive.

2. If a person claims to be repentant then we should remember the words of John the Baptist who insisted that his hearers should produce fruit in keeping with repentance. It is dishonouring to Christ when people are baptised in spite of the fact that they show no credible evidence of a living faith or repentance from a sinful life.

3. Baptism should only proceed when the realities represented are indeed realities, namely a living union with Christ.

4. The grand design of Christianity is the destruction of sin and an end to lawlessness. A whole world of sin and lawlessness is buried and left behind when a person is joined to Christ. This union is portrayed in the burial and resurrection represented by baptism.

5. The fact that Christ is alive now and forever is the guarantee that all those joined to him now will live forever. In baptism the candidate is raised out of death to walk in newness of life, that is, eternal life.

6. The only credible evidence that we are partakers of the benefits of the death and resurrection of Christ is our death to sin and our walking in newness of life.

7. The church must withdraw from and disown hypocrites who profess to believe but who discredit and dishonour Christ by their sinful lives.

8. Those who live in union with Christ, who love him and serve him, and are determined to obey his precepts, can derive the greatest possible comfort from his promises that they will never perish, but enjoy his company and the company of the redeemed forever on the new earth.

Positional sanctification and Holiness teachings

Diametrically opposite to positional sanctification is the notion that justification and sanctification are separate and come by two separate experiences. This is the idea that justification is by faith and later sanctification is received separately by faith, these being two separate gifts of God.

In this chapter I have shown that justification and positional sanctification are the bedrock upon which progressive sanctification proceeds. I have sought to show that progressive sanctification involves many disciplines and is comprehensive in nature. It is a full-time business. Once a man is set apart in Christ the good work of the Holy Spirit begins and will go on throughout one's life. It is a gross over-simplification to think that victory over sin and perfection can take place in a single post-conversion experience. This shallowness is illustrated by the newly wed young convert whose besetting sin was a bad temper. He attended a Holiness meeting where the preacher promised perfect holiness to those who would stand up and then come to the front for prayer, which act would seal the reception of the gift. The young man had no doctrinal teaching and this sounded like a wonderful bargain. He hastened home to his wife with the glad news that he was perfectly sanctified. She too had little doctrinal knowledge and was so happy with the prospect of a perfect husband that she forgot that the dinner was in the oven. It was badly burned whereupon the 'perfectly sanctified' young husband lost his temper! The young couple looked at each other in dismay. Both realised that the experience had had a very short life-span!

B B Warfield points to the fact that we can trace 'entire instantaneous sanctification' back to John Wesley. Warfield suggests 'There is no element of his (perfectionist) teaching which afforded him greater satisfaction.' John McClintock, a Methodist leader of that time, was triumphal in his boasting about perfectionist teaching: 'We are the only church in history, from the apostles' time until now, that has put forward as its very elemental thought … the holiness of the human soul, heart, mind and will.' Another leader, Olin Curtis, wrote: 'Wesley had almost the same epochal relation to the doctrinal emphasis upon holiness that Luther had to the doctrinal emphasis upon justification by faith, or that Athanasius had to the doctrinal emphasis upon the Deity of our Lord.'[6]

'In the early 1740s Wesley spelt out this "full salvation" as freedom from self-will, evil thoughts, and even from temptation itself. He later conceded that the claim was "too strong", yet he continued to insist: "Christian perfection implies deliverance from all sin."'[7]

A mighty resurgence of perfectionist teaching took place in America during the 1830s and 1840s. The name most associated with this Holiness Movement was Charles Finney. Arminianism is the soil out of which Perfectionism as a system grows. Finney was as Pelagian in his views as it is possible to be and Pelagian soil is even more fertile as soil for perfectionist teaching to grow.[8]

Oberlin College in North Ohio developed into a famous institution from which perfectionist teachings emanated. Books on Perfectionism by Finney and his colleague Asa Mahan became very popular. A fortnightly magazine *The Oberlin Evangelist* with a circulation of 5000 propagated the doctrine of Perfectionism which taught, 'There are two kinds of Christians, a lower kind who have received only justification, and a higher kind who have also received sanctification.'[9]

In his book *Views of Sanctification* Finney declared, 'Entire and permanent sanctification is attainable in this life ... It is self-evident that entire obedience to God's law is possible on the ground of natural ability. To deny this is to deny that man is able to do as well as he can.'[10]

Finney denied the doctrine of original sin. He began his ministry in the Presbyterian denomination but soon took every opportunity to oppose the Reformed teaching. He spoke and wrote against the Calvinistic tenets of the Westminster Confession of Faith. He left Presbyterianism and joined the Congregationalists. According to Iain Murray his teachings on Perfectionism were by no means original but were derived in considerable measure from Nathaniel William Taylor who was the foremost figure of the Yale Divinity School which was established in 1822. Taylor moved away from the Puritan view that insists on the bondage of the unregenerate man together with his immediate responsibility to repent and believe. Finney followed this trend and was determined 'to make regeneration so easy that men may not be discouraged from attempting to do it'.[11]

Denial of original sin led Finney to reject the whole concept of the doctrine of the bondage of the will. According to Finney the source and reason for salvation is the will of man. This exaltation of man's will has led to the statement that I heard frequently in my early Christian experience: 'There is only one thing that our omnipotent God cannot do and that is to force the will of man.' The sovereignty of God in election and effectual calling is a subject that requires careful study. To ascribe supreme power to the will of fallen man is ludicrous. The supremacy of the human will plays an important rôle in Finney's thinking. For him conversion was nothing more than the sinner's yielding to the truth and making his decision. The altar-call was to be used to induce this. Those pastors who did not employ the new measures and whose churches did not follow Finney's revivalist methods he regarded as failures.

Over the second half of the nineteenth century a landslide took place away from the old Calvinistic doctrines and practices.

Gradually real heaven-sent revivals were replaced by man-made revivalistic movements. It became the custom in some parts of the USA to advertise revivals ahead of time as though they can come by human organisation. As this system has run its course it has become patently obvious that the huge number of decisions registered are in fact just that, decisions, not regeneration.

On the back of what historically speaking can be regarded as a spiritual tsunami came a wholly different view of sanctification, namely the view that by complete surrender a life of victorious holy living could be procured immediately. The first Holiness camp meeting took place in New Jersey, USA, in 1867. The movement sometimes referred to as the 'Higher Life Movement' spread rapidly. The principal promoter of the Holiness Movement in Britain was a high-powered American Robert Pearsall Smith, a Quaker glass manufacturer from Philadelphia who wrote a book with the title *Holiness through Faith* (1870). He spoke with great effect at Oxford and Brighton in 1874 and 1875. This paved the way for Britain's annual Keswick Convention which began in 1875. My copy of Ryle's *Holiness* (fourth edition published by EP and dated 1987) has a scintillating preface by J I Packer in which he points out that Ryle in his introduction laments the pervasive influence of Pearsall Smith. This influence brought about the birth of the famous Keswick Movement. In recent times Keswick has retreated from Holiness Higher Life doctrine. According to J I Packer Smith suddenly returned to the USA in 1875. 'This was explained as due to a collapse of health (though his son later wrote that he was under threat of exposure for his esoteric habit of bestowing holy kisses upon evangelical ladies, which, understandably, had occasioned some jealousies, if no more).'[12]

Anyone exploring this subject can surf the internet and locate at least twenty 'Holiness' denominations. These include the Salvation Army and the Church of the Nazarene. Holiness teaching focuses on spiritual experience as the source of holiness. The baptism of the Holy Spirit is regarded as a second blessing after conversion and this is purported to deliver the believer from the desire to sin and take him or her to a higher plane. When this does not work then the solution is urged by way of a further crisis experience. We have to be careful not to be derogatory about spiritual experiences *per se* especially since the Bible recounts a wide diversity of them. However the fact is that the New Testament never commands, urges, prescribes, or even suggests a second special gift of sanctification experience after conversion.[13]

Positional sanctification means that once we are in Christ we must apply to ourselves all the disciplines of the Christian life and get on with the hard work of holy thinking and holy living. There are no easy short cuts or secret routes which lead to cloud nine. Holiness teachers are numerous and they vary in their emphases. They all confuse the texts about positional sanctification and interpret them, not as something already attained, but as something to be sought after, a higher life to be attained by spiritual experiences. The way to gain 'the experience' is to attend special meetings where altar-calls are made for those to come forward who are seeking 'entire sanctification'.

In the third chapter of his letter to the Philippians the apostle Paul rejects any idea of perfect holiness in this life. 'Not that I have already obtained all this, or have already been made perfect, but I press on to take hold of that for which Christ Jesus took hold of me. Brothers, I do not consider myself yet to have taken hold of it. But one thing I do: Forgetting what is behind and straining towards what is ahead I press on toward the goal to win the prize for which God has called me heavenward in Christ Jesus' (Phil 3:12-14).

In this same passage Paul declares: 'I want to know Christ and the power of his resurrection and the fellowship of sharing in his sufferings, becoming like him in his death, and so, somehow, to attain to the resurrection from the dead' (Phil 3:10-11). In Romans chapter eight and 1 Corinthians chapter fifteen Paul affirms his absolute certainty about the resurrection to come and about his own place in it. Why then does he say, 'and so, somehow, to attain to the resurrection from the dead'? Discussing this question in his commentary on Philippians Moisés Silva suggests that the most common solution is to see in the expression *ei pōs katantēsō* (if somehow I may reach), not at all a note of 'uncertainty but rather humble expectation and modest self confidence' (Müller). For Paul the life of faith was a life of perseverance requiring discipline and watchfulness. He avoided presumptuousness and complacency.

---

1   John Murray, *Collected Writings*, vol 2, Banner of Truth, 1977, page 277.
2   As we have seen the Hebrew verb *qadosh* means separate or set apart. The New Testament verb *hagiazō* means to set apart, so the adjective *hagioi* (plural of *hagios*, separated) means, when used as a noun, separated ones, saints.
3   Union with Christ simultaneously achieves both justification and positional sanctification. Justification is forensic and has to do with law. Christ alone by his active and passive obedience has merited the justification of those joined to him by faith. Progressive sanctification is never to be regarded as contributing merit toward our justification. That Christians are holy people provides evidence that their faith is genuine.
4   In the case of senility or Alzheimer's disease intellectual faculties decline. We must resist over-idealising progressive sanctification. In many lives a peak is reached and then no further growth is evident. It is comforting to know that however steep decline may be through frailty the Holy Spirit has a firm grip on his people and will never ever leave or forsake them.
5   Charles Hodge, *Commentary on Romans*, Banner of Truth, page 202.
6   B B Warfield, *Perfectionism*, P and R, 1958, page 350.
7   Iain Murray, *Wesley and the Men Who Followed*, Banner of Truth, 2003, page 235.
8   Erroll Hulse, *Who Saves, God or me?* Evangelical Press, 2008. In the chapter 'Arminianisms' I trace out the nature of Pelagianism and various forms of Arminianism.
9   B B Warfield, *Perfectionism*, P and R, 1958, page 67. This volume is a classic in which the author both describes the historical development of the 'Higher Life Movement' and analyses the doctrine of Charles Finney and Asa Mahan.
10 Keith J Hardman, *Charles Grandison Finney*, Evangelical Press, 1990, page 343.
11 Iain Murray, *Revival and Revivalism*, Banner of Truth, 1994, pages 259-261.
12 J I Packer, preface to *Holiness* by J C Ryle, Evangelical Press edition, 1987.
13 Erroll Hulse, *Crisis Experiences*, Carey Publications.

The Personality of the Holy Spirit

The Holy Spirit being the third Person of the Godhead possesses equally all the attributes of deity. He is all-knowing and all wise. He was the mastermind and immediate agent in creation. He was in total control of the creation of the universe and of this world (Gen 1:2). There is no place in which the Holy Spirit does not have immediate intelligent understanding (Ps 139:7-16).

The Holy Spirit's relationship to the Father is expressed in 1 Corinthians 2:10,11: 'The Spirit searches all things, even the deep things of God. For who among men knows the thoughts of a man except the man's spirit within him? In the same way no-one knows the thoughts of God except the Spirit of God.'

As promised by Jesus the Holy Spirit has come as Paraclete which means the one who comes alongside to comfort us (John 14:16,17). 'And I will ask the Father, and he will give you another Counsellor (*paraklētos*) to be with you for ever— the Spirit of truth. The world cannot accept him, because it neither sees him nor knows him. But you know him, for he lives with you and will be in you' (John 14:16-17). He works in the souls of sinners to convince them of their sinfulness, 'He will convict the world of guilt in regard to sin and righteousness and judgment' (John 16:8).

The personality of the Holy Spirit is seen in the way he inspired the Holy Scriptures, 'Above all, you must understand that no prophecy of Scripture came about by the prophet's own interpretation. For prophecy never had its origin in the will of man, but men spoke from God as they were carried along by the Holy Spirit' (2 Peter 1:20,21; cf 2 Tim 3:16).

The Holy Spirit teaches (Luke 12:12), he guides into truth (John 16:13), he performs miracles (Acts 2:4; 8:39), he gives gifts to believers (1 Cor 12:11), he calls missionaries into service (Acts 13:2) and he installs men as pastors of churches (Acts 20:28).

⟿ Chapter 7 ⟿

The Work of the Holy Spirit
in Our Sanctification

T he work of the Holy Spirit in sanctification follows directly
onwards from the supernatural work of regeneration. As
the new birth embraces the whole man, mind, affections
and will, so sanctification embraces that renewed soul in the whole
of his being.

The Holy Spirit indwells the believer. Jesus said, 'And I will ask the
Father, and he will give you another Counsellor to be with you
forever – the Spirit of truth. The world cannot accept him, because
it neither sees him nor knows him. But you know him, for he lives
with you and will be in you' (John 14:16,17).

The indwelling activity of the Holy Spirit is described in Romans
8:1-27 which passage of Scripture can aptly be titled, 'Life in the Spirit'.

The Person of the Holy Spirit is described as, 'the Spirit of life' (8:2),
'the Spirit of God' (8:9), 'the Spirit of Christ' (8:9), and 'the Spirit of
sonship' (8:15). As 'the Spirit of life' he initiates eternal life and then
develops it. He comes from the Father to assure believers that they
are sons and daughters by adoption together with all the privileges
that involves. He is called 'the Spirit of Christ' because he comes
from Christ to apply all the benefits of Christ's perfect and complete
work on our behalf. He who indwells believers forever cares for them
comprehensively. His work is all-embracing. By the Holy Spirit my

whole person is united to Christ and by the Holy Spirit my whole person is united to God the Father. Authors vary in the way they expound the Spirit's work. Edwin H Palmer has twelve chapters including one on the Holy Spirit and common grace.[1] A W Pink has twenty-three chapters.[2] The principal work of the indwelling Spirit can be comprehended under the following headings:

1. The Holy Spirit anoints
2. The Holy Spirit assures
3. The Holy Spirit inspires prayer
4. The Holy Spirit purifies
5. The Holy Spirit transforms

1. The Holy Spirit anoints

In the Old Testament the *anointing* that a king or priest received was symbolic of the grace of God being poured out on him to enable him to fulfil his vocation. We will see that the apostle John uses this symbol of anointing to show how all believers are enabled to understand biblical truth and live by it.

When Jesus prepared his apostles for the time of his departure he promised the coming of the Holy Spirit whom he described as 'the Spirit of Truth'. He would come and guide them into all truth (John 14:26). This understanding is given not only to the apostles but to all those in union with Christ. 'But you have an anointing from the Holy One, and all of you know the truth' (1 John 2:20). This refers to an ability to grasp the teachings of Scripture. The Holy Spirit of Truth who inspired the Scriptures applies their meaning to believers. They are all spiritually equipped to grasp the Word. Following the new birth they soon learn to live by the Word. Peter reminds us that new-born babies crave their mother's milk. He uses that illustration with regard to spiritual growth. Newborn believers must crave spiritual milk so that they can grow. The time comes when they can eat meat because they have an overall grasp of biblical teaching (Heb 5:14).

The anointing given at the new birth is an enlightenment and understanding that is given and which develops. It includes an understanding of the nature of Christ. Believers appreciate that Jesus is the God-man. This was the particular concern of the apostle John when he wrote: 'As for you, the anointing you received from him remains in you, and you do not need anyone to teach you. But as his anointing teaches you about all things and as that anointing is real, not counterfeit – just as it has taught you, remain in him' (1 John 2:27). The background to this is that there was a heresy called gnosticism. The Gnostics denied that Jesus came in the flesh. To them the flesh was intrinsically evil which it is not. The Gnostics denied the manhood of Jesus. Jehovah's Witnesses and Mormons deny the deity of Jesus. The anointing given to true Christians is an anointing of discernment. They embrace the truth that Jesus is both God and man and love that truth.

When John says, 'You do not need anyone to teach you,' he is not denying that we need preachers and teachers. We certainly do and we are grateful for them (Eph 4:11). John's reference is to the heresy of the Gnostics. We might say today that we do not need the Jehovah's Witnesses to come and teach us and confuse us with their fatally-flawed teaching. The Holy Spirit has anointed us and we are able to discern the saving doctrine of Christ.

The knowledge which the Holy Spirit imparts enlightens and at the same time humbles the believer. As we will see, the knowledge he imparts is knowledge which is transforming in its effect.

Preaching is the primary instrument in conveying and impressing biblical truth into the souls of Christians. Preaching is unique because it addresses souls in their wholeness of mind, heart and will. Its purpose is to move to dedication and motivate action. Lecturing is for the mind. At university students attend lectures in order to gather and formulate information upon which they will be examined. A proficient lecturer will be lucid and interesting and will hold the attention of his students. But it is a purely intellectual exercise. It is disappointing and distressing when those who purport to be gospel preachers simply deliver materials in the form of lectures. Our lives are changed through preaching not lectures. While there is value in well-structured teaching that is not the same as preaching with the unction of the Holy Spirit. This subject receives little attention. Iain Murray devotes a chapter to it in his book with the title *Lloyd-Jones Messenger of Grace*.[3]

2. The Holy Spirit assures

The Holy Spirit assures believers of their adoption into God's family. This is affirmed in Romans 8:16-17:

> 'For you did not receive a spirit that makes you a slave again to fear, but you received the Spirit of sonship. And by him we cry, "*Abba*, Father." The Spirit himself testifies with our spirit that we are God's children. Now if we are children, then we are heirs – heirs of God and co-heirs with Christ, if indeed we share in his sufferings in order that we may also share in his glory' (Rom 8:15-17).

There are two subjects to consider here. The first is the meaning of adoption and the second is the assurance of our adoption.

First we consider the meaning of adoption

Adoption in apostolic times usually took place in early youth or adulthood, not infancy. Under Roman law adoption was a legal act by which a man chose someone outside his family to be an heir of his inheritance. A remarkable example of adoption in those early years was the adoption by the Emperor Julius Caesar of Octavius, who became Emperor Augustus and who reigned over the Roman Empire for 41 years. Augustus is referred to by Luke (Luke 2:1). The same principle is followed in the way believers become children of God. This is through the gracious act of God the Father. Psalm 103 anticipates this reality when it declares, 'As a father has compassion on his children, so the LORD has compassion on those who fear him; for he knows how we are formed, he remembers that we are dust.' The Confession of Faith describes adoption as follows: 'They are pitied, protected, provided for, and chastened by God as by a Father. He never casts them off, but, as they remain sealed to the day of redemption, they inherit the promises as heirs of everlasting salvation.'[4] The Greek word translated adoption consists of a compound of two words, *huios* (son) and the verb *tithēmi* the placing of a son.

The privilege of adoption excites admiration and wonder, which is expressed by the apostle John: 'How great is the love the Father has lavished on us, that we should be called children of God! And that is what we are! The reason the world does not know us is that it did not know him. Dear friends, now we are children of God, and what we will be has not yet been made known. But we know that when he appears, we shall be like him, for we shall see him as he is. Everyone who has this hope in him purifies himself, just as he is pure' (1 John 3:1-3).

The nature of sons is given to us in the new birth by the Holy Spirit. The Spirit imparts assurance of our privilege as sons (Rom 8:15-17), a privilege which was described by Professor John Murray as 'the apex of redemptive grace and privilege'. He comments further and says, 'It staggers imagination because of its amazing condescension and love.'[5] The special character of adoption is expressed by John, 'Yet to all who received him, to those who believed in his name, he gave the right to become children of God – children born not of natural descent, nor of human decision or a husband's will, but born of God' (John 1:12,13).

The superlative nature of the Father's love for his children is expressed by the prophets. Isaiah assures eunuchs who are faithful that while they do not have a family of their own on earth yet they have the assurance of adoption. 'To them I will give within my temple and its walls a memorial and a name better than sons and daughters' (Isa 56:5). God's love in adoption is described by Zephaniah, 'The LORD your God is with you, he is mighty to save. He will take great delight in you, he will quiet you with his love, he will rejoice over you with singing' (Zeph 3:17).

The work of the Holy Spirit in the Old Testament era was the same in regeneration, sanctification and adoption as in the New Testament except that there was not the clarity that we have now. Those were preparatory times. Clarity and greatly increased cogency came at the time of Pentecost and thereafter.

'Adoption brings blessings into every part of a believer's life. It affects his relationship to God, to the world, to his future, to himself and to brothers and sisters in God's family.'[6] Adoption provides the Christian with enormous resources of re-assurance and comfort. The believer's relationship with the world is often a troubled one because the world does not understand believers just as the world did not accept Jesus and his teaching. Adoption gives the Christian hope. He cherishes the hope of a glorious future. Adoption affects the believer's personal life radically. In the Sermon on the Mount Jesus instructs us to how to live in our relationship to our Father. All our thinking and reasoning must be in relationship to the Father.

Special attention is devoted in Scripture to adoption and how that relates to relationships in the Christian family. There is a massive emphasis on love. The new commandment is that we should love one another (John 13:34). In his tests of assurance John places love for our brothers and sisters in Christ in the front rank. If we do not pass that test then we are deceived and can be sure that we are not children of God at all.

Second we consider the assurance of our adoption

It is one thing to be adopted and another to be assured of that. There are degrees of assurance. The best definition I have ever read of assurance comes from Thomas Brooks in his classic work with the title *Heaven on Earth*. 'Now assurance is a reflex act of a gracious soul, whereby he clearly and evidently sees himself in a gracious, blessed and happy state; it is a sensible feeling, and an experimental discerning of a man's being in a state of grace, and of his having a right to a crown of glory.'[7]

It is the work of the Holy Spirit to give this assurance which is clearly expressed when Paul writes, 'Now it is God who makes both us and you stand firm in Christ. He anointed us, set his seal of ownership on us, and put his Spirit in our hearts as a deposit, guaranteeing what is to come' (2 Cor 1:21,22).

This assurance is given directly to the soul and also indirectly so we have what we call direct assurance and inferred assurance. Direct assurance is expressed in Romans 8:16, 'The Spirit himself testifies with our spirit that we are God's children.' Also 'We know that we live in him and he in us, because he has given us of his Spirit' (1 John 4:13 *cf.* 3:24). In other words we know by the Spirit's testimony inwardly to our souls that we are God's children. Paul confirms the experience of the Holy Spirit when he writes, 'And hope does not disappoint us, because God has poured out his love into our hearts by the Holy Spirit, whom he has given us' (Rom 5:5).

John writes specifically for those who struggle with lack of direct assurance. His purpose is plain when he asserts, 'I write these things to you who believe in the name of the Son of God so that you may know that you have eternal life' (1 John 5:13). The apostle provides three ways to encourage assurance. These come in the form of three tests. First there is the doctrinal test, second the moral test and third the social test.

As we have already seen, the doctrinal test concerns faith in Christ as the God-man. Since I believe that profoundly I must surely recognise that I would never have discovered that on my own. It is because I am born again. 'Everyone who believes that Jesus is the Christ is born of God.' That saving faith is the gift of God and the work of the Spirit. Then there is the moral test. 'We know that we have come to know him if we obey his commands' (1 John 2:3).

The Holy Spirit and sealing

'He set his seal of ownership on us, and put his Spirit in our hearts as a deposit, guaranteeing what is to come' (2 Cor 1:21,22). Sealing has to do with ownership. Parcels used to have red wax melted over the cords tying them and then the seal (name) of the owner was pressed onto the red wax. When a believer is regenerated God the Father sets his seal of ownership on that person. At the same time the Holy Spirit takes up residence in that believer. The seal is seen by God and by the angels and often by believers who recognise that seal of ownership in each other. Ephesians 1:13 says, 'Having believed, you were marked in him with a seal, the promised Holy Spirit.' The Greek text has *pisteusantes esphragisthēte* 'Believing you were sealed.'[8]

3. The Holy Spirit inspires prayer

Prayer is the essence of Christian existence.[9] Prayer is the channel along which the processes of progressive sanctification proceed. Paul exhorts that prayer must be 'in the Spirit'. 'And pray in the Spirit on all occasions with all kinds of prayers and requests. With this in mind, be alert and always keep on praying for all the saints' (Eph 6:18).

Unceasingly the Holy Spirit inspires prayer in the Church. An example of this phenomenon is the widespread prayer movement that developed before the 16th-century Reformation known as the *Devotio Moderna* (*devotio* 'devotion' or 'love for God') and known also as the Brethren of the Common Life. Foremost leaders of this extraordinary movement were Gerhard Groote (1340-1384) and Florentius Radewijns (1350-1400). In small communities and among lay-people this movement became strong in the Netherlands and the Rhineland. The *Devotio Moderna* was noted for its emphasis on prayer.[10] This movement which prepared the way for the great 16th-century Reformation is a reminder of the importance of the church prayer meeting. That meeting (today it often comes in the form of a house-group) is the arena where believers learn from the prayers of others. That is how they learn to pray themselves. I remember well after conversion the first prayer meetings I attended. I trembled in fear lest I was called on to pray. A start has to be made some time and usually the first prayer is halting and brief. This way of learning to pray applies especially to those who have not had the advantage of being brought up in praying households.

Most Christians confess that maintaining prayer is difficult especially when we note the high standard set by the apostle Paul. His fervency and consistency can be seen in his prayers for Timothy. 'Night and day I constantly remember you in my prayers' (2 Tim 1:3). Paul reminds us that prayer must not only be 'in the Spirit', but it must be continual (Col 4:2; 1 Thess 5:16). This requirement of prayer is for all seasons as we see from Philippians 4:6,7: 'Do not be anxious about anything, but in everything, by prayer and petition, with thanksgiving, present your requests to God. And the peace of God, which transcends all understanding, will guard your hearts and your minds in Christ Jesus.'

The Scriptures anticipate that there will be difficulty in prayer especially in times of trial, stress, fatigue and spiritual warfare when we sometimes feel that we can barely whisper a prayer (Isa 26:16). It is at times of sufferings and groanings that the assurance of Romans 8:26-28 is wonderfully helpful: 'In the same way, the Spirit helps us in our weakness. We do not know what we ought to pray for, but the Spirit himself intercedes for us with groans that words cannot express. And he who searches our hearts knows the mind of the Spirit, because the Spirit intercedes for the saints in accordance with God's will.'

'The children of God have two divine intercessors. Christ is their intercessor in the court of heaven (*cf* Rom 8:34; Heb 7:25; 1 John 2:1). The Holy Spirit is the intercessor in the theatre of their own hearts (*cf* John 14:15-17). Too seldom has the intercessory activity of the Holy Spirit been taken into account. The glory of Christ's intercession should not be allowed to place the Spirit's intercession in eclipse.'[11] The groanings described in Romans 8:26 are the groanings of which the Holy Spirit is the author. They are not articulated but they have very real meaning. Martin E Leckebusch has composed an excellent hymn expressing the work of the Holy Spirit in prayer. The concluding verse reads:

> Holy Spirit, you will be
> One who intercedes for me!
> You alone can understand

> What the mind of God has planned:
> And within his will you lead
> All for whom you intercede.[12]

When low and feeling prayerless how, to use the metaphor of flight, do we get off the ground? The method I use is to recall the way our Lord taught his disciples to pray, saying, 'Our Father in heaven, hallowed be your name' (Matt 6:9-13). That immediately reminds me of my relationship of adoption with the Father, my union with Christ and my union with the Holy Spirit by indwelling. I then express gratitude for that and remind myself of the nature of such an amazing privilege. Remembering the necessity of reverence, humility and confession of sin, I then launch out from there into the exercises of prayer which I daily set for myself. This is normal for all believers but we are not always successful. There are distractions which have to be resisted. Prayer takes energy and for myself I rest in prayer when tired rather than wrestle.

Every Christian has to find his or her own way in the life of prayer and practise disciplines and patterns which are beneficial. We need constantly to be sensitive to the inward call to prayer. When prompted we must respond. When the Holy Spirit is poured out freely in grace and supplications we must make the most of that. When farmers reap their crops they intensify their activity of reaping before adverse weather hinders them. When the Spirit is poured out believers should maximise the opportunity for intercession (Zech 12:10). The gift of being able to lead a congregration to the throne of grace and heavenly courts is rare today. May the Holy Spirit who sustains all the Lord's people also be generous in supplying the gift of public prayer to the churches.

4. The Holy Spirit purifies

The cleansing from sin or purification of believers is achieved through the mortification of sin which is essential. Chapter nine is devoted to this theme.

5. The Holy Spirit transforms

This reality is described by Paul when he writes, 'And we, who with unveiled faces all reflect the Lord's glory, are being transformed into his likeness with ever-increasing glory, which comes from the Lord, who is the Spirit' (2 Cor 3:18). Chapter ten expounds this important subject.

1   Edwin H Palmer, *The Holy Spirit, His Person and Work*, P and R, 1974.

2   A W Pink, *The Holy Spirit*, Baker Book House, 1970.

3   Iain Murray, *Lloyd-Jones, Messenger of Grace*, Banner of Truth, 274 page hardback, 2008.

4   *A Faith to Confess*, The Baptist Confession of Faith of 1689, chapter 12, Carey Publications, distributed by Evangelical Press.

5   John Murray, *Redemption Accomplished and Applied*, Banner of Truth, page 134.

6   Joel Beeke, *The Epistles of John*, Evangelical Press, page 114.

7   Thomas Brooks, *Heaven on Earth*, Banner of Truth paperback, page 14.

8   The aorist participle with the aorist verb indicates contemporaneous action. A similar construction is *apokritheis eipen* (Matt 19:4) 'he answering said', and *ēgeiren autēn kratēsas* 'taking hold of her hand he raised her' (Mark 1:31).

9   Don Garlington, *Calvin's Doctrine of Prayer*, Banner of Truth magazine, issue 323-324.

10 Betty I Knott, Introduction to *The Imitation of Christ* by Thomas à Kempis, Collins paperback, 1963.

11 John Murray, *Romans*, Eerdmans, page 312.

12 PRAISE! 604

Regeneration

Kirk Wellum, Principal of the Toronto Baptist Seminary writes as follows:

'It has been said that the Church is only a generation away from extinction.' In other words, unless the Church is constantly renewed by the power of God it will cease to exist in the world. This need for ongoing renewal is due to the fact that the true Church is composed of regenerate Christians who have been born again by the saving power of God. The regenerate nature of the Church means that the Church must be reborn in each generation or it will become extinct with the eventual passing of Christians from this world into the next.

'Churches that live beyond the spiritual experience of their members only do so as organisations. Unless God continually renews local congregations it is only a matter of time until they cease to be churches in the New Testament sense as "outposts of heaven". There may be services of Sunday, mid-week prayer meetings, Bible studies and other gatherings throughout the week but no real spiritual life.

'Budgets may be met, missionaries supported, weddings and funerals conducted and all the outward trappings of church be in place but unless God is pleased to add new believers to the church and unless he regenerates our children and grandchildren, our days are numbered as a local expression of the body of Christ. It does not matter how well organised we are, or what degree of blessing we have known in the past, if we are to continue we need God to move among us in regenerating power and grace today.'

To be sure these observations are designed to move us to be faithful in using the means of grace especially prayer and preaching and look to the Lord to honour his own Name and glory in the building up of his Church by regenerating sinners.

Chapter 8

The New Birth

John Owen wrote a masterful treatise on the Person and Work of the Holy Spirit which forms volume three of the sixteen volume set of his Works published by the Banner of Truth. In it Owen provides this outstanding definition of sanctification.

> 'Sanctification is an immediate work of the Spirit of God on the souls of believers, purifying them and cleansing their natures from the pollution and uncleanness of sin, renewing in them the image of God, and thereby enabling them, from a spiritual and habitual principle of grace, to yield obedience unto God, according unto the tenor and terms of the new covenant, by virtue of the life and death of Jesus Christ. Or more briefly: It is the universal renovation of our natures by the Holy Spirit into the image of God, through Jesus Christ.'[1]

Regeneration, the new birth, is instantaneous. It is complete and not capable of degrees whereas sanctification is progressive. Growing in grace and in knowledge is what sanctification is all about. It is vital to keep these differences in mind. It is important to observe that the whole person is affected in regeneration, mind, affections, conscience and will. All is changed in the new birth. The mind of enmity to God is changed to love for God. The whole nature is renewed in regeneration. From that moment the work of progressive sanctification begins. As the whole nature was affected in the new birth so now in progressive sanctification the whole nature is affected.

So widespread is confusion about the new birth that I will expound that fully in this chapter and then in the next continue with the theme of the work of the Holy Spirit as he works in a regenerate person in the whole of his nature.

So what is the new birth? Let us go back to what Jesus taught about this as he did on a memorable occasion when he was visited by Nicodemus, a member of the ruling class of seventy Jews known as the Sanhedrin.

It is generally accepted that Nicodemus made his visit when it was dark at night because he did not want to be seen visiting Jesus. When he knocked on the door that night he did not know he was making history. The apostle John tells of this in his Gospel chapter three.

The first sentence from the lips of the Master directed to Nicodemus concerned the absolute necessity of the new birth. 'I tell you the truth, unless a man is born again, he cannot see the kingdom of God' (John 3:3).

To put the scene in a modern context, imagine any well-known bishop coming to Jesus to discuss his miracles, to be told within sixty seconds, 'You must be born again!' The comparison is worth pondering because today well-known bishops are often involved in politics and church affairs and never seem to mention the paramount need of the new birth. Nicodemus represented the Pharisees who sought to establish their own righteousness in the place of the righteousness provided by God (Rom 10:1-4).

It is impressive that Jesus used a double emphasis when he said, 'Truly, truly, I say to you!' which is the way the ESV translates the Greek *amēn amēn*. Amen so let it be is an emphasis. Jesus is recorded as repeating *amēn amēn* three times to Nicodemus, twice in asserting the necessity of regeneration (verse 3 and verse 5), and then in stressing the fact that the ruling class to which Nicodemus belonged did not receive the apostolic testimony that Jesus is the Son of God (verse 11). The 'you' of verses 7 and 12 is plural pointing to the Sanhedrin. Note that Jesus talks about 'our testimony' which suggests the presence of disciples. 'Our testimony' reminds us of the words of John in the opening verses of his first letter, 'The life appeared; we have seen it and testify to it, and we proclaim to you the eternal life, which was with the Father and has appeared to us.' The 'you' and 'us' in John 3 contrast those who receive Christ and those who do not. 'His own people received him not. But to all who received him, who believed in his name, he gave power to become children of God; who were born, not of blood nor of the will of the flesh nor of the will of man, but of God' (John 1:11b-13 RSV). The reason behind believing and receiving is the new birth.

Three main features stand out in John 3:1-19.

First, there is the necessity of the new birth, immediately asserted, like a bolt of lightning. Nicodemus was astounded. Hence Jesus said to him, 'Don't marvel that I say to you, you must be born again!' (verses 1-11).

Second, the incarnation is presented in vivid fashion. No one has ever ascended to heaven to be equal with God and so be able to tell the world what to do. Lucifer attempted that but was cast down (Isa 14:13 ff). The only one ever to come from the dominion of God to men is the Son of Man. He descended from heaven only to be raised up, not to heaven, but as the sacrifice for sin, a stark silhouette against the sky, the God-man nailed to a cross! (verses 13 and 14).

Third, the way of salvation is by faith. Nothing can be done to contribute to new birth. But there is a work to do. Faith is that work. Believing is the way set before Nicodemus. With regard to merit, faith is not a work for it is only the instrument by which we receive Christ and his righteousness. With regard to activity, faith is a work because it involves hearing, thinking, digesting, meditating, reflecting, discussing, reading and possibly agonising.

Verse five says the most about regeneration, 'I tell you the truth, no one can enter the kingdom of God unless he is born of water and the Spirit. Flesh gives birth to flesh, but the Spirit gives birth to spirit. You should not be surprised at my saying, "You must be born again." What is it to be born again? Why of the Spirit? And why of water?

1. What is it to be born again?

First it is needful to appreciate the concept of birth referred to. Nicodemus was baffled by the idea. Jesus however was saying that just as natural birth brings a soul into the world for the first time so one born spiritually enters the world of the kingdom for the first time. Natural birth never ceases to amaze those who witness it. When an infant enters this world he sees and hears and feels and cries. Before him is the whole process of growing into the world with its different spheres of experience and responsibility: language, education, work, culture, home-life, friends, music, politics, joys, dangers and pains. Into this complex world a new person is born and will now have to make his or her way.

The parallel is the same for the kingdom of God. The soul that is born again of the Spirit is given a whole new life. He now sees what he was blind to before. The spiritual realm to which he was formerly indifferent now surrounds him. New affections fill his soul, new ambitions take hold of his mind. There is a complete readjustment of values and a total change in his appraisal of people. In short he has been born into a new world. He is now a citizen of the kingdom which is destined to overcome all other kingdoms and endure forever. His mind now comprehends spiritual realities in a personal way which relates to himself (see verse 12). Especially does he appreciate the miracle of the incarnation (see verse 13), and the atonement (see verse 14).

The new birth consists of the spiritual renewal of the whole person, affections, mind and will. Especially is there illumination, the opening of the eyes. How do you explain the colours of a rainbow to one who is blind? How do you explain the difference between purple and red and yellow? The issue is one for sight, not words.

Essentially the new birth is brought about by union with Christ. The first experience of that union is illumination by which we know the one with whom we are united. We know him as human and divine, yet one person (1 John 5:1). To illustrate the matter I refer to two very close friends, One is Chinese and has come from the heartland of China. The other is a black man from Africa. Each has unique character qualities which I seldom see in Europeans. Each is absolutely unique in personality. Now if I desired with all my heart to be Chinese and thereby possess qualities I do not have what could be done about becoming Chinese? I could change my dress and learn the language but I could never get those distinctive qualities of character and nor would I ever look like anything else but a European. Only being born all over again would suffice. Or say I wanted to be like my black friend and wished with all my heart to be able to sing like he does and speak Zulu like he does. What could be done? Even given the longevity of Methuselah I could not change my skin or my voice, or eyes, or my facial features, or my character. There is no other way. I would need to be born again.

The parallel holds with spiritual new birth. It is a work of exceeding great wisdom and might which is compared to the raising of Christ from the dead (Eph 1:20). When Jesus was raised from the dead additional properties were added and interwoven with his humanity. He is the firstborn from the dead (Rom 8:29). The promise is that we will all be made like him (1 Cor 15:49). In declaring new birth to be from God James says we are the firstfruits (Jas 1:18). We should note that we are firstfruits of a coming cosmic regeneration which will be instantaneous and universal, not by a natural process but by a supernatural act of creation (cf. Rom 8:23; Matt 19:28; 2 Peter 3: 10-13 with Col 3:10; Eph 2:10; 2 Cor 5:17).

2. Why born of the Spirit?

The wind blows wherever it pleases. You hear its sound, but you cannot tell where it comes from or where it is going. So it is with everyone born of the Spirit. There can be no doubt that the sovereignty of the Holy Spirit is mainly in view here together with the mysterious way in which he works, mysterious because we can clearly observe the effects but we cannot see that energy causing the effects. That energy is invisible. We see the trees moving but we cannot see the power that moves them. However, there is more in this reference to the wind than the sovereign will of the Holy Spirit and the mystery of his might to work where he wills, when he wills, and with what power he wills.

The terms used take us back to Ezekiel 37, the description of the valley of dry bones and the spiritual rebirth of the captive people of Israel. In Hebrew the word for spirit is *ruah* and is the same as wind or breath. 'I will make breath (*ruah*) enter you, and you will come to life' (Ez 37:5). The words 'Spirit', 'breath' and 'wind' are synonymous. The Holy Spirit can be prayed to because he is God the Spirit (Ez 37:9,10). He it is that quickens the dead bones and brings them together. He raises them up to be a living, mighty army. Consider the stupendous wisdom and power involved in not only reconstructing the dead bones correctly but the creative power in making all the internal organs, sinews and muscles, eyes and ears, whole perfect bodies, yet inanimate for they must be made to breathe and live. The purpose of the vision was to illustrate the tremendous power of the Holy Spirit in raising the Babylonian captives to spiritual life and then taking them back to the promised land. However it is impossible not to be reminded by the passage of the literal resurrection of our bodies in the great day when the trumpet will sound. The Holy Spirit who commences his good work in us will complete it in that great day (Phil 1:6).

Jesus asserts the sovereign omnipotence of God the Holy Spirit, who is like the wind which moves in a way totally beyond the control of human beings. Like the wind he is sometimes like a gentle breeze, but at other times he is a mighty wind of revival. At Pentecost he came audibly. 'Suddenly a sound like the blowing of a violent wind came from heaven and filled the whole house where they were sitting' (Acts 2:2). When he is about to regenerate a multitude he comes first to prepare the way with teaching. The same Spirit who raises dead souls to life first creates the praying and preaching conditions conducive to his work. This is characteristic of all the revivals in the history of the Church.

3. Why born of water?

What did this reference to water mean to Nicodemus? He was an expert in Mosaic rites and ceremonies. He would be familiar with the washing of bodies to represent the need for cleansing since the Jews regularly practised bodily ablutions or immersions known as Mikvah. Nicodemus would know about John the Baptist and his baptismal practice to symbolise repentance and the washing away of sins. But all the water in the world and all the washing in the world cannot regenerate. Scathingly Jeremiah reminded the Jews of his day that even if they added soda and used an abundance of soap, the stain of their guilt would remain (Jer 2:22).

Baptists of many denominations practise immersion for baptism but they use the water exclusively as a portrayal for burial and for the washing away of sin (Acts 22:16). They employ water only after a credible testimony of faith has been given. The idea that the water itself regenerates is repugnant to them. The Holy Spirit alone is the regenerator. The whole idea of referring to the wind is designed to show that there is no way that the Spirit is tied to human means. Such a notion is hostile to the teaching of our Lord. Water can only be used as a teaching symbol and we should not even begin to think that the Holy Spirit is tied to or restricted by human actions.

So what is this water that regenerates? What did it convey to Nicodemus? There was a water quite apart and quite different from the waters used for washings such as the water used to fill the great laver or bath of the temple for the priests to wash in (2 Ch 4:1-6). The water not used for washing or bathing purposes was the ceremonial water. This water was mixed with the ashes of the red heifer sacrificed annually and kept specially for sprinkling to symbolise cleansing from uncleanness. It was called 'the water of cleansing for purification from sin' (Num 19:9).

The details of this ceremonial water are provided in Numbers 19:1-10. A red heifer was sacrificed and made a whole burnt offering. The ashes were then to be taken and mixed with water to be used for sprinkling. It is never easy to interpret details with regard to the different sacrifices and it is unwise to be dogmatic. However I would suggest that while at least five different sacrifices are described in the opening chapters of Leviticus, we have in the whole burnt offering of the red heifer a kind of summary of all the sacrifices. This was not a male but a female carefully chosen, quite different from all the other animals of sacrifice. There was an emphasis on the fact that the whole sacrifice was consumed in the fire. Even the cedar wood, hyssop and scarlet wool were thrown on the burning heifer. We see a type of Christ our sacrifice offered once and for all for our sins. The once-for-all satisfaction rendered by Christ is stressed in Hebrews 9:11-14, 9:26-28 and 10:11-18. The ashes of the heifer sprinkled on those who are unclean are referred to in the first of those passages namely Hebrews 9:13.

In Hebrews 10:14 the doctrines of the new birth and the atonement are brought together. We read that 'by one sacrifice that he has made perfect forever those who are being made holy', which declaration is followed by a description of the new birth which lies at the heart of the new covenant (Heb 10:15-18).

The conclusion to which I come is that the water of regeneration referred to is the water of sprinkling which is applied by God. In the Old Testament parallel describing regeneration and the wind, namely Ezekiel 36 and 37, we read:

> 'I will sprinkle clean water on you, and you will be clean…I will give you a new heart and put a new spirit in you' (Ez 36:25,26).

It is vital that we note this sprinkling is the act of God, not man. 'I will sprinkle!' Not you! '*I will* sprinkle clean water on you, *I will* cleanse you, *I will* give you a new heart' (Ez 36:25ff, italics mine).

Especially we should note that the cleansing is simultaneous with regeneration because at the same time he says, 'I will give you a new heart and put a new spirit in you' (Ez 36:26).

On what basis does the Holy Spirit regenerate the polluted guilty sinner? The answer is that he proceeds to work on the grounds of the only acceptable sacrifice made once and for all by the Lamb of God. The ashes of the heifer mixed with water symbolise the meritorious cause of the new birth. The ashes of the once-for-all sacrifice represent all the merits of Christ applied to us. This reasoning is in line with the central teaching of the New Testament that our salvation is by virtue of union with Christ in his death, burial and resurrection (Rom 6:1-10). It is through union with Christ that we are born again. Through the powerful work of the Spirit that union takes place.

Helpfully George Smeaton in his book *The Doctrine of the Holy Spirit* suggests that the water referred to, containing the ashes of the red heifer, points to the meritorious cause of the new birth while the spirit referred to refers to the efficient cause of the new birth.[2]

Viewing John 3:5 then, I would suggest that to be born of the Spirit is a reference to the effective cause of regeneration while the reference to the water is a reference to the meritorious cause of regeneration. The new birth does not take place arbitrarily. The reason behind it is the sacrifice which is applied by God himself. In the sprinkling upon the guilty sinner of the ashes of the perfect sacrifice mixed with water, his guilt is removed. The foundation is established for his justification which is declared by God the Father (Rom 8:33).

It is important to be clear about the water because confusion has reigned when water has been taken to mean the literal means of regeneration. In another way confusion has prevailed when regeneration has been regarded as having its source in the human will. When the truth is overthrown in a violent way we call it heresy. Let us look now at two major prevalent heresies.

The heresy of baptismal regeneration

Failure to appreciate that the sprinkling of the ashes mixed with the water is administered in the spiritual sense only by God according to his own sovereign purpose and timing, has resulted in the most appalling muddle. From the time of Augustine the water of John 3:5 has been taken to refer to baptism which has led to the doctrine of baptismal regeneration. J C Ryle (1816-1900) bishop of Liverpool was an exceptional bishop in the Church of England. He emphatically preached the necessity of the new birth. J C Ryle wrote commentaries on the Gospels. In his comments on John chapter three he rejects the idea that the water referred to in verse 5 is a reference to baptism. He lists several scholars who do the same. I will now make a brief survey of the confusion that has developed. This is important. I will be as brief as possible.

The Roman Catholic Church has developed a complicated ceremony in which salt and oil are used and when eventually the baby is baptised the claim is made that regeneration has taken place in the moment of the action of the water contacting the baby. This in Latin is called *ex opere operato,* which means in the action the operation takes place.

Now if we reflect on this the reality is that the Roman Catholic Church in the form of its clergy has taken the place of the Holy Spirit. This dogma usurps the sovereignty of the Spirit taught by Jesus in John chapter three. Not only so it also leads to the absurdity of confining regeneration to all those who have received the Roman rite. This excludes all the rest of us who have not received the rite! This rite also infers that all the babies so sprinkled are regenerate. But we only have to visit prisons to discover that a high proportion of the inmates are Roman Catholics who show not the slightest evidence of spiritual rebirth.

C H Spurgeon exposing the similar doctrine of baptismal regeneration espoused by Anglo-Catholics points to the drunkard reeling down the street, the pest of the neighbourhood, worse than a brute, on his way home to beat his wife. Regenerate indeed!

By the sixth century the Greek Orthodox Church reached a form for their baptismal service which has continued to the present. Included in the service is the consecration of the water three times, the priest breathing upon the water and making the sign of the cross three times over it as he prays that it will become the water of the washing of rebirth. The candidates are then immersed after which they are robed in white clothing, The priest then gives thanks in prayer to God 'who even at this moment hast been pleased to give new birth to these thy servants'.

According to the Anglican Book of Common Prayer which appeared in 1552 the baptism of infants was to be by immersion, after which the priest was to thank God for having been pleased 'to regenerate this infant with your Holy Spirit, to receive him for your own child by adoption, and to incorporate him into your holy congregation'. If infants are sickly then sprinkling can take the place of immersion. This means that 99.9 percent of infants in England have been judged as sickly!

Luther's second baptismal liturgy came to be widely used in Germany. The form of service which included a prayer of exorcism to drive out the unclean spirit from the infant concluded with the godparents holding the baby up in the font, the minister putting a white robe on the child and saying, 'The almighty God and Father of our Lord Jesus Christ, who has regenerated you by water and the Holy Spirit, strengthen you' etc.

John Calvin in his commentary denies that Jesus is referring to baptism in John 3:5. The Presbyterian constituency has avoided the heresy of baptismal regeneration and viewed the water of baptism as a sign. Presbyterians have thought in terms of the promise of regeneration to come later. They base this upon the covenant of grace and the fact that God deals with families. Reformed Baptists accord with covenant teaching but confine the sign and seal of baptism only to those who show evidence of having been brought into the new covenant by regeneration.

The heresy of decisional regeneration

The idea that a man is regenerated when he makes a decision for Christ has invaded the Southern Baptist Convention of America, regarded by some as the largest evangelical denomination in the world. This idea predominates. In most SBC churches the altar call is regarded as essential because it epitomises the notion that coming to the front to make a decision is the way of the new birth. In my book 'The Great Invitation' I describe the history and development of the invitation system.[3] In some churches this system has become what I have suggested is the new evangelical sacrament. Those who practise this do so with the idea that regeneration can be produced simply by using the right methods.

Professor Tom Nettles who teaches Church History at Southern Seminary, Louisville, Kentucky, grew up in the SBC. As a child he walked the aisle almost every Lord's Day. One day his father said to him, 'Son, you don't have to go up to the front every Sunday!' This is apt because it points to the fact that you can only be born again once. You cannot be born over and over again every Sunday by going to the front in response to the altar call.

The heresy of decisional regeneration is now prevalent. According to those who practise this method the Holy Spirit is the servant of the will of man. Only when man decides can the Holy Spirit give the new birth. This contradicts the teaching of Paul in Ephesians 2:1-10 that man is dead in sin. The heresy is that the will of man is sovereign and that the Holy Spirit strives with the sinner but cannot regenerate until that sinner decides for God. This turns our Lord's teaching upside down so that man is the author of his own new birth. This has deceived millions who have never been humbled for their sins, have never repented, have never turned from their sins, but have presumed themselves to be born again on account of a mere one-time decision.

As with most heresies truth is mixed with error. It is true that the Holy Spirit strives with sinners. He does 'convince the world of sin and righteousness and judgment' (John 16:8-11). The work of the Holy Spirit does not stop short with preparation. He accomplishes his work of regeneration when he is ready. In that, as our Lord makes plain, he is sovereign as the wind. Men can catch the wind as with sailing ships or windmills but they cannot create wind or control it.

In decisional regeneration original sin is denied. In the fall man became utterly indisposed and disabled with regard to spiritual issues. The sinner is corrupt in his affections. His affections govern his will. He will not obey because he has no heart to obey. It will be helpful now to define the new birth and relate it to other aspects of salvation and in this way make the teaching more clear.

The new birth defined and related to other aspects of salvation

Regeneration is a supernatural work of the Holy Spirit in which there is wrought an instantaneous change of disposition in the sinner. This spiritual birth is of the whole person bringing illumination or spiritual sight to the mind to embrace Jesus as the Son of God. It consists especially in a change of heart whereby the affections are transformed to love God and his people. The law of God and a divine nature are established in the heart. This new disposition enables the born again soul to live in a loving relationship with God.

The new birth takes place as the Holy Spirit applies the truths of Scripture to the conscience. Hence Peter and James speak of being born according to the Word of truth (1 Peter 1:23 and James 1:18). Sinners never come of themselves but must be drawn. There is a preparation by the Spirit prior to regeneration in which knowledge is imparted by the means of grace.

The actual change is by an act of power within the soul. Hence most are not able to pinpoint the precise time although they may discern the hour, or day or week. Some have no idea at all of the time but nevertheless evidence in their lives the fruit of the new birth. The Holy Spirit can regenerate infants or anyone else without the use of means as we see from John the Baptist who was filled with the Holy Spirit from his mother's womb. Yet we must be careful to avoid the idea that the Holy Spirit will work without the gospel. The Savoy Declaration of the Congregationalists of 1658, based on the Westminster Confession, added a whole chapter with the purpose of thwarting the assumption that God will save people apart from the gospel and preaching. That same chapter became chapter twenty of the Baptist Confession of Faith of 1689.

In the 1689 Confession chapter ten the new birth is referred to under effectual calling in which 'God takes away their heart of stone and gives them a heart of flesh'. It is through the new birth that faith is created which unites the soul to Christ. The same new birth results in repentance whereby the sinner turns from his ungodly and unrighteous ways.

Upon the basis of that union with Christ by faith justification and adoption follow. The same Holy Spirit who gives new birth indwells the regenerate to enable them to be children of God (John 1:12,13; Rom 8:15,16; Gal 4:6). While regeneration refers exclusively to the Spirit's work the term conversion is used to describe what we experience when we are turned around to repent and believe the gospel.

By union with Christ believers are set apart in an initial act of definitive sanctification. Upon that foundation there follows the work of progressive sanctification whereby through the renewing of their minds sinners are more and more conformed to the image of Christ (Rom 12:1ff; 8:29; 2 Cor 3:18 and 7:1). The mighty work of regeneration which marks the initiation of progressive sanctification in believers is ultimately consummated in the glorification of their bodies in the great day of resurrection (Phil 1:6).

All those born again are equally regenerate although some make more rapid progress in holiness of life than others. It is important to realise that every redeemed person, from Abel to Abraham to David to Malachi, all the redeemed in the Old Testament up to the time of Pentecost were regenerated. Not one person will be in the new world we call heaven without having the nature of heaven. The difference between the Old Testament (the book of promise) and the New Testament (the book of fulfilment) is that that which was obscure has now become clear and more powerful.

Have you been born of water and the Spirit?

Have you been born again? Your response may be that you have not. You may, like Nicodemus, ask how you can be born again. It is beyond our scope to say how the Holy Spirit in a moment creates spiritual life in the soul of a sinner, but we can know the way in which Jesus guided Nicodemus. That was a crucial time for Nicodemus for we observe that he did come to believe. This is evident from his courageous action reported in John 19:39.

We see that the instruction of Jesus was designed to make a twofold impact on Nicodemus. First there was the destruction of his self-righteousness, and second, there was the priority of faith, believing in God's provision of atonement.

First, if as Jesus said, the new birth belongs entirely to the realm of the Spirit, does that not leave all unregenerate people in a state of utter helplessness? In our fallen state we are hopeless. We have no power at all to regenerate ourselves. Yet it is intolerable to live with the prospect of eternal ruin and misery.

A great favour was done to Nicodemus in showing him that so long as his religion bolstered his self-righteousness it was useless. His false hopes were killed stone dead so that now he might look to the true and only source of salvation.

Hence it is not surprising that the way of salvation is set before him in the clearest way. Nicodemus was urged to come to the light of truth. Like the Israelites in the wilderness he was to look away from himself and look up to God's provision of healing. He was to concentrate on believing. 'Whoever believes in him shall not perish but have eternal life' (John 3:16).

The truths of God's sovereignty and human responsibility are placed side by side. First Nicodemus is assured that the new birth can come only by the will of God. But then he is pointed to his own responsibility and urged to look only to the sacrifice and to believe. Further on in John's Gospel we read, 'All that the Father gives me will come to me, and whoever comes to me I will never drive away' (John 6:37). Here again is sovereignty alongside human responsibility. I am responsible to go to him. If I go to him he will not drive me away. Similarly when we read Romans 9 we are humbled by the absolute sovereignty of God in salvation, yet immediately, lest we despair, we find exhortations to believe in chapter ten. We are called to put the promise to the test: 'The same Lord is Lord of all and richly blesses all who call on him, for Everyone who calls on the name of the Lord will be saved' (10:12,13).

Have you been born of the Spirit? Have you been cleansed once and for all by the atoning work of Christ? Your response may be that you hope so but you are not sure. You may say that you believe. You do look to the Cross alone for salvation. Yet you are not at all sure that you are born again. You may ask how you can be sure.

The apostle John helps answer your question for in his first letter he describes the signs of the new birth, three signs or tests, doctrinal, moral and social. The regenerate person believes that Jesus is the Son of God (1 John 5:1). He loves sincerely the spiritual family (1 John 3:10; 3:14-17; 4:11-21; and 5:1). At the same time he lives a holy life (1 John 2:28-3:3; 3:7-10; and 5:18). A holy life is the essential characteristic of a true Christian.

---

1   John Owen, *Works*, vol 3, page 386.
2   George Smeaton, *The Doctrine of the Holy Spirit*, Banner of Truth, 1961, page 171.
3   Erroll Hulse, *The Great Invitation, Examining the use of the altar call in evangelism*, Audubon Press, 182 pages, 2004.

John Owen on the Mortification of Sin

For those new to this subject I commend highly a book written by Richard Morley. He has used the title *The Enemy Within* and sub-title *Straight talk about the power and defeat of sin*. This work is firmly based on Owen's *The Mortification of Sin*. It is published as a 150 page paperback by P and R, USA.

The Banner of Truth abridged and paraphrased paperback version of *The Mortification of Sin* by John Owen runs to 130 pages and is highly commended.

A new edition of three works by John Owen has been published consisting of *The Mortification of Sin*, *On Temptation* and *On Indwelling Sin in Believers*. The section *The Mortification of Sin* is fairly short comprising about 90 pages. These were published between 1656 and 1668. The title given to this work is *Overcoming Sin and Temptation*. It is edited by Kelly M Kapic and Justin Taylor, and is published by Crossway Books, 452 pages paperback, 2006.

The work by Kapic and Taylor is not a modern English version, an abridgement or a simplified version of the original works of Owen. Rather, it is a new edition of Owen with various features to help the modern reader to digest and understand Owen. These features include: clearer chapter divisions, highlighting of important points, overviews of each work, footnotes explaining obsolete words, a glossary of obsolete words, and outlines of each work. The English is partly modernised with regard to 'thee and thine', 'hath and wast' etc.

Chapter 9

Holiness and the Mortification of Sin

No statement on the subject of mortification is clearer than that by Paul in Romans.

> *For if you live according to the sinful nature, you will die; but if by the Spirit you put to death the misdeeds of the body, you will live* (Rom 8:13).

This can be divided as follows:

1. The duty prescribed: *to mortify the misdeeds of the body*.
2. It is by believers: *by the Spirit you put to death*.
3. Mortification is a matter of life or death: *you will die,… you will live*.

To mortify can be defined as 'to put to death or crucify any living thing or principle, to take away its strength so that it cannot act according to its nature', or, 'to mortify is to extinguish and destroy all that force and vigour of corrupted nature which inclines to earthly, carnal things, opposite to that which is spiritual, heavenly life and its actings, which we have in and from Christ'.[1] This killing of sin is also urged by Paul in Colossians: 'Put to death, therefore, whatever belongs to your earthly nature: sexual immorality, impurity, lust, evil desires and greed' (Col 3:5).

However there is a qualification in mortification and that is that complete killing of sin or the absolute destruction of sin in this life is impossible. Mortification is not eradication. Mortification as stated above is rendering the power of sin useless. Indwelling sin is a reality producing conflict which is explained in Romans chapter seven.

Note the reference to the body in Romans 8:13, 'the misdeeds of *the body*'. Paul's emphasis on the body is affirmed in another place where he says, 'I beat my body and make it my slave' – beat: *hupōpiazō*, meaning to treat severely, to strike under the eye so as to make it black and blue, by violent and repeated blows I subdue the flesh and bring it into subjection (1 Cor 9:27). The ESV translates, 'But I discipline my body and keep it under control, lest after preaching to others I myself should be disqualified.' Helpfully Peter Naylor comments, 'Paul's physical body, though not intrinsically evil, is the seat of much that is sinful (*cf* Rom 8:13). Here, the sense is that even legitimate desires are to be abandoned should necessity arise.'[2]

Romans 8:13 is a categorical statement. It is death or life. I am alarmed when I observe the hazards surrounding young people who have recently come to faith. The contemporary godless, reckless, secular environment is similar to the description given of the world before the flood. 'The LORD saw how great man's wickedness on the earth had become, and that every inclination of the thoughts of his heart was only evil all the time' (Gen 6:5). How will young believers survive spiritually unless they have this knowledge about mortification?

Using metaphors Jesus taught mortification of sin in a vivid way: 'If your hand causes you to sin, cut it off. It is better for you to enter life maimed than with two hands to go into hell, where the fire never goes out. And if your foot causes you to sin, cut it off. It is better for you to enter life crippled than to have two feet and be thrown into hell. And if your eye causes you to sin, pluck it out. It is better for you to enter the kingdom of God with one eye than to have two eyes and be thrown into hell, where 'their worm does not die, and the fire is not quenched' (Mark 9:43-48). Hell is not metaphorical. It is real.

Jesus is not advising the amputation of limbs. He is commanding mortification which is putting sin to death. He is also emphasising the fact that failure to do this will result in eternal hell. That is a plain way to state essential truth. In another place Jesus uses the metaphor of the vine. 'I am the true vine, and my Father is the gardener. He cuts off every branch in me that bears no fruit, while every branch that does bear fruit he prunes so that it will be even more fruitful' (John 15:1,2). If there is not fruit-bearing (and fruit-bearing is impossible if sin is not mortified) that branch is cut off. In other words there can be no salvation without mortification.

We will now consider reasons why we never cease to attend to this work of mortification. Sin always remains in us while we are in this life. Paul reminds us of that when he describes the incessant warfare between the flesh and the Spirit. 'For the sinful nature desires what is contrary to the Spirit, and the Spirit what is contrary to the sinful nature. They are in conflict with each other, so that you do not do what you want' (Gal 5:17). The misdeeds of the body encouraged by the sinful nature refer to all evil actions as listed in Galatians 5:19-21 – sexual immorality, idolatry, hatred, jealousy, fits of rage, selfish ambition, drunkenness and so on. To mortify or to put to death means to deprive of life or power. By plunging the knife into the heart of a beast it is slaughtered. To mortify is to ruthlessly put to death, to deprive the sinful nature of its lust.

Sin, if not continually mortified, will bring forth great, cursed, scandalous, and soul-destroying sins. We see that in King David who committed adultery with Bathsheba and then murdered her husband Uriah. The reason why no lust should be left unmortified is that every lust has the capacity to grow to a deadly proportion, to be strident, to be imperious, to be vile and to aim at its height. 'When tempted, no-one should say, "God is tempting me." For God cannot be tempted by evil, nor does he tempt anyone; but each one is tempted when, by his own evil desire, he is dragged away and enticed. Then, after desire has conceived, it gives birth to sin; and sin, when it is full-grown, gives birth to death' (James 1:13-15). Resentment can grow into rebellion. Hurt feelings can develop into hateful, unforgiving attitudes which can turn into anger and violence such as the striking of another person. Every lust ultimately aims at its maximum expression. When anger has been subdued it can lie dormant for a while and then flare up again. Paul speaks of the conflict that is waged continually in believers between the Spirit and the flesh (Gal 5:17).

Gospel ministers must be careful to exercise this necessity of mortification. Satan aims to bring them down. Over the years it has been the cause of deep distress to observe some of the most gifted pastors fall into adultery which forever destroys their calling and usefulness. The root cause of this tragedy is lack of attention to mortification of sin.

Observe the deceitfulness of sin. It gradually prevails to harden man's heart to his ruin (Heb 3:13). 'Sin's expression is modest at the beginning but, once it has gained a foothold, it continues to take further ground and presses on to greater heights. This advance of sin keeps the soul from seeing that it is drifting from God. The soul becomes indifferent to the nature of sin as it continues to grow. This growth has no boundaries but utter denial of God and opposition to him. Sin proceeds to gain strength by degrees; it hardens the heart as it advances. This enables the deceitfulness of sin to drive the soul deeper and deeper into sin. Nothing can prevent this but mortification. Mortification withers the root and strikes at the head of sin every hour. The best saints in the world are in danger of a fall if found negligent in this important duty!'[3]

The Holy Spirit and our new nature are given to us to oppose sin and lust (Gal 5:17; 2 Peter 1:4). Only those who are in Christ and who have the gift of the Holy Spirit, that is, his indwelling power, can effectively mortify sin. That is why I have included a chapter on the new birth. Regeneration is the renewal of the whole person in a creative act by the Holy Spirit. Sanctification is the ongoing work of holiness in the whole nature of that person. Mortification is an essential part of the sanctification process. Note the order employed, 1. *You* must mortify lust. 2. You must mortify lust *by the Spirit*. It is *not* a matter of its all being done for us while we are passive. Not at all! By the enabling of the Spirit *we* wage war.

Some lusts are more prevalent than others. This is the reason why the Bible lays strong emphasis on the necessity to mortify sexual lust. It is crystal clear that sexual sin is in the front rank of sins to be mortified. There are passages which demonstrate this.

First when Paul declares that the will of God is our sanctification he immediately applies that first to sexual sin. 'It is God's will that you should be sanctified: that you should avoid sexual immorality; that each of you should learn to control his own body in a way that is holy and honourable, not in passionate lust like the heathen, who do not know God' (1 Thess 4:3-5).

A second passage is the already quoted passage namely Colossians 3:5 where Paul exhorts as follows: 'Put to death, therefore, whatever belongs to your earthly nature: sexual immorality, impurity, lust, evil desires and greed, which is idolatry.'

A third passage is much more detailed and in it the apostle explains why sexual sin is crippling. 'Do you not know that the wicked will not inherit the kingdom of God? Do not be deceived: Neither the sexually immoral nor idolaters nor adulterers nor male prostitutes nor homosexual offenders nor thieves nor the greedy nor drunkards nor slanderers nor swindlers will inherit the kingdom of God. And that is what some of you were. But you were washed, you were sanctified, you were justified in the name of the Lord Jesus Christ and by the Spirit of our God' (1 Cor 6:9-11). Observe here that when Paul describes some of the converts at Corinth he refers first to sexual sinners of different kinds and then goes on in the same chapter to explain explicitly why sexual sin is so staining and damaging.

'The body is not meant for sexual immorality, but for the Lord, and the Lord for the body. By his power God raised the Lord from the dead, and he will raise us also. Do you not know that your bodies are members of Christ himself? Shall I then take the members of Christ and unite them with a prostitute? Never! Do you not know that he who unites himself with a prostitute is one with her in body? For it is said, "The two will become one flesh." But he who unites himself with the Lord is one with him in spirit. Flee from sexual immorality. All other sins a man commits are outside his body, but he who sins sexually sins against his own body. Do you not know that your body is a temple of the Holy Spirit, who is in you, whom you have received from God? You are not your own; you were bought at a price. Therefore honour God with your body' (1 Cor 6:13-20).

Addiction to drugs involves the abuse of the body. Those who are converted out of the drug scene often need medical help in the transition from addiction to freedom. The spiritual part of this begins with regeneration and directly following that the Holy Spirit imparts a revulsion for the addiction. That revulsion will not remove the physical craving for the drug which in many cases is cocaine. There will be a fierce battle of mortification. Enabled by the Holy Spirit and with the help and encouragement of others the addiction can be killed off. Yet ongoing watchfulness will be required lest depression or peculiar temptations prompt the desire to return to the drug scene and the whole cycle of abuse will be continued. Alcohol addiction is similar to drug addiction and the same principles of mortification by the Spirit apply.

Careful attention must be paid to that which falls short of mortification. Much sin is avoided because of fear of the consequences and the damage that will be done to one's reputation, the damage done to one's family or to others. But mortification is not resisting sin on that account but is rather a matter of seeing sin for the evil that it is and killing it in its roots. Thus Joseph did not say to Potiphar's wife, when she sought constantly to seduce him, that they must not do this because it was dangerous in its consequences. No! Joseph went boldly to the very source of the matter and declared, 'How then could I do such a wicked thing and sin against God?' (Gen 39:9).

If sexual sin is not mortified in its roots then when a strong temptation comes in the form of opportunity which seems safe (nobody will find out) then that unmortified lust will break out with a power that it did not seem capable of before and with rage' will plunge its victim into sin.[4]

There are sins that can become so powerful as to virtually take possession of the soul. An example of sin left unmortified and which grew into soul-killing dimensions is seen in Achan. Achan in spite of the clearest warnings was overcome by covetousness (Josh 7:19-26). Similarly it was the sin of covetousness that overcame Judas Iscariot who sold our Lord for thirty pieces of silver. That he had not mortified this sin can be seen in the fact that he was in the habit of stealing from the offerings. Ananias and Sapphira were overcome with the sin of lying. They had left covetousness unmortified. This had grown to such proportions that together they were prepared to deceive the apostles (Acts 5:1-11).

Simon Magus although baptised as a believer did not mortify the sin of covetousness and love of money. He sought to use his newly found religion to enrich himself in a way which is very common in some countries. Peter rebuked him: 'May your money perish with you, because you thought you could buy the gift of God with money! You have no part or share in this ministry, because your heart is not right before God. Repent of this wickedness and pray to the Lord. Perhaps he will forgive you for having such a thought in your heart. For I see that you are full of bitterness and captive to sin.' (Acts 8:20-23). As wealth increases in China the love of money may prove to be a far greater danger to the Christians there and be more damaging to them than the harm caused by persecution from the Communist regime.

Mortification must be comprehensive. This can be illustrated by the Passover. Every year at Passover time (our Easter time) the Orthodox Jews hunt high and low in their houses to get rid of all remnants of old bread or crumbs. This they do in accordance with the commands of Exodus 12:14, 15. We are not obliged to do that now because Christ our Passover has been sacrificed for us (1 Cor 5:7). Christ has fulfilled all the figures and types of the Old Testament. Spiritual lessons however still apply. As we see from the teaching of 1 Corinthians 5:6-8 we are now to hunt high and low and search out and get rid of all evil thoughts, all hatred, resentments, sinful imaginations, crude adulterous lusts, covetousness, jealousies and pride. All malice and all immorality are to be purged out. All pornography of the heart is to be thrown out and burned. The question is, how can we achieve this? How can we overcome those evil thoughts when they invade our minds or when they spring up from corruption within ourselves?

Mortification must be informed by the moral law of God or the Ten Commandments which is why I have devoted a chapter to that subject. The most lucid commentary ever written on the meaning and application of the commandments in daily life is the Larger Westminster Catechism. The best available extended exposition and modern day application of each question in the catechism is in a commentary on the Westminster Larger Catechism by Johannes G Vos edited by G I Williamson.[5]

False mortification

The most common form of false mortification of sin is found in the Roman Catholic Church. I witnessed this personally during five years of boarding school in a Roman Catholic High School. Every Friday the more zealous Roman Catholic scholars would go and confess their sins to the priest. But this and all the other religious observances such as the Mass did nothing to change them. It was simply a constant repetition, sinning and then confessing. Martin Luther exhausted himself seeking salvation with confessions and penances.

Mortification is only achieved by the power of the Holy Spirit. To illustrate the point there is a well-known Italian politician who is a notorious adulterer. His wife has sued for divorce but said she will consider having him back if he is counselled by a sex counsellor and also if he spends a few days in a monastery to correct his adulterous behaviour. That is like placing Elastoplast strips over a raging internal infection. Nothing is achieved until that sin is seen as God sees it and the love and enjoyment of that particular sin mortified by the enablement of the Holy Spirit. By the power of the Spirit the struggle involved can be likened to crucifixion in which those crucified resisted with all the physical power they could muster. With all energy they resisted having their hands and feet being nailed to a wooden cross. But once so nailed by their hands and their feet the power to harm others physically was over.

They could curse and swear but the body was rendered powerless. That is what must be done to sin. It can involve a fierce struggle, a struggle in which the indwelling power of the Spirit is essential.

Another false form of mortification is perfectionist teaching. This seems less common than it used to be. This is the idea that by having a power experience called the baptism of the Spirit sin can be eradicated. That is an illusion. It is not long before sin will be on the rampage again which will prove that only disciplined mortification by the Spirit works effectively. There is the notion of complete surrender: 'Let go and let God'. Romans 8:13 lays the responsibility to mortify sin squarely with us. *You* must do this. There is no easy formula to take the place of the duty of mortification.

Cheating or avoiding mortification of sin takes place when professing Christians avoid mortification by making up their own commandments. In my pastoral experience I have noted this with the now over-hyped subject of homosexuality. I have found in some instances that the battle involved with homosexuality has been joined and victory won. This was evidently the case at Corinth when Paul says, 'And that is what some of you were' (1 Cor 6:11). Today it is politically correct to condone homosexual practice. But where will we be if we re-write the laws of God? That is self- deception.

Indwelling sin always remains ready to launch another attack. This can be illustrated by Special Services soldiers who are carefully chosen for their exceptional physical abilities, endurance and daring courage. After selection they are trained to perform amazing feats. For instance they can penetrate behind enemy lines and cause havoc. They blow up installations, disguise themselves and hide cleverly. After a diligent search the enemy gives up and concludes that they have escaped. *But they have not escaped.* They lie low and then strike again as opportunity affords. It is a deception to imagine that indwelling sin will disappear. Cornelius van Til was a professor of Apologetics at Westminster Seminary and widely appreciated for his skills in interpreting Scripture. When he was in his seventies he was asked in a question and answer time in a conference, 'Dr van Til, isn't there a sense in which as you get older, sins that once bothered you no longer do so?' Van Til, shaking his finger, answered the question energetically: 'Young man, that is incipient perfectionism. The greatest battles I have now are the sins of my youth!' [6]

Heman the Ezrahite wrote Psalm 88. In it he tells of his struggle which is grim from beginning to end. This psalm stands out in the Psalter for unrelieved suffering. In it we discern the voice of our suffering Redeemer. Here is the wrath of God. Yet through it all is perseverance in vehement prayer. Those who suffer identify with this psalm. Some Christians especially in lands of severe persecution endure trials which are almost beyond belief. Yet it is not all grief and pain. Paul and Silas having been beaten and thrust into prison sang praises to God. So persecuted believers often testify to much joy in their tribulations (1 Peter 1:7-9). The Christian life consists of what I call a confluence (mixture) of experiences. Yes, mortification of sin is essential and can involve a fierce battle, but there are at the same time rich blessings of spiritual victory and joy. Mortification of sin makes way for transformation and for the fruits of righteousness which result in joy. The promise is, *you will live.*

A Christian can only be happy on condition that sin does not have dominion over him (Rom 6:14). Jesus said, 'Then you will know the truth, and the truth will set you free' (John 8:32). This freedom can only be maintained by perpetual vigilance and mortification of any sin or lust that may arise. The peace and happiness of a Christian depends upon this freedom from sin. This is the life abundant, which Jesus promised (John 10:10). A Spirit-filled life in which sin is mortified will be crowned with eternal and joyful life when the race is completed.

---

1   John Owen, *Works*, vol 3, page 540.
2   Peter Naylor, *1 Corinthians*, An Evangelical Press Study Commentary, 2004, page 241.
3   John Owen *The Mortification of Sin*, Banner of Truth paperback, page 8.
4   *Ibid*, page 34.
5   Johannes G Vos, *A Commentary on the Westminster Larger Catechism*, edited by G I Williamson. Introduction by W Robert Godfrey, P and R, 2002, 614 pages.
6   Peter Golding, Banner of Truth magazine, issues 321 and 322, two articles on John Owen and Mortification of Sin.

Transforming Sinners into Saints

Robert Carver is a secular writer. He is the author of *The Accursed Mountains, a* book describing his journeys in Albania.

The word accursed is appropriate to describe a land where everyone steals and is proud of it. Carver describes the mountainous parts of Albania as accursed because, 'Girls are kidnapped at fifteen and sold into prostitution. Lying is normal and the government steals more than anyone else. People traffic in guns, drugs and false identity papers and go to richer countries deliberately to rob and pillage. Wife beating is normal and rape and buggery are meted out to anyone not protected either by guns or their family. Sadistic torture by the police is routine and everything from a school certificate to a doctor's degree can be bought for cash. Blood feuds and revenge killings paralyse whole swathes of the land.'

In this prevailing accursedness Carver was deeply impressed by evangelical missionaries who are in the business of ministering in such a way as to see the Lord transforming benighted sinners into saints. Carver admits that he could not tolerate to live for six months in conditions of such terrible misery and darkness but these missionaries live there for years on end.

There is no other religion that transforms the lives of sinners and turns them into saints. By contrast it is all too evident that some extremist religionists believe in killing infidels by suicide bombers and certainly do not entertain the idea of patiently working for their transformation.

Enver Hoxha boasted in 1967 that all religion in Albania, a country of about three million, had been eliminated. It is never wise to pronounce the funeral of God's kingdom. Some estimate that there are now about 170 evangelical churches in Albania.

The above description is likely to anger some patriotic Albanians. In spite of Carver's depiction of Albanian depravity we are sure that God's common grace extends over much of that country as it does universally.

Robert Carver, *Journeys in Albania, The Accursed Mountains*, 349 page, illustrated paperback, Flamingo, 1998.

Chapter 10

Holiness and Transformation

G od has predestined that we be conformed to the likeness of Christ (Rom 8:29). The Holy Spirit gradually and progressively effects this transformation to the likeness of Christ which is described by Paul: 'And we, who with unveiled faces all reflect the Lord's glory, are being transformed into his likeness with ever-increasing glory, which comes from the Lord, who is the Spirit' (2 Cor 3:18).

Transformation is expressed by Paul when he commences the applicatory section of his letter to the Romans: 'Therefore, I urge you, brothers, in view of God's mercy, to offer your bodies as living sacrifices, holy and pleasing to God – this is your spiritual act of worship. Do not conform any longer to the pattern of this world, but be transformed by the renewing of your mind. Then you will be able to test and approve what is God's will, his good, pleasing and perfect will (Rom 12:1,2). Christians are in union with Christ and now it is consistent that they follow the way of transformation.

The practical means for transformation is the renewing of our minds. *metamorphousthe* (metamorphosis in English) is a command – you be transformed! (Rom 12:2). This transformation denotes a change which is inward, permeating and thorough. The only other place where the term metamorphosis is used is in Matthew 17:2 to describe the transfiguration of Christ. From within the whole being of our Lord was irradiated with glory. Metamorphosis is illustrated by the development of the butterfly. A tiny egg hatches into a caterpillar. The caterpillar feeds on leaves and grows until it is ready to spin round itself a cocoon. Inside that cocoon it becomes a chrysalis. In due time the butterfly emerges from the chrysalis. There are beautiful butterflies. The contrast between a caterpillar and a butterfly illustrates what we mean by metamorphosis.

Two similar verbs appear in the text – *metamorphousthe* be transformed and *mē syschēmatizesthe* be not conformed. Both are present, passive imperative verbs. Watchfulness is needed to avoid being shaped by this present evil world.[1] We are being transformed by the Holy Spirit who is working in us. At the same time we are fully responsible in advancing this work through the exercise of our minds. We are not simply passive. As it says in Philippians 2:12, 'Continue to work out your salvation with fear and trembling, for it is God who works in you to will and to act according to his good purpose.'

How are we to respond to this transformation? We are to test what is the good, pleasing and perfect will of God. 'Good' means free from the connivance of evil. 'Pleasing' describes a quality which is recognised by the world as Peter says, 'Live such good lives among the pagans that, though they accuse you of doing wrong, they may see your good deeds and glorify God on the day he visits us' (1 Peter 2:12). 'Perfect' as a description follows from the combination of the two preceding descriptions of good and pleasing.[2] 'Test what the will of God is as men test out coins or metals by accepting the genuine and rejecting or throwing out the spurious.'[3]

The burden of the apostle is that believers will resist conformity to the world and resist being shaped by the thinking and habits of the world. The nature of the world without God is developed in the chapter on worldliness. Natural man, whose mind is at enmity to God and who cannot be subject to the law of God, is shaped inwardly and constantly by the ethos and ways of the world.

The way in which Christian transformation is advanced is by the renewing of the mind. In some churches there is a subtle down-playing of the mind through the influences of the world. The idea prevails that it is feelings and emotions that count and not doctrinal teaching. The temptation is for preachers to go along with this culture and rely on anecdotes and stories to entertain their congregations. The gift of intellect is a superlative gift of God and that gift needs to be developed to the full and used to advance in knowledge and theological understanding. There is a balance to be maintained as gospel preachers have to reckon realistically with the limitations of their hearers. Illustrations help but the aim is transformation of people through the renewing of their minds.

In his sermons on Romans 12:1,2 Dr Martyn Lloyd-Jones stresses that transformation is based on the great change that has taken place in the new birth. Jesus demanded not a change of behaviour, but transformation of character.[4] The Christian minds the things of the Spirit, something he never did before. He ceases minding the things of the flesh, a thing he always did before (Rom 8:5,6). As a son of God he is led by the Spirit of God in his very mind (Rom 8:14). His use of his body shows it.[5]

This emphasis on transformation which follows regeneration is supported by Jesus' teaching concerning the tree and the fruit: 'Watch out for false prophets. They come to you in sheep's clothing, but inwardly they are ferocious wolves. By their fruit you will recognise them. Do people pick grapes from thornbushes, or figs from thistles? Likewise every good tree bears good fruit, but a bad tree bears bad fruit. A good tree cannot bear bad fruit, and a bad tree cannot bear good fruit. Every tree that does not bear good fruit is cut down and thrown into the fire. Thus, by their fruit you will recognise them' (Matt 7:15-20).

James takes this further and refers to a spring of water. 'Can both fresh water and salt water flow from the same spring? My brothers, can a fig tree bear olives, or a grapevine bear figs? Neither can a salt spring produce fresh water' (James 3:11,12).

Isaiah gives us a metaphorical description of the transforming effects of this gospel which are far-reaching and extend eventually over all the earth:

> The wolf will live with the lamb,
> the leopard will lie down with the goat,
> the calf and the lion and the yearling together;
> and a little child will lead them.
> The cow will feed with the bear,
> their young will lie down together,
> and the lion will eat straw like the ox.
> The infant will play near the hole of the cobra,
> and the young child put his hand into the viper's nest.
> They will neither harm nor destroy on all my holy mountain,
> for the earth will be full of the knowledge of the LORD
> as the waters cover the sea (Isa 11:6-9).

It is important to discern when Isaiah is using metaphor and when he is not. For instance note metaphor and poetry in 55:12, 'You will go out in joy and be led forth in peace; the mountains and hills will burst into song before you, and all the trees of the field will clap their hands.'

On Isaiah 11:6-9 Matthew Henry is emphatic when he affirms the spiritual meaning of this poetry and expounds as follows:

'Unity and concord; these are intimated in these figurative promises, that even the wolf shall dwell peaceably with the lamb. Men of the most fierce and furious dispositions, who used to bite and devour all about them shall have their temper so strangely altered by the efficacy of the gospel and grace of Christ, that they shall live in love even with the weakest, and such as formerly they would have made an easy prey of. So far shall the sheep be from hurting one another, as sometimes they have done (Ez 34:20,21) that even the wolves shall agree with them. Christ, who is our Peace, came to slay all enmities and to settle lasting friendships among his followers, particularly among Jews and Gentiles, when multitudes of both, being converted to the faith of Christ, are united in one sheepfold, -- they that inhabit the holy mountain shall live as amicably as the creatures did that were with Noah in the ark and it shall be a means of their preservation for they shall not hurt or destroy one another as they have done.'

In Galatians 5:22,23 Paul describes the fruit of the Spirit as follows:[6]

> Love – inner disposition of esteem and care for others
> Joy – the awareness that one is loved with an everlasting love
> Peace – inner tranquillity and rest in justification by faith
> Patience – the practice of perseverance in difficulty or affliction
> Kindness – an active practical care of others
> Goodness – benevolence shown in good works
> Faithfulness – cleaving to God and his truth
> Gentleness – mildness and tenderness toward others
> Self-control -temperance

In his second letter Peter exhorts as follows: 'For this very reason, make every effort to add to your faith goodness; and to goodness, knowledge; and to knowledge, self-control; and to self-control, perseverance; and to perseverance, godliness; and to godliness, brotherly kindness; and to brotherly kindness, love' (2 Peter 1:5-7). The text is accurately translated by the ESV 'Make every effort to supplement your faith.' These virtues[7] are present in all believers and need to be strengthened. We can view them as follows:

> Goodness – excellent moral energy motivating good works
> Knowledge – the knowledge of eternal life (John 17:3)
> Self-control – resisting temptation
> Perseverance – endurance
> Godliness – culture of the inward life of holiness
> Brotherly kindness – practical caring for the Christian family
> Love – love in all our behaviour according to 1 Corinthians 13

Note that Paul places love at the beginning and Peter at the end. Both include self-control; otherwise the fruit in the Galatians passage is different from the virtues in 2 Peter 1:5-7.

Renewal is another word used to describe the idea of advance and progress. For instance we have 2 Corinthians 4:16, 'Therefore we do not lose heart. Though outwardly we are wasting away, yet inwardly we are being renewed day by day'; and Colossians 3:10, 'And have put on the new self, which is being renewed in knowledge in the image of its Creator.'

Conformed to the likeness of Christ – in the beautiful proportion of his character

In what ways are we made like Christ? The answer surely is that we are conformed to him in the attributes of love, meekness, humility, patience, gentleness, a love of righteousness and a loathing of evil and so on. As Jonathan Edwards asserts in his treatise *The Religious Affections*, there is a beautiful symmetry in all the attributes of Christ-likeness. There is salt and light in the Christian as well as love, sweetness and compassion. These with the virtues mentioned above are constituent characteristics in transformation.

Jonathan Edwards expresses this reality as follows: 'The Spirit that descended on Christ, when he was first anointed of the Father, descended on him *like a dove*. The dove is a noted emblem of meekness, harmlessness, peace and love. But the same Spirit that descended on the head of the Church, descends to the members. 'God hath sent forth the Spirit of his Son into their heart' (Gal 4:6) – to cite Edwards: 'There is every grace in them which is from Christ; grace for grace; that is grace answerable to grace: there is no grace in Christ, but there is its image in believers to answer it. The image is a *true* image; and there is something of the same beautiful proportion in the image, which is in the original; there is feature for feature, and member for member. There is symmetry and beauty in God's workmanship.'[8]

The wonder of God's workmanship, when he creates us in Christ Jesus is that he makes us like himself in true righteousness and holiness (Eph 2:10 and 4:24). Just as in a normal physical birth all the features are there, so in the spiritual birth all the heavenly features of Christ are present. As in physical birth we bear all the features of the earthly man Adam so in spiritual birth we bear all the celestial characteristics of the heavenly last Adam, that is, Christ.

These features include love for God, understanding and a hunger for his truth, humility, meekness, faith, hope, purity, peaceableness, joy, forgiveness, patience, gentleness, tenderness, perseverance, self-control, knowledge, brotherly kindness and compassion. These characteristics are compiled from passages of Scripture such as Romans 5: 1-9, Matthew 5: 1-12, Colossians 3: 12-15, and the two examined above namely Galatians 5:22, 23, and 2 Peter 1: 5-7.

As we study the person of Christ we see not only perfection of detail in his virtues of patience, love, humility, compassion, meekness and so on, but we are struck by the beautiful symmetry and proportion of all the features together. In physical terms a truly lovely countenance is the result of a number of beautiful features in proportion with an emphasis on proportion. As in the physical, so in the spiritual, it is the symmetry or proportion of graces or features that explains the beautiful form.

The word *eikōn* in Greek literally means image, '*image* of Christ'. None of us knows what he looked like when he was here or what he looks like now. The Father's purpose is to make us like his Son in inward disposition and character. The divine sculptor is the Holy Spirit. We should derive tremendous encouragement from the fact that the Holy Spirit is wise, powerful and constant in his working within us (2 Cor 3:18; 2 Thess 2:13, Phil 2:12,13).

The lovely symmetry and proportion and perfection of all the graces and virtues characterises Jesus the perfect man. None of our graces are perfect but the wonder of possessing them all is a thrilling fact. We should be deeply concerned that the proportion is maintained and that the improvement of all the graces, one by one, should contribute to our being conformed more and more to the likeness of Christ. Some graces are more prominent than others and affect the others in a pervasive, strengthening way. I will comment on just two graces namely humility and love.
Conformed to the likeness of Christ – humility

In Romans chapter twelve where Paul begins his application to the life of believers in the Church he starts with humility. This includes a modest realistic opinion of oneself. In the New Testament humility takes on an active meaning, best illustrated by Christ who humbled himself to become man and yet again when he submitted himself to death – even so desperate a death as crucifixion. In action he humbled himself to be his Father's servant and to do all his will. He even humbled himself to serve his disciples by washing their feet (John 13:4).

Pride lay at the root of the fall of the archangel Lucifer. Pride lay at the root of the fall of Adam. Pride brings destruction to the human race. The Nazi regime was built on national pride namely the absurd notion of racial superiority. By nature fallen man imagines himself superior to others. Conversion to Christ changes that. As Christ came to outcasts, to lepers and to the weak, so his followers interest themselves in the poor. Instead of thinking themselves superior to other racial groups they now rejoice in the international Church made up of members from all nations and languages, all of them united in Christ.

When a person has his eyes opened to see his guilt before God, the debt he has incurred and his spiritual wretchedness, this strikes at the heart of self-righteousness and pride. Never again has he reason to exalt himself above others. Christ came from glory and from the highest place of power and authority yet he humbled himself to work among sinners. The humility of Christ was a great incentive for the needy to approach him. His meekness and humility are held out as an encouragement to come to him. 'Come to me, all you who are weary and burdened, and I will give you rest. Take my yoke upon you and learn from me, for I am gentle and humble in heart, and you will find rest for your souls' (Matt 11:28,29). The word translated 'gentle' (*praus*), in the NIV is rendered 'meek' in the KJV. Divine power belonged to Christ, yet under provocation he was meek.

3. Conformed to the likeness of Christ – love

The same Holy Spirit who creates a new nature in us develops the graces of that new nature – all the graces, including the foremost of them, namely, love. As God's sons and daughters we love him and we love each other. Humility paves the way for love. For instance, when Saul of Tarsus was humbled and converted he immediately began to love those whom he had formerly hated and persecuted.

Love is the fulfilment of God's law (Rom 13:10). Love disposes us to all proper acts of esteem and care toward God and our fellow creatures.

1 Corinthians 13:4-7 describes the behaviour of love. Love is a way of life. 'Love is patient, love is kind, it does not envy, it does not boast, it is not proud. It is not rude, it is not self-seeking, it is not easily angered, it keeps no record of wrongs. Love does not delight in evil but rejoices with the truth. It always protects, it always trusts, always hopes, always perseveres.' This should be a description of you if you are a Christian.

How can love be built up in us? How can we resemble Christ in love? The apostle John points to the Father's love as the pattern. He gave his Son as a propitiation for our sins (1 John 4:10). This should motivate us to love one another. As far as John is concerned, the sure sign of a Christian is that he loves those who are born of God (1 John 3:14,23; 1 John 4:12; 1 John 5:2).

The measure or degree of love is seen when we are put under pressure or provocation. It is also seen when we meekly bear wrongs from others. Peter tells us that Christ 'committed no sin and no deceit was found in his mouth. When they hurled their insults at him, he did not retaliate; when he suffered, he made no threats. Instead, he entrusted himself to him who judges justly' (1 Peter 2: 22,23).

To undergo such an ordeal on our behalf showed the full extent of his love. Can our love be like his? The Holy Spirit does engender within believers a love of the same kind, even if not of the same strength or power. Heaven is a world of love and the transforming work going on in us is preparing us for that. Christ is the King of love and we are being conformed to his likeness.

The question of our conformity to the likeness of Christ is a very important one. As expressed above the overall, beautiful symmetry or proportion of graces involved in transformation is vital. As you examine your life can you give attention to points of weakness? It is most encouraging to know that the Holy Spirit is always at work in transforming believers to the likeness of Christ.

---

1   In his commentary on Romans Thomas R Schreiner (Baker Book House, 1998) draws attention to the fact that both verbs *syschēmatizomai* and *metamorphousthe* denote that which takes place from within. William Hendriksen in his commentary on Romans (Banner of Truth, 1981) disputes on theological grounds that *syschēmatizomai* in this context is inward and argues correctly in my view that transformation is wholly from within while conformity to this world is something that tempts us from without.

2   F L Godet, *Romans*, Kregel, 1977, page 428.

3   R C H Lenski, *Romans*, Augsburg Publishing House, 1936, page 751.

4   Martyn Lloyd-Jones, *Romans*, chapter 12, Banner of Truth, page 103.

5   *Ibid*, Lenski.

6   The Greek words used are *agapē, chara, eirēnē, makrothumia, chrēstotēs, agathōsynē, pistis, prautēs, egkrateia.*

7   The Greek words used are *aretē, gnosis, egkrateia, hypomonē, eusebeia, philadelphia, agapē.*

8   Jonathan Edwards, *The Religious Affections*, Works, vol 1, Banner of Truth, pages 304 and 309.

Holiness According to Peter

Teaching on sanctification throughout the New Testament shows that personal holiness applies to every part of life and to all conditions. Peter's focus on sanctification is set within an environment of suffering and serious impending persecution which would eventually end in martyrdom for him (1 Peter 4:12 and 2 Peter 1:14). He nevertheless asserts that there is joy inexpressible to be experienced in our trials and in his letter he stresses holiness: 'But just as he who called you is holy, so be holy in all that you do.' (1 Peter 1:15). The ESV translates 'all that you do' as 'in all your conduct'. That is helpful as it points to our way of life as we live before a pagan world. 'Keep your conduct among the Gentiles honourable' (ESV 2:12). It is here that Peter's practical approach takes off with the theme of living the Christian life before a watching world, this emphasis being brought out very well in the NIV, 'Dear friends, I urge you, as aliens and strangers in the world, to abstain from sinful desires which wage war against your soul. Live such good lives among the pagans that, though they accuse you of wrong, they may see your good deeds and glorify God on the day he visits us.'

The day he visits us may be a time of revival when those for whom we have prayed for so long are converted.

Peter also emphasises that the life of holiness includes submissiveness to God-given authority. We are to submit to our rulers. Peter goes further and urges that slaves submit to their masters with all respect. The reason is plain, which is that they might commend themselves to God in maintaining the graces of the Christian character. Peter also stresses the vital importance of wives submitting to unbelieving husbands that 'they may be won over without words by the behaviour of their wives' (1 Peter 3:1-7).

Chapter 11

The Death and Burial of the Old Man

We sometimes read of those who, converted by the gospel, are rejected by their own families. In some cases a converted husband is rejected by an unbelieving wife, or vice versa. 'John is simply not the same person,' declares Jane. Even though John may improve by way of being more considerate and kind, the change is so profound that Jane is correct when she maintains that her husband is a different person. Jane's interest in the Church is zero. To her John is now a religious fanatic. He insists on going to church three times a week! But it is not only that. Jane protests that John is no longer interested in dances and parties. He has abandoned his old social life. Jane is right. The old John has died. He will never live again. John is a renewed person with a new disposition. He has a new set of affections and a new spirit. This is reflected in his new horizon of interests.

We have seen from the chapter on the new birth that John is born again. He is a new creation in Christ and all things are now new (2 Cor 5:17). Since John is still capable of sin of all kinds, to what do we attribute that sin? It will help to establish a basic principle and then examine the relevant Scriptures on this theme.

The unity of a man

It is a commonly held idea that the struggle in the Christian is between two people, the old man and the new man, as though the believer is a kind of split personality. We must repudiate completely the idea that the Christian is two people, an old man and a new man. It might be convenient to blame our sins on the old man and attribute credit to the new man, but the fact is that a person is always one, not two. In creation man is essentially one. For the purposes of study we can follow the example of Thomas Boston who made an analysis of man by dividing him up into constituent parts: mind, affections, conscience, will and memory. This can be found in his famous book *Man's Fourfold State* which is found in volume eight of his Complete Works. Such considerations are important and useful. We can learn much from the procedure but it is important to remember that man is one in the unity of his being.

The death of the old self and the emergence of the new

Having stressed the unity of a man in his being or make-up it is necessary to stress the importance of using the right terms. In the KJV of Ephesians 4:24 we read 'put off the old man' which is a literal translation of *ton palaion anthropon,* the old man. However it is better to use the terms 'the old self' and 'the new self' and to use them consistently which is the case in the NIV, the NASB and the TEV. This avoids the idea of any person being two people at the same time like Jekyll and Hyde. Some would use the term 'schizophrenia' as they think that conveys the idea of a split personality. Schizophrenia is a complex illness and we should avoid that idea in this context. A born-again person is changed but is still the same person with the same natural temperament, the same personality and the same natural gifts. It is important to avoid over-rating what occurs in the new birth, but also avoid underrating what takes place.

Relevant Scripture passages

'For you died, and your life is now hidden with Christ in God,' declares Paul to the Colossian believers (Col 3:3). Then further on he appeals to them on the grounds that they have taken off the old self and put on the new self (Col 3:9,10). In determining the extent to which a person has died and has been changed through the new birth (regeneration) we can survey the Scripture passages as follows:

1. Through the new birth the old self dies once and for all (John 3:1-15) together with John's statements in his first letter (3:2,3; 3:7-10; 4:7-9; 5:1-4; 5:18). Also Titus 3:4-7, Ephesians 2:9,10 linked with 4:24, 2 Corinthians 5:17 and 1 Peter 1:23.
2. Christians are required to live according to the new self. Colossians 3:8,9 and Ephesians 4:20-24 speak of the old self and the new self in the context of an old sphere of outlook and practice left behind for a new sphere.
3. Christian baptism symbolises the burial of the old self and the resurrection of the new self (Rom 6:1-6; Col 2:11,12).
4. Conflict takes place in the new self due to remaining sin (Rom 7:14- 25; Gal 5:16,17).

1. Through the new birth the old self dies once and for all

Regeneration can be defined as that change brought about in a man by the powerful creative work of the Holy Spirit whereby his whole nature is made spiritual. His eyes are opened to the truth. The old enmity to God is completely removed. He is enabled to love God and embrace the revelation of God in Scripture. No part of man is excluded in this change. It is a renewal of the affections and of the mind, of the will and of the conscience. As we have seen this is achieved by union with Christ. That union means that the regenerated person now shares the mind of Christ and is enabled thereby to will and do God's good pleasure (Phil 2:13).

When we view the scriptures describing the new birth and its consequences we see that Jesus spoke of the new birth as 'a seeing' (John 3:3), an illumination of the mind whereby the kingdom of God can be seen (comprehended) and believed. In his first letter John insists that the new birth brings a person to believe in the deity of Christ (5:1), to moral obedience (he cannot go on sinning, 3:7-10 and 5:18), and to love for fellow believers (3:14; 4:7-12).

The new covenant is described as the writing of God's law on the heart and mind (Jer 31:33; Heb 8:10). 'I will give you a new heart and put a new spirit in you; I will remove from you your heart of stone' (Ez 36:26). The outcome is adoption, 'you will be my people, and I will be your God' (verse 28 cf. Rev 21:3; Rom 8:15,16). The giving of a new heart is God's workmanship and is like a new creation. For 'we are God's workmanship, created in Christ Jesus to do good works' (Eph 2:10). This creation is 'to be like God in true righteousness and holiness' (Eph 4:24). It is brought about through spiritual union with Christ.

An act of creation has taken place. The Revised Version of 1881 has a marginal note for 2 Corinthians 5:17 which states it well, 'Wherefore if any man is in Christ, *there* is *a new creation.*' 'A new nature has been created which now relates to the new world. *Ktisis,* 'creation' refers to the making of a new creation, which centres in Christ and of which the believer becomes a part.[1] The Christian now relates to that new sphere and to every part of that new sphere. 'Therefore, if anyone is in Christ, he is a new creation; the old has gone, the new has come!' (2 Cor 5:17).

The Christian belongs to the coming new world order, the eschatological (coming) macrocosm. Peter confirms this in describing the Christian's inheritance that can never perish or fade (1 Peter 1:3-5). He describes the seed by which we have been born again as imperishable (1 Peter 1:23). That seed is God's Word and what that Word creates cannot perish (John 10:28). It stands forever for it is God's will and promise. The sons of God now await their glorification, the redemption of their bodies together with the glorification of the entire creation (Rom 8:18-25). The old self dies in the transition by new birth from the old order of sin to the new sphere of glory. By the new birth that person can never be what he was before. He possesses a new disposition which pervades the entirety of his being. The old self has died. The new self now lives.

2. Christians are required to live according to the new self

The New Testament is consistent in speaking of the death of the old self as something which took place in the past, a definitive act, something decisive. The birth of the new self is also definitive, something definitive as a specific point in time. 'It is no more feasible to call the believer an old man and a new man, than it is to call him a regenerate man and an unregenerate.'[2] Observe the use of the past tense employed in Colossians 3:9,10: 'Do not lie to each other, since you have taken off your old self with its practices and have put on the new self, which is being renewed in knowledge in the image of its Creator.'

Paul's appeal is an ethical one. I used to walk in the world of rage, malice, slander, filthy language, but then there was the transition. Now as a renewed person I have nothing in common with the ungodliness and sinful practices of that former life. Note the apostle's reference to what happened in the past. As a decisive event the old self was put off. The figure used in the text is that of clothing. Paul's reference is probably to proselyte Jewish baptism in which stripping off of clothing was required because it was essential to them that every part of the body be touched by water. The idea of stripping off filthy clothes and being clothed with the garments of God's righteousness is familiar in the Old Testament (Zech 3:3; Isa 61:10; Ps 132:9 and 16). The death of the old man and the birth of the new man is in the past. It can never be repeated.

On first reading the parallel passage in Ephesians 4:22-24 seems to contradict the above concept of the death of the old self once and for all. The text seems to be suggesting that putting off the old self is a continual duty, something that goes on and on as a process. In a thorough exegesis of this passage Professor John Murray provides his own translation which clearly brings out the tenses used in the Greek text of verses 20-24.

> 'But you have not so learned Christ, if so be you have heard him and have been taught by him as the truth is in Jesus, so that you have put off, according to the former manner of life, the old man who is corrupted according to the lusts of deceit, and are being renewed in the spirit of your mind, and have put on the new man who after God has been created in righteousness and holiness of the truth.'[3]

The believer is exhorted to observe what has occurred in the past and to act consistently with that. He is being urged to be what he truly is, that is, the new self. He is not being asked to be involved in a process of taking off and putting on, but rather to take note of the fact that he has already been brought into the realm of the new life. 'To put off' and 'to put on' are aorist infinitives which convey the meaning of a decisive event. The use of these as imperatives is very rare. There is no reason to take the text as an exhortation to keep on doing something which has been done once and for all. The verb 'you have not so learned' points to something which has been done and understood.

What takes place in the new birth is fully expressed in spiritual baptism which in turn is symbolised in water baptism, to which subject we now turn.

3. Christian baptism symbolises the burial of the old self and the resurrection of the new self (Rom 6:1-6 and Col 2:11,12)

Firstly we look at Romans 6:1-6 concentrating on verses 3 and 4

When confronted with the idea that a free justification might lead to a careless attitude toward sin, Paul reminds his readers of their baptism and what it signified. The basic meaning signified is union with Christ in his death and resurrection. 'Or don't you know that all of us who were baptised into Christ Jesus were baptised into his death? We were therefore buried with him through baptism into death in order that, just as Christ was raised from the dead through the glory of the Father, we too may live a new life' (6:3,4).

The apostle's appeal to baptism certifies that the readers were aware of the place and importance of baptism.[4] But what exactly did the Christians at Rome understand by this reference to their baptism? Paul says it was a burial. The word baptism was the best word to use to describe a burial because it conveys the concept of totality. The word *baptizo* is an intensive form of the word *bapto* which means to dip or to dip into a dye. *Baptizo* conveyed more than the idea of dipping or submerging; it went further to give the idea of perishing or destruction, the sinking of a ship.[5]

Does the burial have to be in water? Baptism in the New Testament symbolises two things: the washing away of sin (Acts 22:16), and union with Christ in his death and resurrection. The latter is more prominent than the former. It could be argued that references to washing could point to an equal status to the symbol of burial and resurrection with Christ. (see 1 Corinthians 6:11, Hebrews 10:22, Ephesians 5:26 and Titus 3 :5). But it is clear that union with Christ in his death and burial and the rising again to newness of life is the central thought of Paul in the Romans 6:1-5 passage. There are at least six other Greek words associated with washing or with ablutions. *Louō* to wash, *plunō* to scour, *niptō* to rinse, *ekcheō* to pour, *ballō* to pour rapidly, *brechō* to moisten. In addition there is the word *rantizō,* which means to sprinkle. Baptism is the only word which can convey the symbolism of burial because of the totality and comprehensiveness it conveys in its meaning. Those who dislike the idea of water immersion need to find a better way of symbolising burial.

Even when used as a metaphor baptism conveys the concept of something which is complete or overwhelming. In referring to his death Jesus said, 'Can you be baptised with the baptism that I am baptised with?' He is using both the verb *baptise*, and the noun *baptism*, in a figurative way to point to that which is catastrophic or overwhelming. The idea of baptism is also used to emphasise union of a complete nature; hence the children of Israel were so closely associated with Moses that Paul says of them 'They were all baptised into Moses in the cloud and in the sea' (1 Cor 10:2).

Therefore to be baptised into Christ's death means that I am plunged into the death of Christ in such a way that the whole of his death was my death too. The next time I see a crucifix, instead of imagining that I see Christ there, I see myself as the victim, or perhaps myself nailed to the other side of the same cross on which he was nailed. What is true of me is true of all believers. 'One died for all, and therefore all died' (2 Cor 5:14).

Paul in reminding believers of their baptism says that in their baptism they were buried with Christ. Here we have the ultimate expression to denote the decease of the old self. The burial was a burying out of sight of the old life. The old self is not only dead, he is buried!

'Burial is the seal set to the fact of death. It is when a man's relatives and friends leave his body in a grave and return home without him that the fact that he no longer shares their life is exposed with inescapable conclusiveness.'[6] The death we died in baptism was a death ratified and sealed by burial which portrays in the most vivid way imaginable that I have died. With the Roman Christians I can look back to my conversion, and my subsequent baptism which took place fairly soon afterwards. My baptism was a literal burial signifying the reality of the death that had taken place. Although there is no tombstone I know the place and can take friends there and show them the burial spot of the old me.

Of the old self I declare with Paul, 'I have been crucified with Christ and I no longer live, but Christ lives in me' (Gal 2:20). 'Our old self was crucified with him so that the body of sin might be rendered powerless, that we should no longer be slaves to sin because anyone who died has been freed from sin' (Rom 6:6,7).

Secondly we examine Colossians 2:11,12.

> 'In him you were also circumcised, in the putting off of the sinful nature (literally the body of flesh), not with a circumcision done by the hands of men but with the circumcision done by Christ, having been buried with him in baptism and raised with him through your faith in the power of God, who raised him from the dead.' Ceremonially circumcision stood for the putting off of the sinful nature. It was a rite which pointed to regeneration, 'The LORD your God will circumcise your hearts and the hearts of your descendants, so that you may love him with all your heart and with all your soul and live' (Deut 30:6). The responsibility to get a new heart was the duty pressed on the people by the prophets (Deut 10:16; Ez 18:31; Jer 4:4). The act of circumcision was performed in such a way that the stripping off of the flesh was performed by the priest as an act

of repugnance. The Greek in Colossians 2: 11 is a compound word meaning 'the entire stripping off' *(apekdusis,* note the double prefix).

In the context Paul is exhorting the Colossians to resist false teachers who were trying to persuade them to receive Jewish circumcision which was the removal of the excess foreskin. The apostle insists that they had already been circumcised with a circumcision of far more significance, that is the spiritual circumcision made without hands, a circumcision brought about by Christ, through his substitutionary death. The believer is united to Christ through Holy Spirit baptism (1 Cor 12:13), a unity with Christ in his death, burial and resurrection. The old unregenerate self is stripped away by union with Christ in his death. It is buried and left behind in the grave, while the new self emerges to walk in newness of life.

Again Spirit baptism is symbolised by water baptism. The Colossians could reflect on their participation in Christ's burial.

'The "putting off of the body of the flesh" and its burial out of sight alike emphasised that the old life was a thing of the past. They had shared in the death of Christ; they had also shared in his burial. 'It is through faith that the believer bids farewell to the old life and embarks on the new; the sacrament of baptism derives its efficacy not from the water nor from the convert's token burial in it, but from the saving act of Christ and the regenerating work of the Holy Spirit, producing faith-union with the risen Lord of which the sacrament is the outward sign.'[7]

'Baptism is the grave of the old man, and the birth of the new. As he sinks beneath the baptismal waters, the believer buries there all his corrupt affections and past sins; as he emerges thence, he rises regenerate, quickened to new hopes and a new life. This it is, because it is not only the crowning act of his own faith but also the earnest of God's Spirit. Thus baptism is an image of his participation both in the death and resurrection of Christ.'[8]

Conclusions up to this point

We conclude from these passages of Scripture that the old self or old man (Rom 6:6; Col 3:9; Eph 4:22,23), which in Colossians 2:11 is also designated 'the body of flesh', KJV (NIV has 'sinful nature'), refers to the godless and depraved fallen nature of a person thinking, speaking and acting according to this present evil world, wholly without God. This is the old Adam, born of the flesh and living for the flesh.

It follows therefore that 'putting off the old man is neither a continuous process nor a present duty but an accomplished fact. It is incorrect, therefore, to speak of the old man as remaining in the believer. The old man has been put off, crucified and destroyed. He is not merely enfeebled and enervated. He is not merely in process of destruction. He no longer exists.'[9]

While we know with relief and gratitude that we bid farewell to the old man who has been destroyed forever and who met his decease in that moment of union with Christ, we hasten on to note full well that remaining sin and corruption are a terrible reality. Sin remains in us who believe and this involves us in a struggle so severe that it can be like a daily death (1 Cor 15 :31).

There is an enormous difference between the spiritual man and the natural man. The contrast is so great that Paul states the matter like this: 'For you were once darkness, but now you are light in the Lord' (Eph 5:8).

4. Conflict takes place in the new self due to remaining sin (Rom 7:14-25 and Gal5:16,17)

Inasmuch as the passage in Galatians describes vividly the depravity of the ungodly life it is similar to Ephesians 4:17-32 and Colossians 3:5-11. The believer has left that evil world behind him; nevertheless there is conflict because remaining sin conflicts with the mind of the Holy Spirit (Gal 5:17). Romans 7:14-25 describes the intensity of conflict that can be experienced. It is mistaken to conclude that Romans 7:14-25 is the perpetual experience of the Christian or that it describes all his experience. See chapter twelve. Conflict is part, *not all,* of his experience. Joy inexpressible is also part of his experience but not all the time. We should note too that much of the conflict described in Romans 7:14-25 is due to deep regret and disappointment with ourselves and our lack of love for God. We experience distress because of the weakness of our spiritual life and we grieve over our sins of omission.

The sins that Christians commit directly, that is, by commission, are not so much against the first table of the law but against the second table. The new self contrasts with the old self because the new self has been fully turned round to love God instead of hating him. Under extraordinary pressures the new self can become angry with God as Jonah was, or speak rashly of God as Jeremiah did, but the regenerate nature does not blaspheme God. Job under conditions of the most aggravating and appalling kind did not blaspheme God. I am not saying that it is not possible but rather that it is entirely uncharacteristic of the regenerate nature, whereas the unregenerate nature constantly curses God.

The clearest distinction is required in the use of terms. We have seen that the old man is the same as the old ungodly self, but what terms do we employ to describe remaining sin? Here are some:

> *My sinful nature,* Romans 7:18.
> *The sinful nature,* Galatians 5:16,17 and 19, Romans 7:25;
> *Sin living in me,* Romans 7: 17.
> *The law of sin as work within my members,* Romans 7:23
> > *Remaining corruption,* Westminster Confession.
> *Sin's corrupt remnants,* The 1689 Confession in modern
> > language *(A Faith to Confess,* Carey Publications).

As observed above remaining sin has more powerful tendencies in some directions than in others and varies from person to person. Paul warns particularly against the tendency to go back to old sins and especially does he warn against lust and the sins of the flesh, (1 Thess 4:3), but also against sins which were formerly prominent such as lying, deception, stealing, slander, malice, rage and anger. That which was indulged before must be completely repented of and forsaken (Eph 4:25-32).

Bunyan's classic *The Holy War* illustrates the subject of remaining sin very well. King Emmanuel has captured the city of Mansoul. He defeats Satan the previous owner and occupier of Mansoul and drives him out. The city is new inasmuch as it is under new management and has new citizens. The layout, the streets and buildings are the same. (A converted man has the same body, temperament and personality as he had before.)In Bunyan's picture of Mansoul the city being captured, the town hall and major installations are taken over: the affections won, the mind occupied, the will conquered, the memory and conscience taken. Yet there are pockets of resistance. In terms of area there are streets and houses and especially basements still occupied by the enemy. The enemy must be located and must be put to the sword. Some sins can offer fierce and determined resistance. The break with the ungodly life is often spectacular and dramatic at first but then there comes a counter-attack. Suddenly the forces of remaining sin fight back with surprising vigour and vengeance.

There can be no compromise with any sin because each sin if indulged can grow and become so powerful as to become scandalous and wreck the testimony of the Christian. Adulterous fantasies if indulged can become tangible adultery and bring havoc not only to the two involved but bring tragic consequences to families, the local church and the cause of Christ. Likewise covetousness if indulged can turn to fraud which is a criminal offence which disgraces the professing Christian and brings the gospel into disrepute.

Final conclusions

The Christian should be greatly encouraged that he can never be the man he was before, yet at the same time he must always have a realistic view of the power and danger of sin that remains in him. He should rejoice that he has been planted together with Christ.

In Romans 6:5 a significant word is used which the KJV translates as plant. 'If we have been planted together in the likeness of his death.' The NKJV, NIV and NASB all use united instead of plant, 'For if we have been united together in the likeness of his death.' The phrase, 'have been united with him' is from a single word *sumpsutoi,* which means 'united by growth.' The word expresses exactly the process by which a graft becomes united with the life of a tree. The concept conveyed is powerful, namely that by this union the old is taken over by the new. The Christian is a transformed person 'possessed of new resources and new defences, living under new constraints and characterised by new attitudes and ambitions.'[10]

The old self has been destroyed in the moment of union with Christ. He no longer exists to bear the responsibility or assume the blame. It is the new self who sins. Indeed this is what Paul is concerned to emphasise, because it declares, as nothing else can, the exceeding sinfulness of sin in a believer. When the Christian sins he sins against the light. His culpability is great because he has all the resources he needs in the Word. He has fellow believers to whom he can turn for fellowship, prayer, sympathy, strength and encouragement.

Mortification of sin is a subject which requires separate treatment yet I would assert here that mortification always concerns remaining corruption not a repeat of being born again. We are baptised into Christ once and for all and hence symbolic baptism is but once. It is possible in times of stress for the Christian to behave like he used to behave when unregenerate, and even have ugly facial expressions which very unhappily might remind those who know him well to recall the former unregenerate person that he was. But whatever grievous lapses there may be he ought to bear in mind always that the old self has died once and for all and that it is terribly inconsistent for him to allow remaining sin to defile and disfigure his testimony.

How great is that act of sovereign mercy that gave us new birth, to bring us to newness of life so we can never again be what we were before.

Born by the Holy Spirit's breath,
Loosed from the law of sin and death,
Now cleared in Christ from every claim
No judgment stands against our name.

In us the Spirit makes his home
That we in him may overcome;
Christ's risen life, in all its powers,
Its all-prevailing strength is ours.[11]

1   Peter Toon, *Born Again,* Baker, 1987, p. 44.
2   Prof John Murray, *Principles of Conduct,* Tyndale, 1957, page 218.
3   *Ibid,* p. 216.
4   Prof John Murray, *Romans,* Eerdmans, 1971, p. 214.
5   cf discussion in *The Illustrated Bible Dictionary*, IVP., vol 1, page 172ff.
6   C E B Cranfield, *Romans*, Eerdmans, 1985, page 132.
7   E K Simpson and F F Bruce, *Commentary on Colossians,* page 235.
8   J B Lightfoot, *Colossians*, Published by Hendricksen, 1982, page 184.
9   Donald MacLeod, *Paul's use of the term 'The Old Man'*, Banner of Truth magazine, number 92, May 1971.
10   *Ibid*, p.16.
11   Timothy Dudley Smith, PRAISE! 688

Holiness According to James

We should note that all teaching in the letters of the New Testament is an extension and elaboration of the teaching of Jesus through his apostles. James has a very distinctive style of his own. For instance he is unique in the way he develops the necessity of controlling the tongue. Isaiah when faced with the glorious holiness of Yahweh in the Temple was immediately convicted about his speech. 'Woe to me – I am ruined! For I am a man of unclean lips, and I live among a people of unclean lips' (Isa 6:5).

'If anyone is never at fault in what he says, he is a perfect man, able to keep his whole body in check' (3:2) 'All kinds of animals, birds, reptiles and creatures of the sea are being tamed and have been tamed by man, but no man can tame the tongue. It is a restless evil, full of deadly poison' (3:7-8).

But essentially that is an extension of our Lord's teaching when he said, 'But I tell you, Do not swear at all: either by heaven, for it is God's throne; or by the earth, for it is his footstool; or by Jerusalem, for it is the city of the Great King. And do not swear by your head, for you cannot make even one hair white or black. Simply let your 'Yes' be 'Yes,' and your 'No' 'No'; anything beyond this comes from the evil one' (Matt 5:34-37).

The outstanding features describing the holy life in James are as follows:

Holiness is:

1. Enduring trials well 1:2-4
2. Controlling the tongue 3:3-12
3. Looking after orphans and widows in their distress 1:27
4. Shunning worldliness 1:27 and 4:4
5. Zeal for good works 2:14-25

✎ Chapter 12 ✎
Holiness and Being a Wretched Man

According to B B Warfield there developed in Germany rationalist teachers such as Ritschl, Wernle, Clemen, Pfleiderer and Windisch who regarded what they termed 'miserable-sinner Christianity' with contempt.[1] These rationalists mounted a full-scale assault against 16th-century Reformation teaching. They regarded the straw man they set up, namely, – the miserable sinner – with extreme distaste and hurled rotten tomatoes at it. It is needful therefore to preface this exposition with a caveat, namely, that Paul in Romans seven is not suggesting that the demeanour of the Christian is one of unmitigated misery and that he is always going around in sackcloth and ashes lamenting his miserable condition. Rather Paul is describing the very real conflict involved in the work of progressive sanctification. It is one of the glories of the Psalms that they describe every kind of spiritual experience from ecstatic joy to deepest depression. Also the Psalms describe battles, struggles and conflicts of all kinds. King David experienced all these. We should not take any one conflict and suggest that all the life of the believer is like that. There is a battle with sin and to that we now turn.

Sanctification and the conflict of Romans 7

Romans chapter 6 presents the main or central passage in the Bible on positional life. 'In Christ', the expression used exclusively by Paul about 150 times, aptly expresses 'positionism' or union with Christ, which is the basis upon which God deals with us. Having marked out the implications of positional sanctification in chapter six the apostle goes on to consider the very important subject of the law of God. Romans chapter two has important references to the law but here in chapter seven we have a thorough treatment. To begin with we are reminded clearly that the law can never justify. We can never be saved by our own goodness. The law is the weapon to show us our sin and need. Without it we might think that we were not sinners at all. By the law is the knowledge of sin. Sin is the transgression of the law. Oh! What fury! What a tempest, earthquake and storm can come to the conscience by the power of the law! By using the law, the Holy Spirit can mightily amaze the conscience. What awakenings of soul and vigorous personal convictions are described in Romans 7:7-13! Paul tells us what the law did to him to awaken him.

Then suddenly at verse 14 there is a change of tense. At this point Paul describes the work of the law, not in terms of what it did to show him that his only hope was Christ, but now in 7:14-25 he provides an intensely personal description of what the law was doing for him as a Christian. 'What a wretched man I am!' (7:24) 'I am sold ... as a slave to sin' (v14). The apostle is describing his experience as a believer. All the way through verses 14-25 he is telling of the conflict present with him. The lesson of Romans 7:14-25 will be lost if we do not appreciate the role of the law in progressive sanctification. But first a problem needs to be removed.

The difficulty that arises in some minds is the question, How can the holy apostle be so bad as to use the language ascribed to the wicked king Ahab? 'There was never a man like Ahab, who sold himself to do evil in the eyes of the LORD' (1 Kings 21:25). How can an advanced Christian talk as though he were Ahab? Once we define exactly what Paul means by *the sinful nature* (vs 22 and 25) and at the same time grasp exactly what he means by 'I *myself in my mind*', we will begin to understand and appreciate this very important part of the New Testament.

A further problem as already indicated above is the apparent contradiction between Paul the victorious and joyful apostle and his lamentation of wretchedness. Indeed how does that wretched state fit with the modern song?

> *I am a new creation, no more in condemnation,*
> *Here in the grace of God I stand.*
> *My heart is overflowing,*
> *My love just keeps on growing,*
> *Here in the grace of God I stand.*

Holiness movements and the advocates of perfectionism miss the inseparable union of justification and positional and progressive sanctification in Romans six. They divide Christians into two camps: those who are justified only and are carnal struggling Christians who fit into the description of Romans 7:14-25, and those who are both justified and sanctified.[2]

The new man and the sinful nature

That Paul 'the new man' or 'new creation' (2 Cor 5:17; Eph 2:10) is speaking is seen by verse 22, 'For in my inner being I delight in God's law.' Such a delight is the exact opposite of the unregenerate person whose mind is at enmity to God's law, is not subject to it, neither indeed can be (Rom 8:7). The new man is the believing Paul who loves God, loves God's laws and loves his people. He loves so much that he strives to do the will of God perfectly. Precisely because of his desires to do what is right he is extremely vexed that he is unable to fulfil the good he aspires to do.

Here is Paul, not the old blaspheming persecutor and hater of the Church, but the new man locked in a spiritual conflict. What is the hindering factor? Answer: *the flesh* (KJV), *the sinful nature* (NIV). It will truly help to understand what 'the flesh' is. This represents all the sinful desires of the flesh and of the mind. A catalogue of these evil propensities is described in Galatians 5:19-21. Here are a few: sexual immorality, idolatry, hatred, jealousies, fits of rage, selfish ambition, dissensions. Do you know these? When a person is born again he is renewed in the whole of his nature, mind, and will. But he is not made perfect. He does not become an angel. He is not yet glorified.

The sinful nature can be defined as that corrupt nature which remains after a man is regenerated. All the evil propensities of the flesh and the mind, the whole range of them, add up to 'the sinful nature'. This layer of desires may be dormant like poisonous snakes in the winter. When warmed by the sunshine of temptation these serpents are dangerous. For example there is the awful power of pride. This remains in the Christian but can be aroused to be a vile and ugly monster. The Christian may feel himself to be truly repentant and humble but let someone come along and tell him what a wonderful, outstanding, magnificent fellow he is, if he is not careful he will accept it and fall into the sin of pride. Pride is very subtle. Remember the kings Uzziah and Hezekiah. Although experienced elderly men they fell grievously into the evil of pride. Both Uzziah and Miriam were afflicted with leprosy as a result of pride.

It is fatal for a Christian to presume that he is free from the dangers of the sinful nature. Remember how David fell into the sins of adultery and murder. I have known fully reformed consistent hard-working pastors who have allowed themselves to backslide and then fall into scandalous sin which has subsequently barred them from the ministry and caused that shadows have been cast over them for the rest of their lives. This does not happen often but sadly it does take place.

I have used the most basic illustrations but am persuaded that Paul was battling with the issue of sin and temptation at a much deeper level, namely that of falling short of the spiritual standards he desired. This brings me to the main purpose of the passage, which is to describe the function of the law in the struggle involved in progressive sanctification. We should remember the experience of Job who is described as 'blameless and upright, a man who fears God and shuns evil' (Job 1:8). At the end of his tribulation Job declared, 'My ears had heard of you but now my eyes have seen you. Therefore I despise myself and repent in dust and ashes' (Job 42:5,6). That is surely the same kind of experience as is described in Romans 7:14-25. Likewise there is the description of the new covenant by Ezekiel. 'I will give you a new heart and put a new spirit in you.' The prophet goes on to describe the blessings bestowed in the covenant but adds, Then you will remember your evil ways and wicked deeds, and you will loathe yourselves for your sins and detestable practices' (Ez 36:26-31). That is very similar in character to Romans 7:14-25.

The power of the law

'Do not covet' declares the 10th commandment. That strikes at the inward man (7:7). The law is holy, righteous and good. All God's laws are just whether expressed in the decalogue or in other ways. His law requires that we love him perfectly and other men as ourselves. Now when we strive after that we find that we simply cannot attain to it. As God's law never changes in its perfection and demands so we find another principle which Paul calls 'a law', – 'a law of sin', – 'a law of selfishness', which is always present. We never seem to be able to witness to the faith the way we would like to.

Especially when we are under pressure or in some trial we make such a hash of things. We feel ashamed. We say, 'That's me! what a wretched creature I am.' The more spiritual we become and the more we grow in grace and in knowledge the higher the standards we set for ourselves and the greater is our disappointment when we fall short of being like Christ in his love, compassion, wisdom, patience and good works. The deeper our understanding of the spirituality of the law the greater our distress when we fall short of what we should be and want to be. As a young believer I often felt proud about my 'good works' but now often feel disgust, shame and repugnance at both self and its performances. First by the express meaning of the passage and second by my own experience I conclude that Paul in Romans 7:14-25 is Paul at his highest and best spiritually. Here we have Paul who clearly sees the beauty of holiness. He strives mightily for it. He knows truly how good and spiritual the law is. He experiences sorrow and frustration that he is hindered from the perfection which he desires.

Let us illustrate the principle. Take prayer as an example. Think of all that we should be in fervent and constant prayer. Then look at our performance! Isn't it wretched? Why is it that we do not have the passion for good and for holiness that we should have? If we take God's law to stand for love (Rom 13:10), think of how far short we fall.

Also consider what zealous faithful church members we should be. Then look at our feebleness. We observe there is nothing wrong with God's requirements. The problem lies in our sinful natures. The laws and precepts of God in general and the Ten Commandments in particular fulfil a vital role in our progress in holy living. Constantly the full measure of what we ought to be must be set before us. We must strive after holiness without which no man will see the Lord. Will this struggle not result in misery and introspection? Certainly not! Obviously we are not beating our breasts in lamentations all the time. Romans 7:14-25 is a vital and integral part of our Christian experience. It describes the reality of the spiritual battle. It is not a constant experience all the time but a component part of our experience, just as there are other components such as love and anger, joy and sorrow. Paul describes his conflict. He is not overwhelmed by it. The battle is a reality.

Help for those who struggle to accept that this is truly Paul

Just how difficult this passage can be for some Christians, even the most gifted, is illustrated by Dr Martyn Lloyd-Jones. He taught that the wretched man of Romans seven represents an unconverted man who is experiencing conviction of sin as the Holy Spirit reveals to him the depravity of his heart.[3] He understood the wretched man of Romans seven to stand for a soul under conviction of sin and on his way to becoming a true believer. Dr Lloyd-Jones is correct in describing the history of interpretation of Romans seven. The early Fathers took the wretched man to be unregenerate. So did Augustine but later he changed his mind and took the wretched man to be Paul the regenerate believer battling with indwelling sin. Almost all the 16th century Reformers and English Puritans such as John Owen and Matthew Henry followed this interpretation. Well-known expositors and commentators of the 19th and 20th centuries who follow the Puritans in their understanding of the wretched man of Romans seven are John Brown, Charles Hodge, Robert Haldane, H Bavinck, Louis Berkhof, G C Berkouwer, F F Bruce, R C H Lenski, Prof John Murray, Cornelius Pronk, Ernest Kevan, J I Packer, Anders Nygren, Leon Morris, C E B Cranfield and G B Wilson. This position is confirmed by the wording of the Westminster Confession of Faith chapter 16 paragraph 4.

John Stott in his commentary on Romans suggests that Roman 7:14,15 describes, 'Jewish Christians of Paul's day, regenerated but not liberated, under the law and not yet in or under the Spirit'. So how would the passage have meaning for us today? Stott answers: 'Some church-goers today might be termed "Old Testament Christians". In "slavery to rules and regulations". '[4] What makes this view untenable is that the section concludes on a high note of thankfulness for deliverance in Romans 7:25.

Douglas Moo in his commentary on Romans concedes that the use of *egō* in verses 14 to 25 is very strong, Paul testifying of himself, but then Moo reasons that Paul is expressing solidarity with Jewish people under the law. 'Paul speaks as a "representative" Jew, detailing his past in order to reveal the weakness of the law and the source of that weakness: the human being, the *egō*.'[5]

Readers of Paul's letter to the Romans do well to delete the chapter headings for chapters six to eight and observe that the same believer is described throughout. 'You have been set free from sin and have become slaves to righteousness' (6:18). Conflict is described in chapter six verse 12 where resistance to sin reigning in 'your mortal body' is urged. Romans 8:13 is an outright command to mortify the misdeeds of the body. A chapter of this book devoted to that essential discipline for every Christian. Chapter seven is unique inasmuch as it provides a complete overview of the rôle of the moral law. Galatians 5:16-18 is correctly regarded as a parallel with Romans 7:14-25 describing the conflict in the soul of a believer: 'So I say, live by the Spirit, and you will not gratify the desires of the sinful nature. For the sinful nature desires what is contrary to the Spirit, and the Spirit what is contrary to the sinful nature. They are

in conflict with each other, so that you do not do what you want.
But if you are led by the Spirit, you are not under law.'

Some suggest that Romans 7:14-25 is a description of a Christian
in bondage and that deliverance consists of moving out of Romans
chapter seven into Romans chapter eight. But 7:25 expresses
gratitude for the deliverance that belongs to the believer in Christ.
Paul having declared, 'So then, I myself in my mind am a slave to
God's law, but in the sinful nature a slave to the law of sin' (7:25),
goes on to say, without any break, 'Therefore, there is now no
condemnation for those who are in Christ Jesus.' The reality is that
all believers experience conflict but at the same time they are held
firmly in the state of justification.

'The man who never strives against the sin which dwells in him, who
indeed is not conscious of any sin to strive against, that is the man
who may begin to question whether he knows anything at all about
the spiritual life. He who has no inward pain may well suspect that he
is abiding in death, abiding therefore under constant condemnation;
but the man who feels daily striving after deliverance from evil, who
is panting, and pining, and longing, and agonizing to become holy
even as God is holy, he is the justified man. The man to whom every
sin is a misery, to whom even the thought of iniquity is intolerable,
he is the man who may with confidence declare, "There is therefore
now no condemnation to them which are in Christ Jesus." Souls
that sigh for holiness are not condemned to eternal death, for their
sighing proves that they are in Christ Jesus.'[6]

For further reading

The most concise and lucid book devoted to this subject is by A
Benjamin Clark. Aptly the title is *Delight for a Wretched Man* and
the sub-title, *Romans seven and the doctrine of sanctification.*[7]

C H Spurgeon was 25 years old when he preached a resounding
sermon on Romans 7:24. In his exposition the young preacher
declared, 'It is my agonising death struggle with my corruptions
that proves me to be a living child of God. These two natures will

never give up; they will never cry truce, they will never ask for a treaty to be made between the two.'[8]

Charles Hodge by way of summary and application in his Commentary on Romans 7:14-25 writes, 'The person here described hates sin, verse 15, acknowledges and delights in the spirituality of the divine law, verses 16, 22; he considers his corruption a dreadful burden, from which he earnestly desires to be delivered, verse 24. These are exercises of genuine piety, and should be applied as tests of character.'[9]

F F Bruce in his commentary on Romans tells of Alexander Whyte who used to have new books brought to him for examination with purchase in mind. If a new commentary on Romans arrived he would open it at chapter 7:14-25 and if the author set up a straw man, (that is if he said that it wasn't really the spiritual Paul speaking), then he would send back the commentary forthwith!

C E B Cranfield goes to the heart of this issue. He maintains that, 'Many commentators have stated confidently that it cannot be a Christian who speaks here. But the truth is, surely, that inability to recognise the distress reflected in this cry as characteristic of Christian existence argues a failure to grasp the full seriousness of the Christian's obligation to express his gratitude to God by obedience of life. The farther men advance in the Christian life, and the more mature their discipleship, the clearer becomes their perception of the heights to which God calls them, and the more painfully sharp their consciousness of the distance between what they ought, and want, to be, and what they are. The assertion that this cry could only come from an unconverted heart, and that the apostle must be expressing not what he feels as he writes but vividly remembered experience of the unconverted man, is we believe, totally untrue.'[10]

William S Plumer's commentary on Romans is helpful. He writes: 'The language is so strong that some have said it cannot possibly apply to the Christian for he is happy and not wretched. Wardlaw well says: "It is truly marvellous that such an argument should ever have been used. One is strongly tempted to suspect that he by whom such an argument could be used can never himself have felt the burden of corruption, the plagues of his own heart. Is it not the very man whose heart is most under the influence of holiness and the love of God that feels most acutely the anguish of a sense of remaining corruption?'"[11]

Thomas R Schreiner's commentary on Romans was published in 1998. He suggests that, 'The struggle with sin continues for believers because we live in the tension between the already and the not yet. The specific texts adduced above (6:12; 8:10-13,23) demonstrate that there is tension between inaugurated and consummated eschatology in believers. Complete deliverance from sin is not available for Christians until the day of redemption.'[12]

---

1 B B Warfield. Perfectionism, P and R, 1958. In an eight page preface, the editor of this volume, Samuel G Craig explains that B B Warfield wrote two volumes on Perfectionism. The first dealt with German rationalists and is not currently in print. The second is the well-known 486 page volume which is the classic work on Perfectionism in the English- speaking world.

2 Benjamin Clark, in his book *Delight for a Wretched Man*, includes the Fellowship Movement, the Sanctification Movement, English Methodism, the Victorious Life Movement, the Keswick Convention and Pentecostalism and much of the modern charismatic movement as following this principle of sanctified and unsanctified Christians. For further discussion of this issue see appendix. *Delight for a Wretched Man* with the sub-title *Romans 7 and the doctrine of sanctification* is published by Evangelical Press, 160 pages, 1993.

3 Dr Martyn Lloyd-Jones preached a series of expositions on Romans at Westminster Chapel from 1955 to 1968. These have been edited and published in eleven bound volumes by the Banner of Truth Trust. They reach the end of chapter 13. In the volume 'Chapter 7:1 to 8:4' (359 pages), Dr Lloyd-Jones defends his interpretation of the wretched man of chapter seven being a man under conviction on his way to be converted. In his ministry Dr Lloyd-Jones placed a much needed emphasis on the importance of experimental Christianity. These volumes are full of excellence. The Doctors' view that the wretched man was an unregenerate man is not convincing as has been demonstrated.

4 John Stott, *Romans*, IVP, 2003, page 209.

5 Douglas Moo, *Romans*, Eerdmans, page 448.

6 I picked this quote up in general reading but did not make a note of its source. The style is Spurgeonic.

7 *Ibid*, Benjamin Clark.

8 C H Spurgeon, sermon 235, *The New Park Street Pulpit*, 1859, Banner of Truth, 1964.

9 Charles Hodge, *Romans*, Banner of Truth, 1972.

10   C E B Cranfield, *Romans*, Eerdmans, 1985, page 169.
11   William S Plumer, *Romans*, Kregel, 1993, page 357.
12   Thomas R Schreiner, *Romans*, Baker Book House, 1998, page 390. Schreiner is very fair in his setting out the views of those who cannot accept that Romans 7:14-25 is descriptive of regenerate souls.

E F Kevan and the Grace of Law

E F Kevan (1903-1965) was a Baptist pastor from 1924 to 1946 before becoming the first principal of the London Bible College. During the period immediately following the World War Dr Kevan with Dr Martyn Lloyd-Jones were outstanding nonconformist evangelical leaders in London. E F Kevan's book *The Grace of Law* is a classic. He shows that the English Puritans contrary to popular opinion succeeded more than any other group of theologians in differentiating between legalism and antinomianism. In this study he explores the indispensable place of God's law in the life of the Christian. Here is a typical statement:

> 'The place of the moral law of God is observable in every department of theology, and particularly Puritan theology. Sin is the transgression of law, the death of Christ is the satisfaction of law, justification is the verdict of the law and sanctification is the believer's fulfilment of the law.'[1]

To further unpack the above statement I observe the following. Without the moral law of God, that is the Ten Commandments, we cannot define what sin is, as the Scripture says, 'Through the law we become conscious of sin' (Rom 3:20). Without the law there is nothing for Christ to satisfy, but the moral law is the measure or rod of Christ's perfections throughout his life. He kept the law for us so that the righteousness of that law can be imputed to us who believe. And how could Christ be sent to the Cross unless it was on account of the transgressions of the holy law of God that we have committed?

Antinomians claim that we are no longer under the Ten Commandments. This position is known in the 21st century as 'New Covenant Theology'. This view is not new. E F Kevan shows that all aspects of this theological territory were covered in nineteen books, for and against, published between 1631 and 1656. The controversy broke out again in 1690 when Richard Baxter wrote a book with the title *The Scripture Gospel Defended*. This led to eight more books being published on this subject between 1690 and 1700.[2]

---

[1]   E F Kevan, *The Grace of Law*, page 21. First published by Carey Kingsgate Press this treatise was republished by Baker Book House in 1976 and again by Soli Deo Gloria Publications in 1993.

[2]   *Ibid* page 35ff.

✎ *Chapter 13* ✐

Holiness and the Reality of Sin

An essential part of sanctification is understanding what sin is.

In an exposition with the title 'Going Soft on Sin' given at the Carey Conference for Ministers in January 2010 John Benton began as follows:

> 'Perhaps understandably, people have always looked for some loophole, some way of avoiding or at least toning down the seriousness of sin and its consequences. And current Western culture puts pressure on the church to play down sin's seriousness and that pressure has grown almost overwhelming.

> 'As we move into the second decade of the 21st century we must give fresh attention to the doctrine of sin, because of course, the whole gospel is predicated upon the fact that people are sinners and need to be saved from sin and its wages. If we go soft on sin, the biblical gospel and the whole necessity for the gospel begins to sink into obscurity.'[1]

Principal reasons which underline the urgent need to be clear about what sin is are as follows.

Firstly, we live in the climate of postmodernism. Western society encourages sin massively and resists definition or clarity about sin.

Postmodernist philosophy is fiercely antinomian, that is anti-law. Right and wrong are judged according to human feelings. The result is a slide into an abyss of lawlessness. The consequences of lawlessness are seen in the alarming increase in family break-up, divorce, crime and overcrowded prisons. An example of a book which deals with this theme is *The Vanishing Conscience* by John F MacArthur Jr, a study which demonstrates that failure to deal with sin as sin lies at the foundation of America's moral collapse.[2]

Secondly, John Benton points out that much which flies under the name of Christianity avoids the subject of sin. The word 'sin' is hardly ever mentioned in the media. When well-known people behave in a scandalous manner that is described as 'mistakes' made by them not sin. A ministry which is weak and flabby on the subject of sin is a useless ministry. A preaching ministry that does not result in conviction of sin is useless. If it does not wound how can it heal? The good news is only for sinners. The unbelieving world caricatures and mocks preachers. They are sometimes depicted as silly, soft and effeminate. At other times the typical preacher is portrayed as one who bellows and raves. The young Spurgeon was by far the most effective preacher of his time but was fiercely ridiculed and opposed in the press. Those truly called know that the Word of God is as sharp as a two-edged sword and that their business is to wield that sword (Heb 4:12).

Thirdly, Christ and him crucified is our theme. Christianity is unique as it alone deals faithfully with the root problem of mankind which is sin. And Christianity is unique as it provides the only effectual remedy for sin. Christ appeared that he might take away our sins. He, who knew no sin, was made to be sin for us that we might become the righteousness of God in him (2 Cor 5:21). The enormity of sin is seen in the death of deaths that was Christ's. Millions of dollars are invested in scientific laboratories to seek solutions for disease but our business as pastors and preachers is to deal clearly and faithfully with sin, its nature, guilt and consequences, and then the remedy which is found uniquely and only in the blood and sacrifice of Christ. 'Look, the Lamb of God, who takes away the sin of the world!' (John 1:29).

Fourthly, without a biblical understanding of sin we cannot deal correctly and faithfully with the great central themes of life, namely, creation and the historic space-time fall of Adam and Eve, the nature of law, the place of conscience, the history of redemption, Christ's active and passive work, regeneration, sanctification, ultimate judgment and eternal heaven and hell.

Fifthly, arising out of the above, no reality is more terrible in all the universe than eternal hell. Sin is the principal issue explaining why there should be such a thing.

The English Puritans were strongest where we are weakest and we can derive much help from their writings on the subject of sin. They dealt with the subject of sin comprehensively. Jeremiah Burroughs in his book *The Evil* of *Evils*[3] declared of sin that it makes a man conformable to the devil, 'for sin is of the same nature as the devil and a furtherance of the devil's kingdom in the world'. Using the Puritan armoury let us proceed on this subject of sin as follows.

The strengths of Puritan teaching:

1. They used God's moral law to define sin
2. They expounded the truth of original sin
3. They stressed the necessity of mortification of sin
4 They warned of eternal punishment

1. The Puritans used God's moral law to define sin

Ralph Venning (1621-1674), a popular preacher in London four years after bubonic plague swept the city in 1665, wrote a book *The Plague of Plagues,*[4] an apt title since there is no plague like the plague of sin which kills every member of the human race. Physical death is the first death. The plague of sin is also responsible for the second death whereby all those who die in their sins are subject to eternal punishment in hell. Venning divides his exposition into four parts, 1. What sin is, 2. The sinfulness of sin, 3. The witnesses against sin, and 4. Application in which he describes the good news of how to escape from the guilt and power of sin.

Venning begins his treatise with definition: 'Sin is the transgression of a law, yea of a good law, yea of God's law. Sin presupposes that there is a law in being, for where there is no law there is no transgression (Rom 4:15). But where there is sin, there is a law, and a transgression of the law. Whosoever commits sin transgresses also the law, for sin is a transgression of the law (1 John 3:4). That this is the sin intended in our text is apparent from Romans 7:7. Now the law not only forbids the doing of evil, whether by thought, word or deed, but also commends the doing of good. So to omit the good command is sin, as well (or ill) as is the doing of the evil that is forbidden.'

Edward Reynolds (1593-1676) was an eminent preacher greatly skilled in the Greek language. He served in the Westminster Assembly and wrote a treatise titled *The Sinfulness of Sin*. This principally consists of an exposition of Romans 7:9: 'Once I was alive apart from the law; but when the commandment came, sin sprang to life and I died.' Reynolds shows that a man may have the law in the letter and yet be without it in power and spirit. But the Holy Spirit takes the law and convinces a man that he is in a state of sin.

He continues: 'Now the law gives life and strength to sin in three ways: First by way of the curse and obligation of it, binding the soul with the guilt of sin to the judgment of the great day. Second by the irritation of the law, "Sin took occasion by the law, and so by the commandment became exceeding sinful." Third by conviction, laying open the wideness of sin to the conscience. As a serpent seems dead in the snow but is revived by heat so sin seems dead when covered by ignorance but when awakened a man finds himself in the mouth of death.'[5]

The majority of Puritans placed much stress on the preaching of the law to bring men to an awareness of sin. William Perkins knew that true repentance was the result of gospel grace, but he opposed those who for this reason would despise the preaching of the law. Anthony Burgess declared that the exhibition of 'the pure, strict and exact obligation of the Law' makes 'all thy deformities' to appear, and so 'in this sense it is good to be a legal preacher, and a legal hearer often'. He considered that this legal preaching was 'the great work that the ministers of God have to do in their congregations in these times. Men must come to the knowledge of sin in themselves, by the Law', and this is no 'easie matter', but 'it is the preaching of the Law of God . . . that will . . . discover to them their hidden and secret sins; never was any brought to a sight of his sinnes, . . . but only by the preaching of the Law of God.'[6]

2. *The Puritans expounded the truth of original sin*

Thomas Goodwin in his great work *An Unregenerate Man's Guiltiness Before God in Respect of Sin and Punishment* proceeds directly to the root of the matter, namely, original sin.[7] Goodwin begins with Romans 5:12: 'Wherefore, as by one man sin entered into the world, and death by sin; so death passed upon all men, for that all have sinned.' Goodwin opens up Romans chapters one to three to show that sin has universally overtaken the world, not one person excepted. Having established the truth of original sin and guilt, Goodwin proceeds to show how corruption has overtaken man in all his faculties, his understanding, affections, conscience and will.

The Puritan doctrine of original sin is expounded among others by David Clarkson, Thomas Watson, John Flavel, John Owen, and later in the same tradition by Thomas Boston and Jonathan Edwards.[8] The clearest definition which sums up the doctrine of original sin is that of the Larger Westminster Catechism, question 25:

> *Wherein consists the sinfulness of that estate into which man fell?*

Answer:

> *The sinfulness of that estate whereinto man fell consists in the guilt of Adam's first sin, the loss of that righteousness in which he was created, and the corruption of his nature, whereby he is utterly indisposed, disabled, and made opposite to all that is spiritually good, and wholly inclined to all evil, and that continually; which is commonly called original sin, and from which all actual transgressions proceed.*

Similar wording is found in chapter 6 of the Westminster Confession, paragraph four. In the 1689 Baptist Confession the same paragraph reads:

> The actual sins that men commit are the fruit of the corrupt nature transmitted to them by our first parents. By reason of this corruption, all men become wholly inclined to all evil; sin disables them. They are utterly indisposed to, and, indeed, rendered opposite to, all that is good.[9]

All born to Adam inherit[10] his guilt and corruption. The clause 'rendered opposite to all that is good' does not mean that every person is as bad as he possibly could be. There is an enormous amount of good in the world. This good we ascribe to the loving kindness of God. We call it common grace. God's common grace is widely misconstrued since it is argued that since there is so much good in the world, this gloomy view of sin which I have been describing cannot be correct. But it is correct. Man's depravity is stark. Recall the two great World Wars of the last century, the holocaust organised by the Nazis (six million perished in the extermination camps plus a further six million who were classed as belonging to undesirable categories), and the Gulag (eighteen million perished in the death camps in the Soviet Union under Stalin). The genocide in Cambodia, Rwanda/Burundi, Yugoslavia, and currently the murders in East Timor, all provide evidence of the depravity of man. World history is a saga of sin and suffering but life would be impossible were it not for the tremendous power exercised by the Holy Spirit to restrain sin and keep it under control.

It can be argued, if man is fallen in all his faculties, why expend effort to persuade him to believe and repent? The answer is that the Holy Spirit uses preaching and literature to invade the dominions of darkness. He is the Spirit of regeneration. He uses the proclamation of biblical truth to arrest and convert. He convinces the world of sin, righteousness and judgment to come (John 16:8).

Adam was given a specific law. He represented the human race. In breaking that law his guilt is imputed to all his descendants.

Thomas Watson suggests that much was involved in that first sin. Included was unbelief, ingratitude, discontent, pride, disobedience, theft, presumption, carelessness (lack of thought or consideration) and murder.[11] Murder, because Adam had been told most clearly that in the day he ate that fruit he would die. In his sin he murdered his posterity. Watson places unbelief at the head of his list. Stephen Charnock in an exposition of John 16:9, 'Of sin, because they believe not on me', asserts unbelief to be the fountain of all sins and suggests that God has to employ the highest means to bring men to a sense of the sin of unbelief.[12] Of all sins unbelief is the most harmful because it is a sin against the only remedy available.

Adam stood in the place of us all in his disobedience and sin. What he did was in effect what all his posterity, each and every one of us, did. Thomas Manton expresses it this way: 'We saw the forbidden fruit with his eyes, gathered it with his hands, ate it with his mouth; that is, we were ruined by those things as though we had been there and consented to his acts.'[13]

Original sin is not an easy truth to grasp. Herman Bavinck, the great Dutch theologian, declares that this question is the second greatest enigma that exists. The origin of being is the first enigma. Bavinck adds that the origin of sin is certainly the hardest cross for man's understanding to bear.[14]

3. The Puritans stressed the necessity of mortification of sin

I have devoted a chapter to this subject and so will be brief here. Owen opens up Romans 8:13 under the following heads, 1. A duty prescribed: *mortify the deeds of the body* 2. The persons denoted *You, if you mortify* 3. *the* promise attached: *you shall live* 4. *the* means employed: if you *through the Spirit* and 5. The condition: *If* you mortify.[15]

Owen stresses that the Christian should all his life make it his business to mortify the power of indwelling sin. 'The vigour, and power, and comfort of our spiritual life depends on the mortification of the deeds of the flesh.' He warns sternly of the power that lies in unmortified sin.

> 'Sin aims always at the utmost; every time it rises up to tempt or entice, if it has its own way it will go out to the utmost sin in that kind. Every unclean thought or glance would be adultery if it could, every thought of unbelief would be atheism if allowed to develop. Every rise of lust, if it has its way reaches the height of villainy; it is like the grave that is never satisfied. The deceitfulness of sin is seen in that it is modest in its first proposals but when it prevails it hardens men's hearts, and brings them to ruin.'

Owen quotes Hebrews 3:13 which tells us that sin deceives – 'the deceitfulness of sin'! Remember how sin deceived the Israelites in the wilderness when they hardened their hearts.

Thomas Manton in an exposition of Romans 6:14, 'For sin shall not have dominion over you; for ye are not under the law, but under grace,' reasons 'There is still sin in us, a bosom enemy which is born and bred with us, and therefore soon will get the advantage of grace, if it be not well watched and resisted, as nettles and weeds, which are kindly to the soil, and grow of their own accord, will soon choke flowers, which are planted by care and industry, when they are neglected and not continually rooted out. We cannot get rid of this cursed inmate till this outward tabernacle be dissolved, and this house of clay be crumbled into dust, like ivy gotten into a wall, that will not be destroyed till the wall be pulled down.'[16]

Mortification of sin extends to thoughts of the mind. Obadiah Sedgwick opens up Psalm 19:13: 'Cleanse me from secret sins.' 'Secret sins will become public sins if they are not cleansed. If you suppress them not in their root, you shall shortly see them break out in the fruit. A fire catches first the inside of the house and if not put out makes its way to the outside, 'Lust when it has conceived brings forth sin' (James 1:15).[17]

Sometimes we are deeply shocked by the falling into sin followed by the complete apostasy of some who have been highly esteemed as preachers and leaders in the Church. This is a reminder that no believer is exempt from the necessity of mortification of sin. Often there is very real pain involved in mortification. Jeremiah Burroughs' principal thrust in his great book *The Evil of Evils* declares that there is more evil in the least sin than in the greatest affliction. He points out that the heroes described in Hebrews chapter eleven chose and preferred the most terrible afflictions rather than to sin by denying their faith.

4. The Puritans warned of eternal punishment

Ralph Venning describes the hell into which Jesus descended in the bearing away of our sins. 'He suffered all kinds of sufferings. He suffered in every part and member of his body from head to foot. He suffered in his soul. He cried out on the cross , "My God, my God, why have you forsaken me?" He had all kinds of aggravating circumstances united in his sufferings.' 'The greatness of Christ's sufferings is a full witness against the sinfulness of sin.'[18]

Christ's achievement to atone for and take away our sin is immense. This is appreciated when we see what every sin deserves. Venning does not shrink from telling of the appalling torments which result from sin. 'Hell is the centre of all punishments, sorrow and pain, wrath and vengeance, fire and darkness,' 'These torments will be without intermission and will be forever . . . there will be aggravations of these torments for those who have lived long in sin, those who have had more opportunity to repent, and more knowledge, and for apostates who have turned their backs on God.'[19]

Ralph Venning displays a wonderful ability to have the text of Scripture exercise its own power. He proceeds:

> The persons sentenced: those on his left hand
> The sentence: Depart from me
> The state they are in: cursed
> The torment: everlasting fire
> The company that is theirs: the devil and his angels [20]

The weight of the guilt of sin is stressed by John Flavel in his treatise on the Soul of Man. 'The guilt of all sin gathers to, and settles in the conscience of every Christless sinner, and makes up a vast treasure of guilt in the course of his life in this world.'[21]

George Swinnock (1627-1673) in a deeply moving exposition on Matthew 25:41 titled 'The sinner's last sentence' exposes the guilt of law-breakers 'He breaks the whole law by breach of any one of them, because he sins against love, and breaks that bond and knot which keeps and fastens the whole law together.'[22] In a sermon on the same text Richard Adams concludes by reminding his hearers that our Lord urged that we are to fear him who is able to destroy both soul and body in hell (Luke 12:5). Adams exhorts to flee speedily from sin by repentance and holds up the superlative love of Christ displayed in undergoing the punishment that was our due. 'O let us now bathe our souls in the blood of Christ that everlasting burnings may not hereafter seize upon us.'[23]

---

1   John Benton is pastor of Chertsey Street Baptist Church, Guildford, Surrey, and is editor of the monthly newspaper *Evangelicals Now*. His exposition 'Going Soft on Sin' is published in *Reformation Today*, issue 234.

2   John F MacArthur Jr. *The Vanishing Conscience*, 280 page hardback, Word Publishers, 1994.

3   Jeremiah Burroughs (1599-1646), *The Evil of Evils – The Exceeding Sinfulness of Sin*. His book first appeared in 1654 and was republished as a handsome bound volume of 341 pages by Soli Deo Gloria, USA in 1992.

4   Ralph Venning (1621-1674) was an outstanding preacher. His book *The Plague of Plagues* was republished with the title *The Sinfulness of Sin* in 1993. Banner of Truth paperback, 283 pages.

5   Edward Reynolds, *The Sinfulness of Sin*, Soli Deo Gloria, 1992, page 114ff.

6   This paragraph is cited from Ernest F Kevan's outstanding book *The Grace of Law* published in 1976 by Baker Book House. A valuable service has been rendered by the publication of a new edition by Soli Deo Gloria.

7   Thomas Goodwin, *Works*, vol 10.

8   David Clarkson (1621-1686), who followed John Owen in his last pastorate wrote on original sin in an exposition of Psalm 51:5, *Works*, vol 1, pages 3-15. Also Thomas Watson, *Body of Divinity*, pages 139-146, John Flavel, vol 6, page 172ff, John Owen, *Works*, vol 2, page 64, and vol 10, pages 68 to 82, in which he shows that Arminians deny the doctrine of original sin. In the tradition of the Puritans see also the *Works* of Thomas Boston, vol 1, pages 1-256. The twelve volumes of Boston's *Works* were published by Richard Owen Roberts, Wheaton, Illinois, USA, in 1980. Jonathan Edwards expounded the doctrine of original sin in depth, *Works*, vol 1 pages 146-233, Banner of Truth edition, 1974.

9   *A Faith to Confess* transposition into modern English of the 1689 Confession published by Carey Publications.

10 Wayne Grudem, *Systematic Theology*, IVP, 1994, page 494ff. Grudem gives sound reasons for using the term 'inherited sin' in lieu of 'original sin'. The phrase *inherited sin* brings home more forcibly the sin that is ours as a result of Adam's fall.

11 Thomas Watson, *A Body of Divinity*, Banner of Truth. Watson's analysis of Adam's sin is highly commended, page 142 ff.

12 Stephen Charnock, *Works*, Parsons edition, 1815, vol 6, page 289ff.

13 Thomas Manton, cited in a bound volume titled *Man's Total Depravity*, written by Arthur W Pink, and published in 1969 by Moody Bible Institute of Chicago.

14 Herman Bavinck, *Gereformeerde Dogmatiek*, 111, page 29.

15 John Owen, *Works*, vol 6, page 5.

16 Thomas Manton, *Works*, vol 1, page 266.

17 Obadiah Sedgwick, *The Anatomy of Secret Sins*, Soli Deo Gloria, 1995.

18 Venning, *ibid*, page 106ff.

19 *Ibid*, page 84ff.

20 *Ibid*, page 71ff.

21 John Flavel, *Works*, vol 3, page 133.

22 George Swinnock, *Works*, vol 5, page 456. The Banner of Truth republished Swinnock's works, five volumes, 1992.

23 Richard Adams, *Puritan Sermons, Morning Exercises at Cripplegate*, Richard Owen Roberts, Wheaton, Illinois, USA, 1981, vol 5, page 471ff.

Wilhelmus à Brakel – the moral law

Wilhelmus à Brakel (1635-1711) born of godly parents served in five pastorates in the Netherlands. His very valuable four volume *Works* have been translated into English and published by Reformation Heritage Books, USA. This is how à Brakel addresses the issue of the moral law of God.

'That the law is and remains a rule of eternal duration is evident for the following reasons:

First, the law of nature remains in force and puts all men under obligation (Rom 2:14-15). Second, the law was solemnly given to the Church without any limitation of time. The law has never been rescinded, neither has a counter law been given. Third, the Lord Jesus declared that the Ten Commandments have not been abrogated, but it remains a binding rule for all times. 'Think not that I am come to destroy the law, or the prophets: I am not come to destroy, but to fulfil. For verily I say unto you, Till heaven and earth pass, one jot or one tittle shall in no wise pass from the law, till all be fulfilled. Whosoever therefore shall break one of these least commandments, and shall teach men to do so, he shall be called least in the kingdom of heaven: but whosoever shall do and teach them, the same shall be called great in the kingdom of heaven' (Matt 5:17-19). It is evident that the reference here is not to the ceremonial law, since Christ, being its embodiment, has abrogated it and the apostles have preached it as having been abrogated. Fourth, the Lord Jesus commands the performance of that which is good since the law requires this (Matt 7:12). Fifth, the keeping of the moral law is proposed and urged everywhere in the New Testament. Here are some of the references: Romans 3:31; 13:8-10; Galatians 5:13-14, Ephesians 6:1-3; James 2:8, 10-11; 1 John 3:4'.

À Brakel follows this (abridged) outline by answering objections, one of which is, Many texts declare that believers in the NT are not under law, the following being the most prominent: Romans 6:14; 7:6; Galatians 3:23-25; 5:18-23 and 1 Timothy 1:9. All these texts are expounded by à Brakel.

Chapter 14

Holiness and the Ten Commandments

The Ten Commandments should have a profound influence in the lives of believers. Not only are the commandments used to bring about a conviction of sin before conversion but as we see from the central passage of Scripture on this subject, namely Romans chapter 7, the commandments are essential in the progressive sanctification of Christians.

In our day there has been a widespread denial of the relevance of the Ten Commandments. The idea has been spread that these commandments were for the Jews and belonged to an ancient legislative system which has little bearing for us today. It has also been suggested that you cannot separate the Ten Commandments from the Jewish ceremonial and civil laws. Prior to the nineteenth century, most, if not all Christians agreed, that the law of God as found in the Ten Commandments was still applicable. However, with the beginning of dispensationalism during the 19th-century all of this was to change. Dispensationalism brought a new doctrine that made a radical distinction between the Church and Israel and the Old Testament and the New. Since the Old Testament was directed primarily to the physical descendants of Abraham and not the New Testament Church, the law of God as found in the Ten Commandments was considered relegated with the ceremonial law.

Basic to the relegation of the Ten Commandments is the contention that you cannot divide the law into moral, ceremonial and civil sections, which is precisely what our Reformed confessions teach.[1] An example of this contention was printed in the Canadian paper *The Gospel Witness*, August 2009. The writer David G Barker states, 'To separate the law into civil, ceremonial and moral components flies in the face of the unity of the law' (cf Gal 5:3). Of course we respect the unity of the law as a whole but that principle must not be used to deny that it is essential to locate the ceremonial law in its entirety and in its constituent parts: tabernacle, priesthood and sacrifices. We must do this because Jesus has fulfilled completely all the typology of the ceremonial law so we will never again have to sacrifice animals, erect a tabernacle and re-establish the Levitical priesthood to serve in it. Also with regard to all civil laws whether in Israel of the past or nations today, civil laws are meaningless unless they are precise. Every law must by its very nature be as clear and explicit as possible if it is to have practical meaning. There are tens of thousands of laws. For instance for centuries in England there have been laws governing the maintenance of roads, pavements and properties. What do you think of a person who, having broken one of these laws, appealed to the magistrate saying, 'Sorry, Your Honour, you cannot divide the unity of law of England into constituent parts and charge me with transgression.' It is the detail of the law which makes it cogent. If you have broken a civil law and have been found guilty of transgression you pay a fine. If you refuse to pay the fine you face a prison sentence. Precise detail is the very essence and nature of all law. It is clarity in respect of detail that makes law viable. We all know what a thirty mile an hour speed limit is and the difference between 30 and 40. Nadab and Abihu were struck dead for their carelessness about detail. They thought it did not matter. But it did matter.

1. The Ten Commandments are unique and separate

If there was ever a time when God stressed something to be special and important it was when he gave Israel the Ten Commandments. Let us recall those actions which pointed to the unique nature of the Decalogue or the Ten Words.

First of all Yahweh made Mount Sinai his throne and surrounded it with thunder, lightning, a thick cloud and an impenetrable darkness. All this was accompanied with a very loud trumpet blast (Ex 19:16). The whole mountain trembled and the smoke billowed from it as it does from a furnace. Then the LORD spoke face to face to the people out of the fire from the mountain (Deut 5:4). This speech was not in a whisper but with a very loud voice to the whole assembly. This event was quite unique. Has any other nation heard the voice of God speaking out of a fire? (Deut 4:33). The most important of all events in history was the coming into this world of Jesus Christ, yet by comparison with Sinai his coming was silent. It was not heralded with trumpets. Certainly it was not a great public event.

Enough has been said to prove that God intended us to note the special nature of the Decalogue. To confirm it all he himself did something further which was quite unique. He wrote these laws on two stone tablets. The two tablets were identical and were engraved on both sides by the fingers of the Lord. And then as if to emphasise once more the separate and special nature of the Decalogue the two tablets, one for the people and one for the LORD by deed of covenant, were placed inside the Ark. This Ark was covered with a solid gold top. To that top were fixed two cherubim of the glory. This gold top was called the mercy seat or literally the place of propitiation (Heb 9:5). The mercy seat represented God's throne, the place from which he could dispense mercy, because Christ himself has satisfied the demands of the moral law. Having fulfilled all those demands he can now justly forgive those who trust in him.

Why is it that the Lord did so much to stress the unique nature of the Decalogue? The answer must surely be that these commandments reflect the holy character of our Triune God.

2. The Ten Commandments reflect the holy character of God

The number ten reminds us of fullness, and when we study the Decalogue we see that every aspect of morality is included. We note this positively because we cannot improve on the command to love God with all our hearts and our neighbours as ourselves.

If we love God with all our minds and hearts it follows that we will not transgress his commands. We note too that the commands concerning our Creator come first, and then those commands which relate to each other follow in logical order. Godliness will always lead to righteousness with regard to our neighbour. Likewise ungodliness will lead to unrighteousness (Rom 1:18).

It is evident that by its very nature the Decalogue is a reflection of the nature of God because it tells us of his love for righteousness and his hatred of iniquity. The Ten Commandments define exactly what sin is. Everyone who sins breaks the law; in fact sin is lawlessness (1 John 3: 4). Since his law reflects his majesty and holiness and purity, to sin is to attack or assault the very nature of God.

Also to be observed is the unity of God's law because if you break one command, you break them all (James 2:10). James, in referring specifically to the Decalogue, calls it 'the royal law'. It is the law of our King. If you put a crack into one of those stone tablets that crack will run right through the whole tablet so that it falls apart. Similarly if one precept is broken it leads to transgression of other parts of God's law. To break one part is effectively to break the whole.

We see that the Decalogue reflects the holy character of God in that life itself is sacred (Commandment 6), as marriage is sacred (Commandment 7), as property ownership is sacred (Commandment 8), as truth is sacred (Commandment 9). That all these things which are holy in God's eyes should be observed from the very depths of the heart is proven by the tenth commandment, you shall not covet, which means that you shall not have evil desires. This reminds us of Jesus and his exposition of some of these commandments in which he proves that all the commandments apply to the hearts of men and point to the evils that spring from fallen hearts (Matt 5:17-30; 15:19).

3. The Ten Commandments transcend time

As the holy character of God is unchanging, so the nature of sin is unchanging. Lying, cheating, adultery or murder were the same in the Garden of Eden as they are today. We know that all desire for sin will be entirely removed so that there will be no transgressions in heaven, but nevertheless were a transgression to be committed in heaven, it would be a transgression of the moral law because sin is the transgression of the moral law. That principle is unchanging.

The New Jerusalem and the world of glory to come will eternally and permanently demonstrate God's great love of righteousness because righteousness will reign there. Likewise hell will permanently and eternally exhibit the fact of God's hatred of transgression and all that does violence to the expression of his holy character.

We can see that while the moral law transcends time and will always be a reflection of God, the ceremonial law was temporary. The ceremonial law with sacrifices and priests and a tabernacle was set up to point sinners to the way of salvation. Those who had transgressed the Decalogue could find the justification which God provides, through the ministry demonstrated by the ceremonial law. All this ceremonial law found its fulfilment in the person and work of Jesus Christ. The old patterns, types and shadows contained in the ceremonial law can serve as illustrations and they can help us to understand the grandeur and glory of Christ's work for us, but essentially the ceremonial law is something of the past.

Likewise the civil law given to the Jews was based upon the Ten Commandments. Of course, I do not deny the connection between the civil law and the moral law, or the connection between the ceremonial law and the Decalogue, but insist on the way in which these are clearly distinguished for us by the way they are expressed in Scripture.

Every civil administration should base its laws on the Ten Commandments. It is not possible for any government to enforce the first four commandments, but certainly commandments 5 to 9 are imperative while the rest are highly relevant for wisdom and observation. No civil administration today is required to follow the theocracy which pertained to Israel, because that was unique. That too has passed away completely and now every nation should base its own administration upon a wise observation and application of the Decalogue.

To sum up then, the ceremonial law, while it has much to teach us, has been fulfilled and completed. The Jewish civil law, while it also has much to teach us, has become part of history, whereas the Decalogue transcends time and must by its very nature always and eternally reflect the holy character of God.

4. The Ten Commandments correspond with the consciences of men

Written in the heart of every human being is what we call natural law. This is the law of the conscience. Paul tells us, 'Indeed, when Gentiles, who do not have the law, do by nature things required by the law, they are a law for themselves, even though they do not have the law, since they show that the requirements of the law are written on their hearts, their consciences also bearing witness, and their thoughts now accusing, now even defending them' (Rom 2:14,15).

Observe that it is specifically the moral law that is being referred to when it comes to convicting men's consciences. Thus when our Lord spoke to the rich young ruler he referred to the commandments. We have just seen that James does the same, and again Paul refers in Romans to the Decalogue specifically, especially to the tenth commandment (Rom 7).

Sometimes the word 'law' is used in Scripture to describe the whole Mosaic system of law (John 1:17; Gal 3:10, 23). Sometimes the word 'law' refers to the Bible as a whole with all its promises and precepts (see Psalms 19 and 119).

We can use the whole Bible to appeal to the consciences of men or we can appeal to the consciences of men with the gospel. All these we may do, but effectively if men are to be convinced of sin, righteousness and judgement to come, they must know the meaning and horror of transgression as being sin against a holy God.

While we know that the consciences of men can be dreadfully seared and hardened and rendered ineffective, nevertheless we also know that all men are born with a natural law, or conscience, which corresponds exactly to the Decalogue. While sinners may strive to suppress the calls and alarms in their consciences when they hear the proclamation of the law, nevertheless we must never underestimate the power that lies in those calls.

We should never set up the law and the gospel against each other. The one is a complete complement of the other. They are twin pillars in the temple of God. In Charles Bridges' book there is a quote in Latin. The author is not named. It reads, '*Qui scit bene distinguere inter Legem et Evangelium, Deo gratias agat, et sciat se esse Theologum,*' which translated means, 'The man who knows how to distinguish between the Law and the Gospel, may thank God, and know himself to be a theologian!'[2]

5. The Ten Commandments serve as a powerful guide for Christians to live by.

It is a vast mistake to think that the Decalogue can be relegated to the ancient past. The relevance of God's moral law is as great now as it ever was, and as Paul shows in Romans 7 is a most powerful means of revealing the perfections that are required by a perfect God.

We should note that it is when our Lord expounded the searching nature of the commands of the moral law that he urged, 'Be perfect, therefore, as your heavenly Father is perfect' (Matt 5:48).

Our union with Christ argues for a greater obligation to please God. If we are married to Christ, then like him we will honour our Father by observing carefully what he loves and what he hates, and by avoiding everything that offends the majesty and holiness of his character.

Also the new privilege of adoption whereby our Father comes into a relationship of care and love for us, which is very intimate, means that we have to live to please him in every possible way.

Furthermore, the privilege of possessing the gift of the Holy Spirit whereby we enjoy his work and person as he indwells, guides and teaches us, means that we have an empowerment and ability which enables us to love God's law from the heart and to keep it.

When Paul says that he is wretched, it is because he feels the grievousness and distress of not living up to the perfection reflected in the Decalogue. Far from becoming enslaved or coming into bondage, he glories in the justification which undergirds the whole process of his progressive sanctification. When he says, 'Christ is the end of the law so that there may be righteousness for everyone who believes' (Rom 10:4), he means that Christ by his active and passive obedience has fulfilled everything required by the moral law. We observe the moral law as Christians not in order to earn our salvation nor in order to contribute toward our justification. We revere and honour the moral law as God's redeemed children. We observe the Ten Commandments because they are right and because we want to live in harmony with our heavenly Father and enjoy his love (John 14:23). That love of delight that the Father has for his children is because they are obedient.

When we say that we keep the commands of Christ we include the new commandment, namely to love one another, as part of the larger commandment of loving God and men. Now the fulfilment of the ceremonial law by Christ and the satisfaction of all the requirements and demands of the moral law by him obligate us more than ever to love as he loved and especially to enjoy that unity and love with his own redeemed family.

There is an emphatic stress at the beginning of the Decalogue that it was because they had been redeemed from the slavery of Egypt that the law was given to them. The law came out of the grace of God. The commandments were given in order that the privileged position of Israel could be maintained. The commandments confirmed the relationship to Yahweh. They also prohibited what might destroy that relationship. In other words it was not by law-keeping that the people were to come to salvation. They had already been redeemed as a people, and now the breaking of the law was forbidden lest their relationship with Yahweh should be damaged. The principle of personal devotion to God becomes the obvious fulfilment of the law. Conformity to the law is accomplished by the gracious work of the Holy Spirit. It is the work of the Holy Spirit to reveal just how much is required by the commandments.

We need to see how each commandment provides a blaze of light as to how we can please Yahweh by loving him and honouring him and by fulfilling his will as it is reflected in his law. In this way we live out our relationship of adoption (1 John 3:1,2; Ps 103:13-18; Eph 1:5).

The Westminster Larger Catechism shows how exceedingly comprehensive each commandment is in its requirement. In the Sermon on the Mount our Lord shows how demanding the law is as it relates to the heart of man. He shows that murder and adultery spring from evil thoughts.

The second commandment is particularly comprehensive when it comes to making an application to the public worship of God. It certainly requires separate treatment, as does the fourth commandment upon which a huge volume of material has been written over the centuries. That the minds of God's people have been so exercised by the Ten Words bears testimony to their mighty power and decisiveness. The Decalogue does not give power. It sheds light. The Holy Spirit empowers, and union with Christ gives strength, and the blessing of adoption by the Father motivates love and obedience.

We ought always to have our minds and hearts open to the bright light of God's truth as it is expressed in those words which were uttered audibly to the people of Israel and transcribed into stone to show that this moral law can never pass away. Their primary use is to convince us of our need. When we have received salvation then the Ten Commandments act as a guide.

---

1   *The Westminster Confession of Fa*ith, chapter 19. *The Second London Baptist Confession of Faith*, chapter 19.

2   *The Christian Ministry,* Charles Bridges, 1967, page 230.

Recommended books

Richard C Barcellos, *In Defence of the Decalogue, a critique of New Covenant Theology*, Winepress publishing, 2001.

Norman Shields, *Pattern for Life*, Evangelical Press.

Horatius Bonar, *God's Way of Holiness*, Evangelical Press.

Samuel Bolton, *The True Bounds of Christian Freedom*, Banner of Truth.

Thomas Watson, *The Ten Commandments*, Banner of Truth.

E F Kevan, *The Grace of Law*, Baker Book House.

John Calvin, *Sermons on The Ten Commandments*, Baker Book House.

Rousas Rushdooney, *The Institutes of Biblical Law*, Craig Press, 1973.

John Owen on Sanctification

John Owen's exposition of sanctification is subsumed under *The Work of the Holy Spirit* which forms volume three of Owen's sixteen volume *Works*. Owen's 285 page exposition includes a shorter 28 page section on The Mortification of Sin which is opened up in much more detail in volume 6. The latter is well known and readers tend to overlook the fact that Owen's main work on sanctification makes up Books 4 and 5 in his work on the Holy Spirit.

John Owen begins his treatise on sanctification with a study of regeneration and from that base explains that sanctification is a progressive work.

> 'Sanctification is an immediate work of the Spirit of God on the souls of believers, purifying and cleansing their natures from the pollution and uncleanness of sin, renewing in them the image of God, and thereby enabling them, from a spiritual and habitual principle of grace, to yield obedience to God, according unto the tenor and terms of the new covenant, by virtue of the life and death of Jesus Christ.'

He expounds Ephesians 5:25-26, 'Christ loved the church and gave himself up for her to make her holy, cleansing her by the washing with water through the word.' Owen strongly asserts the responsibility of believers in the progress of sanctification and among many texts cites 2 Corinthians 7:1.

On Ephesians 1:4, 'For he chose us in him before the creation of the world to be holy and blameless in his sight,' Owen comments: 'The doctrine of God's *eternal election* is everywhere in Scripture proposed for the *encouragement* and *consolation* of believers, and to further them in their course of *obedience* and *holiness*' (*Works* vol 3, page 597, Owen's italics).

✦ *Chapter 15* ✦

Holiness and Character Building

The early life of Joseph was one of severe affliction. What a desperately bitter experience was his as the following scriptures remind us.

'So when Joseph came to his brothers, they stripped him of his robe – the richly ornamented robe he was wearing – and they took him and threw him into the cistern. Now the cistern was empty; there was no water in it. ... Judah said to his brothers, "What will we gain if we kill our brother and cover up his blood? Come, let's sell him to the Ishmaelites and not lay our hands on him; after all, he is our brother, our own flesh and blood." His brothers agreed. So when the Midianite merchants came by, his brothers pulled Joseph up out of the cistern and sold him for twenty shekels of silver to the Ishmaelites, who took him to Egypt' (Gen 37:23-28).

'When his master heard the story his wife told him, saying, "This is how your slave treated me," he burned with anger. Joseph's master took him and put him in prison, the place where the king's prisoners were confined' (Gen 39:19,20).

'The chief cupbearer, however, did not remember Joseph; he forgot him' (Gen 40:23).

Joseph's hope of release from prison was dashed.

How are we to view Joseph's afflictions? Can they be classified as chastisement? That is an important part of every Christian's experience. I maintain that these bitter experiences are much better described as 'character building' rather than chastisement. Joseph was being prepared for the tremendous authority that he would wield as prime-minister of Egypt which then was probably the most powerful nation on earth. He was humbled by terrifying and painful experiences. When high office and illustrious privileges came to him he was well equipped to handle them. He was able to avoid taking revenge on his brothers. He was able to receive honour without falling into the deadly sin of pride.

We can be sure that in his life as a slave and then as a prisoner there was much correction experienced. To what extent should we apply the famous Hebrews passage to the life of Joseph? That passage reads as follows:

> In your struggle against sin, you have not yet resisted to the point of shedding your blood. And you have forgotten that word of encouragement that addresses you as sons:
>
> "My son, do not make light of the Lord's discipline,
> and do not lose heart when he rebukes you,
> because the Lord disciplines those he loves,
> and he punishes everyone he accepts as a son.'"

Endure hardship as discipline; God is treating you as sons. For what son is not disciplined by his father? If you are not disciplined (and everyone undergoes discipline), then you are illegitimate children and not true sons. Moreover, we have all had human fathers who disciplined us and we respected them for it. How much more should we submit to the Father of our spirits and live! Our fathers disciplined us for a little while as they thought best; but God disciplines us for our good, that we may share in his holiness. No discipline seems pleasant at the time, but painful. Later on, however, it produces a harvest of righteousness and peace for those who have been trained by it' (Heb 12:4-11).

This passage in Hebrews is partly a citation of Proverbs 3:11,12. Job 5:17-21 is similar where Eliphaz declares: 'Blessed is the man whom God corrects; so do not despise the discipline of the Almighty. For he wounds, but he also binds up; he injures, but his hands also heal. From six calamities he will rescue you; in seven no harm will befall you. In famine he will ransom you from death, and in battle from the stroke of the sword. You will be protected from the lash of the tongue, and need not fear when destruction comes.' Eliphaz was correct in observing that our suffering as believers must always be viewed in the context of God's over-ruling love, protection and care.

In times of tribulation the believer is subject to deep heart-searching. The inevitable thought is, What have I done to deserve this? Is God punishing me? But more often the mind is set on thinking about what I am supposed to be learning from this bitter experience.

A present day example of this is a teenager who has professed faith in Christ. He suffered a serious injury and could not play football which he loved dearly. He had been playing football on the Lord's Day. The thought arose, Was this punishment for what he had done? When I was asked about this I suggested that the Lord is never vindictive and certainly never punitive. Christ is the only sin-bearer. We do not atone for our sins by suffering. The affliction of not being able to play football due to injury will lead to heart-searching. The correct line of thought must surely be, How can I make the best of this setback? How can I live through this part of my life with God's glory in view? How can I come through this with profit? Perhaps I can improve in my academic work. In other words, how can this adverse providence be a character building exercise?

In a closer look at the Hebrews 12:4-11 passage, most of which is cited above, I plead that the word 'chastisement' is inadequate. The NIV and ever more popular ESV do not follow the KJV but translate the Greek word *paideia* (verse 7) as discipline. The NLT translates the word as 'divine discipline'. As Peter Golding suggests, 'Although discipline is more accurate it still does not convey the fullness of meaning that is in the original. When we speak of a parent chastising a child, we naturally tend to think of the child being punished for a particular misdemeanour – disobedience say. That element is included but it is clearly not the main emphasis. The Greek word (*paideia*) literally means child-training. It means "to instruct, educate, rear, mentor and discipline a child", with all that that involves: everything necessary to produce a full and rounded maturity, both negatively and positively. So the term has a much wider scope than punishment, or even discipline. If this is not grasped it can lead to a concept of chastisement which is synonymous with punitive; and at worst a failure to distinguish between the retributive anger of God, and his fatherly discipline. And the difference between the two is not a line, but a chasm.'[1]

Helpfully Simon Kistemaker says here on the word discipline (*paideia*), 'The concept *discipline* in ancient Israel was not limited to describing physical punishment but included the concept of *education*. That is the father as head of the household taught his children the law of God, the tradition of the elders, and the skills of a trade. Education was meant to inculcate obedience to God's law, respect for authority, and a love for their national heritage.'[2]

From this I am persuaded that the best way of viewing this section of Hebrews is to interpret discipline as character training. The exercise is wholly within the sphere of our adoption as sons and daughters. Adoption is the highest privilege we possess. Our Father's purpose is to work all things together for our good, that is for us who are the called according to his purpose (Rom 8:28). This is all about progress in holiness, as the text says, 'God disciplines us for our good, that we may share in his holiness' (Heb 12:10). 'To become partakers of his holiness is to have my mind brought to his mind, my will brought to his will: to think as he thinks, – to will as he wills – to find enjoyment in that in which he finds enjoyment. This is man's profit. This is the perfection of his nature, both as to holiness and happiness. This is to live the life of angels, to live the life of God; to partake of his holiness is to enter into *his* joy.'[3]

What human father worthy of his rôle is not passionately concerned about the character building of his children? In that process much constant correction is par for the course. Says daughter Caroline to her brother David, "Dad wants to see you in his study." Replies David, "Why? What's wrong?" Caroline: "He knows that you were lazy yesterday and didn't do your homework!" David: "Shall I say I had a headache?" Caroline: "That's no good; he knows you were playing computer games."

Apart from our Lord the most complex example of character building in Scripture is Job. The book opens with an emphasis on the near perfect character of Job. Then unfolds a series of disasters. God permits Satan to strip Job of all his prosperity and then worse still all his children. To lose one child is exceedingly grievous: to lose all one's children in a stroke who can bear? Job was stunned but retained his faith. 'At this, Job got up and tore his robe and shaved his head. Then he fell to the ground in worship and said, "Naked I came from my mother's womb, and naked I shall depart. The LORD gave and the LORD has taken away; may the name of the LORD be praised"' (Job 1:20,21).

More was to come. At the next assembly in heaven God was vindicated by Job's faith and integrity. Then Satan, the advocate of malice, applied for a fresh trial of Job's faith. He was given permission to make a savage attack on Job's body. Job was afflicted from top to toe with unsightly, agonising, humiliating boils. Job's wife found both him and his believing attitude repugnant. She goaded him to curse God and die! Job cursed the day of his birth but he did not blame God. More was to come. Job's three friends caused more grief than relief. In addition to all his sufferings Job's spiritual comfort dried up. He felt the absence of the supportive work of the Holy Spirit. He complained that he was a deserted soul. 'But if I go to the east, he is not there; if I go to the west, I do not find him. When he is at work in the north, I do not see him; when he turns to the south, I catch no glimpse of him' (Job 23:8,9).

As the chapters unfold Job's three friends (comforters so-called) tried their best to find out what secret or hidden sins of Job might explain these extraordinary painful experiences. But Job had *not* neglected the poor. He had *not* been guilty of lascivious thoughts. The real reason for his tribulation was known to the principalities and cosmic powers (Eph 6:12). Job had done nothing to deserve the calamities that came upon him. Yet he was aware that his character was being built up through his trials. 'But he knows the way that I take; when he has tested me, I shall come forth as gold' (Job 23:10).

At the end of it all Job made this confession: 'My ears had heard of you but now my eyes have seen you. Therefore I despise myself and repent in dust and ashes' (Job 42:5,6). Highly rated for his godliness before his trials Job showed afterwards that he had advanced in maturity, humility and understanding. In the end he did not receive an answer to his question, Why all this pain? Instead he was taken for a trip to the equivalent of the Kruger National Game Park to view God's wonderful created animals. If Job did not know how these magnificent creatures were created then how could he possibly understand the mystery of providence?

In the whole saga of Job there is not a hint of chastisement. It is all about character building. Believers are never punished in a punitive or retributive sense. Jesus alone has made propitiation for all our sins so that the guilt of them is removed from us as far as the east is from the west (Ps 103:12). Believers from time to time are chastised for their disobedience and persistent sins. We know that was not the case with Job who was the subject of character training through afflictions which made no sense to him.

Trials which seem to make no sense at all are common. Job's trials were like that. Often the bad behaviour of God's people is a trial hard to comprehend. Contradiction from the secular world is to be expected. That is normal. But arguments and divisions among God's people can cause great hurt. Differences there will always be because we are all fallible but we need a loving and generous attitude to prevail when we have to agree to differ.

The matter of chastisement in no way applies to Jesus. His experience was one of perfect divine unity, love and harmony with his Father. Yet in Hebrews 5:8 we are reminded that he learned obedience from what he suffered. He suffered in anticipation of the ordeal that was coming. Ever closer that ordeal loomed. In the Garden of Gethsemane the immediate prospect of death on a cross as the sin-bearer nearly killed him. All the way through his life he was preparing to make the supreme sacrifice.

Does God get angry with his people? He certainly does! Remember the example of Moses. When Moses was stubborn the Lord's anger burned against him (Ex 4:14). Later Moses said, 'The LORD was angry with me because of you, and he solemnly swore that I would not cross the Jordan and enter the good land the LORD your God is giving you' (Deut 4:21). When Aaron compromised miserably and made the golden calf, 'the LORD was angry enough with Aaron to destroy him' (Deut 9:20). Collectively the idolatry and unfaithfulness of Judah was such that 'in furious anger and in great wrath the LORD uprooted them from their land' (Deut 29:28; Jer 25:8-11). Nowhere is the blatant unfaithfulness of Israel more graphically described than in Ezekiel 16. 'I will bring upon you the blood vengeance of my wrath and jealous anger' (Ez 16:38). This is further described in Psalm 78. The Lord 'unleashed against them his hot anger, his wrath, indignation and hostility' (Ps 78:49). National idolatry was corrected during the time of the exile. With the return from captivity in Babylon in mind, Daniel confessed fully the collective sins of the people and prayed for their promised restoration and return (Daniel chapter 9).

We can easily fail to recognise God's high purpose of discipline or character building. The author of Hebrews suggests that we can make light of it. Instead of heart-searching improvement some adopt a stoical attitude which braces the soul to endure hard times but they fail to engage in heart-searching self-examination. Instead of taking it to heart the lessons are shrugged off. The other negative response is to sink down in discouragement and be despondent. This can lead to neglecting the means of grace, Bible reading, meditation, intercession, fellowship at the prayer meetings and attendance at Lord's Day services. All of these are designed to help us through testing times and assist us in making needed improvements. The exhortation in the text says, 'So take a new grip with your tired hands and stand firm on your shaky legs' (Heb 12:12 NLT).

John Owen, the Prince of the Puritans, who wrote the most extensive commentary ever on the Hebrews letter makes this application: 'It is an act of spiritual wisdom, in all our troubles, to find out and discern divine paternal chastisements; without which we shall never behave ourselves well under them, nor obtain any advantage by them.'[4] He then goes on to explain the benefits of heeding chastisements and thereby yielding fruit, the fruit of righteousness and peace.

The painful times we experience can be viewed in the light of Jesus' teaching. 'I am the true vine, and my Father is the gardener. He cuts off every branch in me that bears no fruit, while every branch that does bear fruit he prunes so that it will be even more fruitful (John 15:1,2).' Our Father is the gardener; we are branches under his care. He watches over our lives. The painful afflictions which cut into our very souls, the taking from us of objects that are dear to us, as when the gardener with his sharp knife removes luxuriant branches from the vine are our Father's prunings! No hand but his ever holds the knife! We are sure, then, that there is never any careless cutting, any unwise pruning, any needless removing of rich branches or growths. We really need to go no farther than this. A strong, abiding confidence that all the trials and sorrows ought to silence every question, quiet every fear and give peace and restful assurance to our hearts in all their pain. We cannot know the reason for the painful strokes but we know that he who holds the pruning-knife is our Father! That is all we need to know. The other thought in the Lord's allegory, is scarcely less full of comfort to a Christian. Jesus says, that it is the fruitful branches which the Father prunes: 'He prunes every branch that produces fruit so that it will produce more fruit.'

Afflictions then have to do with character building and fruitfulness. He does not prune the fruitless branches. He cuts them off altogether as useless, as mere cumberers, absorbing life and yielding nothing of blessing or good. Some Christians have the impression that their many troubles indicate that God does not love them, that they cannot be true Christians. This teaching of

Christ shows how mistaken they are. Chastening shows that the Father is pruning fruitful branches to make them more fruitful! All whom the Father loves he chastens! It is the fruitless branch that is never pruned; the fruitful branch is pruned, and pruned not by one without skill, not by an enemy but by the wise Father! Thus we see how we may rejoice even in our trials and afflictions!

'One who was altogether ignorant of the art and purpose of pruning, who should see a man with a sharp knife cutting off branch after branch of a luxuriant vine, would at first suppose that the pruner was ruining the vine. So at the time it seems but by and by it appears that the prunings have made the vine more fruitful. In the season of vintage the grapes are more luscious, with a richer flavour in them because of the cutting away of the superfluous branches. In like manner, if an angel who had never witnessed anything of human suffering, and who knew nothing of its object, were to see the Father causing pain and affliction to his children, it would seem to him that these experiences could be only destructive of happiness and blessing; but if the angel were to follow those chastened lives on to the end, he would see untold blessing coming out of the chastenings! The Father was but pruning the branches that they might bear more and better fruit! We should never lose sight of the divine purpose in all trials to make our lives more fruitful.'[5]

The Puritan giant William Gouge in his commentary on Hebrews reminds us of James who exhorts sufferers to rejoice in their afflictions. He goes on to observe that it is staggering to think that the Holy Spirit can 'raise joy out of that which is not joyous.'[6]

There is much remaining sin in the form of bad attitudes and unacceptable behaviour that has to be dealt with. Another Puritan Joseph Symonds puts it in this quaint way: 'There are many things in the saints that are very repugnant to that filial state in which they are set by grace.'[7]

Paul declared that it was the aim of the apostles to 'present everyone perfect in Christ' (Col 1:28). It is certainly the purpose of our heavenly

Father to conform us to the likeness of his Son (Rom 8:29). Suppose professing Christians are worldly and lukewarm. Is that not repugnant to God? That was the main problem in the church at Laodicea (Rev 3:14-22). Our Lord says, 'Those whom I love I rebuke and discipline' (Rev 3:19). He takes measures to move them out of their comfort zone and shake them out of their worldly careless attitudes.

In our contemporary, Western, postmodern, politically correct consumer-society, the philosophy often prevails that the chief end of man is his own comfort and happiness. Happiness and holidays are the aim and it is heresy not to enjoy yourself. Some of that outlook penetrates the churches so it is not surprising that the Lord takes measures to awaken his people out of their lukewarm state.

One of the most pernicious errors ever to invade so-called evangelical churches is the health and wealth movement, 'The Name it and Claim it' teaching. All sickness can be healed by faith. If healing does not take place the sick person is blamed for not having enough faith!

It is not our happiness and comfort that is the main concern with God. It is holiness. Trophimus was left sick at Miletus (2 Tim 4:20). Paul's request that the thorn that pained him be removed was declined (2 Cor 12:7-10). It was not a simple matter of 'Name it and Claim it'. All the ground we have covered in this chapter shows that we who believe are subjects of character building. We are subject to discipline and correction.

We must sail through stormy seas. We learn all through the voyage of life. Peter speaks of 'an inheritance that can never perish, spoil or fade, kept in heaven for you, who through faith are shielded by God's power until the coming of the salvation that is ready to be revealed in the last time. In this you greatly rejoice, though now for a little while you may have to suffer grief in all kinds of trials. These have come so that your faith which is of greater worth than gold, which perishes even though refined by fire, may be proved genuine and may result in praise, glory and honour when Jesus Christ is revealed (1 Peter 1:4-7).

1   Peter Golding, *Hebrews 12:1-11: Towards a Theology of Chastisement.* This
     is an unpublished 17 page manuscript written in 2009, cited here with
     permission.
2   Simon J Kistemaker, *Hebrews*, Baker Book House, 1984, page 376.
3   John Brown of Edinburgh, *An Exposition of Hebrews*, 1862, republished by
     the Banner of Truth, 1961, page 628.
4   John Owen, *Hebrews*. I have the 16 volume Banner of Truth set of Owen's
     Works, but my set of Owen on Hebrews was published in the USA by the
     National Foundation for Christian Education, which company published
     Owen's seven volumes on Hebrews in four volumes. These quotes are from
     vol 4, page 266.
5   J R Miller, *Looking at the Right Side*, 1888.
6   William Gouge, *Hebrews*, vol 3, page 197, James Nichol, 1867.
7   Joseph Symonds, *The Case and Cure of a Deserted Soul*, 1671, Soli Deo Gloria,
     reprint 1996, page 322.

Holiness and Islam

Islam has no Saviour. The Qur'an refers to the 'balance' in which Allah on the Day of Judgment will weigh the deeds of every single individual. The good deeds will be placed in one pan of the balance and the evil deeds in the other. If the good deeds are heavier the believer may have a chance to go to paradise. If the individual's evil deeds are heavier he will be cast into the fires of hell.

There are five pillars to be followed. The first is profession of faith (Shahada). 'There is no deity but Allah and Muhammad is the Messenger of Allah.' The second pillar is formal prayer five times a day. Tradition prescribes a precise pattern of actions and recited words which must be followed exactly. The third pillar is the giving of alms for which there are detailed and strict regulations. The fourth pillar is fasting. Fasting takes place mainly in the month of Ramadan. The fifth pillar is pilgrimage (Hajj). At least once in a lifetime a spiritual journey must be made to the holy city of Mecca. A small number of radical Sunnis and Shias advocate Jihad as a sixth pillar. Those who die in Jihad are considered martyrs and are promised an immediate place in paradise.

There is no doctrine of inward transformation wrought by the Holy Spirit in Islam. The entire basis of Islam is works- orientated. The Bible declares: 'Therefore no-one will be declared righteous in his sight by observing the law; rather, through the law we become conscious of sin' (Rom 3:20).

There are superstitious aspects within Islam similar to Roman Catholicism (attaching virtue to physical objects such as relics). For instance if only a person can touch the tomb of Muhammad then all the sins of that person will be forgiven.

Chapter 16

The Word
the Instrument of Sanctification

Sanctify them by the truth; your word is truth (John 17:17)

This petition in John chapter seventeen lies at the heart of the great high-priestly prayer of Jesus. Jesus is our great high priest. All believers are priests in the sense that all have equal access to the throne of grace but Jesus is special as he is divine. He fulfils the type of the high priest in the Old Testament tabernacle who represented the twelve tribes. Jesus represents all his redeemed people. In this last great recorded prayer Jesus' paramount concern is for the unity of all his people. This unity is unity in the truth. He prays that this unity will be complete so that the world may know that Jesus is truly sent from the Father (17:23).[1] Unity contributes in a major way to the witness of the Church. Disunity is extremely harmful to that witness. The unity prayed for is a spiritual unity which our Lord likens to the unity of the Trinity.

The perfection or completeness of unity with each other is brought about by the indwelling of Christ by the Holy Spirit. The question of unity is closely related to that of progressive sanctification which is the full-time concern or business of all believers. With this comment on the context we will now look in more detail at verse 17.

John 17:17 can be divided as follows

1. The work to be done *Sanctify them*
2. How this work is to be achieved *by the truth*
3. The instrument by which this work is achieved *your word is truth*

1. The work to be done: Sanctify them

'Sanctify' is an aorist imperative which is emphatic. It means sanctify them completely. This strong imperative suggests all the sanctifying activity of God from the time of a believer's being set apart in Christ, (which as we have seen is the first meaning of sanctify), through the whole process of progressive sanctification to its completion when the believer will be perfect in glory.

The Westminster Larger Catechism has an excellent definition of progressive sanctification:

> 'Sanctification is a work of God's grace, whereby they whom God hath, before the foundation of the world, chosen to be holy, are in time, through the powerful operation of his Spirit applying the death and resurrection of Christ to them, renewed in their whole man after the image of God; having the seeds of repentance to life, and all other saving graces, put into their hearts, and these graces so stirred up, increased and strengthened, as that they more and more die to sin, and rise to newness of life.'

Christians are described as those who are being made holy. 'By one sacrifice he has made perfect for ever those who are being made holy' (Heb 10:14). Progressive sanctification or holiness applies to all those who are in Christ without exception. Paul expresses his burden for progressive holiness when he says that his aim in the ministry is to 'present everyone perfect in Christ' (Col 1:28).

2. How this work is to be achieved by the truth

I take the truth here to mean the teaching of the gospel. Jesus said, 'If you hold to my teaching, you are really my disciples. Then you will know the truth, and the truth will set you free' (John 8:32). The truth here consists of the basic facts of the gospel. It is a helpful exercise to compile a list of summaries of saving truth which are found in the New Testament. A good example is 1 Corinthians 15:1-8 where Paul explains briefly how we are saved through faith in the life, death and resurrection of Christ. Another is Paul's introduction in his letter to the Romans: 'I am not ashamed of the gospel, because it is the power of God for the salvation of everyone who believes: first for the Jew, then for the Gentile. For in the gospel a righteousness from God is revealed, a righteousness that is by faith from first to last, just as it is written: "The righteous will live by faith"' (Rom 1:16,17).

Examples of statements which describe salvation from the Old Testament are Genesis 15:6; Proverbs 3:1-6; Isaiah 53:4-6; Jeremiah 31:31-34 and Ezekiel 36:25-29, and from the New Testament: Matthew 7:24-27; Luke 24:45-49; 1 Timothy 1:15-17; Hebrews 7:23-28; 1 Peter 1:3-9; 2 Peter 1:5-11, 1 John 1 and Revelation 22:12-17.

The Holy Spirit uses the words and meaning of Scripture to convince of sin and to regenerate sinners. 'He chose to give us birth through the word of truth' (James 1:18). Peter expresses this same truth when he writes, 'For you have been born again, not of perishable seed, but of imperishable, through the living and enduring word of God' (1 Peter 1:23). The same word is the instrument of progressive sanctification as Peter says, 'Now that you have purified yourselves by obeying the truth so that you have sincere love for your brothers, love one another deeply, from the heart ' (1 Peter 1:22).

This leads us directly to the next principal issue in our understanding of John 17:17.

3. The instrument by which this work is achieved: your word is truth

The instrument of our sanctification is the Bible. As the truths of the Bible are understood and acted upon so our lives are transformed. We have already examined Romans 12:2, 'Do not be conform any longer to the pattern of this world, but be transformed by the renewing of your mind.' The Word is the instrument of renewing the mind. It is through our minds that our affections are stirred to love and obey God's will for us. It is through our minds that we are motivated to serve God in practice. Psalm 119, placed in the centre of the Bible, is an acrostic poem in which each of the twenty-two Hebrew letters is used eight times in each section. The theme of the psalm is the believer's relationship to Scripture. Every part of his life is to be permeated with and governed by Scripture.

Now why should God change our lives by a book? Why should the Bible be the instrument? Why does he not speak to us audibly as he did at different times to Moses? Why does he not use dreams as he did in the life of Joseph? Or why does he not use visions as he did when he called Ezekiel to the ministry of teaching his people in the exile in Babylon? We should note that these direct communications were extremely rare and mark those times when God intervened in a major way in history and especially at times of major transition in the history of his people. No, he does not use direct speech or dreams or vision because the clear written Word is the best and most reliable way for us. 'It is written: "Man does not live on bread alone, but on every word that comes from the mouth of God"' (Matt 4:4). God teaches and guides his sons and daughters through the instrumentality of a book, the Bible.

The primary methods ordained of God in mediating the substance of the Bible to us are preaching and reading. Called preachers expound and apply the Bible and they are acutely aware that without the work of the Holy Spirit the Word will not be heeded and will not convict. What about those who are not blessed with faithful preaching of the Word? They read and meditate on the Word and are thereby instructed by it. And what of those who cannot read? When Tyndale's New Testament reached the English people, those who could not read would gather round a reader and listen. The words were so precious that they memorised paragraphs. What about those who do not have the Bible? That is tragic! The apostle Paul says, 'How, then, can they call on the one they have not believed in? And how can they believe in the one of whom they have not heard? And how can they hear without someone preaching to them? And how can they preach unless they are sent? As it written, "How beautiful are the feet of those who bring good news!"' (Rom 10:14,15).

Using the conversation between Abraham in heaven and the rich man in hell (see Luke 16:19-31) Geoff Thomas warns against low views of the Bible:

'This rich man, then, grew up in the synagogue, memorising the Scripture, hearing it week by week. But he never obeyed it, nor did he love it, finding it boring. He never dreamed for a moment that he would end up in hell. He never thought that one day there would be a great chasm fixed between himself and Abraham. There are many like him who hear the Word of God preached with the Holy Ghost sent down from heaven. Judas heard it; Ananias heard it; Sapphira heard it; Demas heard it; the Judaisers heard it – but all were lost. Now, you see what the rich man is saying from hell – "If the Scriptures are the only thing that you are going to give my brothers, well ... I had them, and what good did they do to me? They did not change me." In fact, he is saying in hell, deep within his heart: "It is perfectly understandable that I didn't believe and that they don't believe – all we had was the Bible. I know my brothers; I am aware how they live; I know where they are going. The Bible is not going to touch them – those kinds of men need something more." In effect, he is saying: "It is excusable; if only I had seen a miracle that thrilled me, I would have believed. If a man had been raised from the dead and spoken to me, then I would have paid attention. If I could have gone to a meeting where amazing things happened, it would have been different. But all I had was the Bible. The Bible!"'

'That is what many people say still. "You don't expect the world to be attracted by the Bible, by preaching the Scriptures, by texts outside chapels, and verses on railway station hoardings, and tracts with Scriptures on them, and memorising the Bible, and lessons from the Bible to children in Sunday School, and camps where young people are taught the Bible, and conferences where the Bible is proclaimed. You don't expect people to be attracted by that? We need concerts! We need drama! We need costumes! We need bands! We need choreography! Bring in the drums and the synthesizers. Send for the clowns! Then the people will come. We need superstars and celebrities to give us their testimonies – not just the Bible alone!" But, you see, Abraham was unyielding. "The Bible is sufficient," he said.'

'Now there are many religious people who argue like that man from hell. The Roman Catholic Church says that the Bible is not enough, we must have Sacred Tradition too. The Quakers say that the Bible is not enough, but there must be an inner voice in the congregation. Modernists say Scripture itself is not enough, it must be interpreted by "the assured results of modern criticism". They say that we must go back to sources "behind" our present Gospel narratives to find the "authentic" sayings of Jesus. Cults say the Bible is not enough, men must obey a Book – the Book of Mormon, or Science and Health With a Key to the Scriptures by Mary Baker Eddy, or the Watchtower's productions of the Jehovah's Witnesses. Many Charismatics say that the Bible is not enough, that it needs to be authenticated by miracles and signs. All such people are saying that the Bible is not good enough. They say: "It's a good start, but it needs a bit of help from us."[2]

The Word is the instrument of salvation and of progressive sanctification. The best way to illustrate this is to take specific subjects that apply to all true Christians as follows:

First the Bible is unique in describing the creation of the world. Then from creation the story of the human race, and especially of Israel, is unfolded so that we have a line of history all the way through. We can see that God is in control from beginning to end. In the Bible we have a solid foundation for our understanding of the sovereignty of God in creation, in providence and in redemption.

The Word is unique in revealing the transcendent holiness and divine attributes of the Trinity. Throughout Scripture we come face to face with the living God and the way he reveals himself in his actions and in his inspiration of the prophetic writers. The immediate effect of that is to humble us and convict us of our sinfulness and unworthiness. A striking example is the calling of Isaiah. He saw the glory of God in the temple. "Woe to me!" I cried. "I am ruined! For I am a man of unclean lips, and I live among a people of unclean lips, and my eyes have seen the King, the LORD Almighty" (Isa 6:1-5).

The Word of God is unique in exposing the origin and appalling consequences of sin. No other book is like this one which faithfully describes sin and its effects. Cain murdered Abel. Then it is reported in Genesis chapter six, 'The LORD saw how great man's wickedness on the earth had become, and that every inclination of the thoughts of his heart was only evil all the time' (Gen 6:5). Then followed the universal flood. After the flood Noah's sin is exposed. New hope for the race of mankind came in the calling of Abraham but not even Abraham's sins are concealed. King David sinned grievously and that is on record too. The fact is that the Bible is unique not only in describing sin as it really is but in providing atonement for sin. When the sinner is forgiven and justified how does he go forward from there? The Bible provides all the teaching required by which believers can live holy lives and make progress in sanctification. All this comes by a knowledge of Scripture. The Word is the instrument of sanctification.

The Word of God is unique not only in explaining the origin of sin but also in defining what sin is in detail. As soon as the children of Israel emerged from Egypt and came into Sinai the Lord gave them the Ten Commandments. These were spoken audibly to them all and the same Ten Commandments were written on tablets of stone to be kept in the ark. The primary importance of the Ten Words as a perfect summary of moral law could hardly be more emphatic. Here is moral law by which not only Israel but all mankind will be judged. This perfect moral law is also written in the consciousness of all mankind (Rom 2:14,15).

The Bible is unique in showing that sin is destructive and damning. Also the Bible alone shows the great difficulty and cost of atoning for sin and the fact that nothing but the ultimate sacrifice of Christ could take away the guilt of our sin (2 Cor 5:21).

The Word of God is unique in describing salvation. Christ is revealed progressively through the Old Testament by way of foretelling what the Messiah will be like in his person and work. For instance his glorious person, his ministry and his perseverance are described by Isaiah in the four Servant passages.[3] When Jesus came to fulfil all these promises there is not one Gospel account to describe him but four so we can view him from every angle. This is germane to our sanctification because as believers we are in union with Christ by faith, and it is from him that we derive our salvation. We are reminded of this every time we come to the communion table and partake of the bread and the wine. But that ordinance too is dependent on the Word of God for its authority. There is no other book which describes the life, death, resurrection, ascension and exaltation of Christ like the Bible. As believers we feast on Christ but that feasting comes through Scripture. Hence Jesus prays, 'Sanctify them by the truth; your word is truth.'

The Word of God is unique in describing the sovereign way in which salvation takes place. 'You see, at just the right time, when we were still powerless, Christ died for the ungodly' (Rom 5:6). We call this free grace. It is unmerited favour freely given without any regard to human merit. When we were dead in sins God raised us up in a spiritual resurrection which is expressed by Paul when he declares, 'For we are God's workmanship, created in Christ Jesus to do good works, which God prepared in advance for us to do' (Eph 2:10). The Father has predestined his people to be conformed to the likeness of his Son (Rom 8:29). 'He who began a good work in you will carry it on to completion' (Phil 1:6). This knowledge of God's sovereign purpose is vital in personal sanctification and it is conveyed to us through the Word.

Why is it that we are not immediately translated to heaven like Enoch and Elijah? Why can't we escape death like they did? The reason is that God's purpose for us is progressive sanctification. We are here to make spiritual progress and grow in knowledge and grace as Peter urges: 'Grow in the grace and knowledge of our Lord and Saviour Jesus Christ' (2 Peter 3:18). When things go wrong and we are disobedient or even rebellious the Lord is patient with us and corrects and restores us. This may take place through chastisement because the Lord disciplines those he loves (Heb 12:1-11). But how would we know all these things except by the Word?

The word is unique in explaining the life of holiness in its every sphere. 'Your word is a lamp to my feet and a light for my path' (Ps 119:105).

Here are some examples.

The Word explains how we should live as husbands and wives and how we should bring up our children. Ephesians 5:22 – 6:4 provides instruction for family relationships. Husbands are to love their wives as Christ loves the Church. Wives are to be submissive to the leadership of their husbands in the Lord. Children are to obey their parents in the Lord. Fathers are to bring up their children in the training and instruction of the Lord. This theme is especially important in days when there is a massive attack on family life. Pastors should preach regularly on the subject of the family. The Church provides a spiritual home for those who are single and live on their own. Here again the New Testament provides all the instruction needed for churches to be well ordered and well led by caring pastors, elders and deacons. The latter attend to the practical affairs of the assembly.

The Word explains how we should exemplify the doctrines of grace. Having been saved by grace we show grace to others. In Colossians 3:12-14 there is this exhortation: 'As God's chosen people, holy and dearly loved, clothe yourselves with compassion, kindness, humility, gentleness and patience.' John Davenant (1572-1641) unpacks the meaning of each word in this passage in a masterly way. His commentary on Colossians is published by the Banner of Truth. Included in this passage is the exhortation to forgive each other even as Christ has forgiven us. On that theme there is nothing to equal the example of our Lord which is described in 1 Peter 2:21-23.

The Scriptures explain the wiles of the devil and how we conduct spiritual warfare. Ephesians 6:12-18 is an important passage since it describes the weapons provided for the conflict. Discipline is a necessity. Holiness includes tears and toil but it is combined with joy, peace and hope. There is the anticipation of the Second Coming of our Lord and the glorious resurrection from the dead. There is the joyful prospect of the New Jerusalem and the new earth in which eternal righteousness will reign. In the meantime there is the privilege of access to the throne of grace in prayer (Heb 12:22-24).

I have sought to show the centrality of the Bible in our lives as Christians and how the Bible is used by the Holy Spirit to achieve progressive sanctification. A Christian's relationship toward the Bible is a telling and crucial factor. How do you relate to the Bible? To love the Bible is to love the Triune God.

The manner in which the Bible was inspired and collated over about 1,400 years and preserved is a marvel. It has survived all its critics. It continues more than ever all over the world in innumerable languages to be the instrument of the new birth and the instrument of sanctification in those who are born again. Do you look for a miracle? Pick up the Bible and you have *the* miracle book in your hands. When John Jewel, one of the great English Reformers who became the bishop of Salisbury, was preaching on the Scriptures he ended with this rousing exhortation: 'Are you a father? Have you children? Read the Scriptures. Are you a king? Read the Scriptures. Are you a minister? Read the Scriptures. Has God blessed you with wealth? Read the Scriptures. Are you a usurer? Read the Scriptures. Are you a fornicator? Read the Scriptures. Are you in adversity? Read the Scriptures. Are you a sinner? Have you offended God? Read the Scriptures. Do you despair of the mercy of God? Read the Scriptures. Are you going out of this life? Read the Scriptures.'[4]

---

1   The periphrastic plural, perfect, passive *ōsin teteleiōmenoi* is pointing to a goal, namely, the goal of complete unity which has ongoing effects. John 17:23 is not easy to understand. Don Carson says in his commentary on John, 'The thought is breathtakingly extravagant.' As we look about today the unity of

individual churches is often in tatters and there are so many denominations it is bewildering for the world to understand. Of these denominations some have moved so far from the Bible that it is difficult to explain to unbelievers that they hardly come into the orbit of John 17 which is a unity of those who are united to the Trinity.

2   Geoff Thomas, *Satisfied with the Scriptures*, 24 page booklet published by Chapel Library, 2603 W Wright St, Pensacola, Florida 32505, USA.

3   Isaiah 42:1-9; 49:1-7; 50:4-11 and 52:13-15 on through chapter 53.

4   *Ibid*, Geoff Thomas.

Two Cities or One?

The famous Hebrews chapter eleven provides a chronicle of Old Testament believers who are commended for their faith. Many of the best known are described including Abel, Enoch, Noah, Abraham, Isaac, Jacob and Moses and some from the books of Joshua and Judges such as Rahab, Gideon and Samson. David and Samuel are included and then reference is made to many un-named who died as martyrs rather then deny their faith.

The chapter concludes with these words: 'These were all commended for their faith, yet none of them received what had been promised. God had planned something better for us so that only together with us would they be made perfect' (Heb 11:39,40).

In the great resurrection day they will be made perfect just as we will be made perfect. All the Old Testament saints will be made one with us. They too will be part of the Bride of Christ. They too will be residents of the New Jerusalem. There will not be two cities on the new earth, one for the Old Testament saints and one for those redeemed in the New Testament era, with perhaps a dualcarriage highway between.

How were the Old Testament believers saved? They were saved by believing in the Saviour to come. The sacrifices instituted in the Old Testament were pointing toward the one great final sacrifice that was to be made by the person of Christ (Heb 10:14). We have the advantage, which they did not, of seeing Christ in the Gospels in the fullness and perfection of his active and passive obedience.

In his great high priestly prayer our Lord prayed for all his people 'to be brought to complete unity' (John 17:23). Such unity forms a powerful testimony to the world. But there is also an eschatological dimension to this prayer of Jesus. Ultimately the whole believing community of both the Old and New Testament epochs will be completely perfected and totally united. That is a glorious prospect to which we look forward by faith and perseverance.

Chapter 17

Holiness and Church Membership

The prominence of the church in sanctification is seen in the way this subject occupies the major sections of application in the New Testament. As soon as Paul reaches his practical application in his letter to the Romans he deals with the relationship of members to each other and the humble submission required of members as they recognise their gifts for the service of the body (Rom 12:1-8). Hebrews 10:19-39 asserts the need for individuals to cleave consistently to the assembly both for the sake of its well-being and for their own sake to guard against falling away. Ephesians 1:11 to 4:16 displays the glorious unity of the Church, which unity brings great responsibility to individual members to maintain that unity. Both apostles Peter and Paul use the illustration of living stones being compacted and cemented together into one building (1 Peter 2:5; Eph 2:20-22).

The divisions at Corinth constrained Paul to urge the vital importance of unity for all the members (1 Cor 12:12-31). Every member is important. One sick member causes pain in the whole body. Every member has a rôle to play which is like the human body in which all the parts are vital. They are all needed. The eye cannot say to the hand, I don't need you!

It is sometimes hurtful when we are subject to reproof or correction. For instance it can be hard for a young believer who imagines that he is a born preacher to discover that the consensus of the body is firmly of the opposite opinion. Humility of mind and heart is a vital and precious part of sanctification. When the bricklayer takes a brick and chops off corners, shaping it up to be fitted in to the rest of the brickwork, that cutting can seem to be rough. But it is necessary. Church discipline in all its aspects, from mild reproof to severe warning, to exclusion from the communion table, is provided to assist and to ensure the integration and sanctification of the members of Christ's body.

Hebrews 10:24 insists on believers observing or considering one another. This cannot be done in absentia. It necessitates regular faithful assembling of ourselves together. Spasmodic attendance often leads to non-attendance and ultimately to the severance of that particular branch from the vine. Dead branches that have dried up are gathered to be thrown into the fire (John 15:6).

How do you grow in affection for fellow members you seldom see? In some churches attendees seem to disappear very quickly after the formal worship. In some assemblies they linger for as long as possible, sometimes until the caretaker urges them to leave. Provision must be made for fellowship. 'May the Lord make your love increase and overflow for each other and for everyone else, just as ours does for you' (1 Thess 3:12). Likewise Peter urged, 'Love one another deeply, from the heart' (1 Peter 1:22).

This love for God's family is an important part of progressive sanctification. At the beginning of our Christian lives we are called into fellowship with the church (Acts 2:41). Professor John Murray shows the gravity of the sin of negligence in failing to be concerned for the sanctification of others:

'If the individual is indifferent to the sanctification of others, and does not seek to promote their growth in grace, love, faith, knowledge, obedience, and holiness, this interferes with his own sanctification in at least two respects. Firstly his lack of concern for others is itself a vice that gnaws at the root of spiritual growth. If we are not concerned with, or vigilant in respect of, the fruit of the Spirit in others, then it is because we do not burn with holy zeal for the honour of Christ himself. All shortcoming and sin in us dishonours Christ, and a believer betrays the coldness of his love to Christ when he fails to bemoan the defects of those who are members of Christ's body. Secondly his indifference to the interests of others means the absence of the ministry which he should have afforded others. This absence results in the impoverishment of these others to the extent of his failure, and this impoverishment reacts upon himself, because these others are not able to minister to him to the full extent of the support, encouragement, instruction, edification, and exhortation which they owe to him.'[1]

The author of Hebrews exhorts that we spur 'one another on towards love and good deeds'. Devoted service comes about by the observation of fellow church members in action. We learn much of the Christian life by seeing others in action. Perseverance is encouraged by observing the patient endurance of fellow believers. We learn how to pray by hearing others in prayer. Faith is increased and strengthened by sharing with those who exercise it. In Hebrews chapter eleven attention is drawn to the example of those who exercised faith in difficult circumstances.

We must never lose sight of the fact that there is only one organisation that is in the very centre of God's purpose. That is his Church, which Christ bought with his own blood. Jesus promised, 'I will build my church, and the gates of Hades will not overcome it' (Matt 16:18).

The Church of Christ is utterly unique. Every believer on earth is required to give total allegiance by way of active membership and practical support to his or her local church.

The nature of the church as a whole in the way it functions has a formative influence on the individual members. I will now demonstrate this by opening up a statement by Paul in his first letter to Timothy.

> I am writing you these instructions so that, if I am delayed, you will know how people ought to conduct themselves in

> God's household, which is the church of the living God, the pillar and foundation of the truth (1 Tim 3:14,15).

The text printed above is one of several which describe the uniqueness of the local church. It is the only place where the living God guarantees his residence. Of course there are churches, which have forsaken the Bible, and so God has forsaken them. *Ichabod* (meaning the glory has departed) is written over them. In this exposition I have in mind churches (sometimes referred to as assemblies), which for all their weaknesses and deficiencies form the body of Christ on earth. These are assemblies where the leaders and members are striving to be faithful to the Bible.

Observe from 1 Timothy 3:15 five ways in which a local Christian church is unique. Each of these impact progressive sanctification:

1. The church is a spiritual household – a family of those called to be saints (1 Cor 1:2)
2. The church is an ordered household with elders and deacons – see context 1 Timothy 3
3. The church is the house of the living God
4. The church is the pillar of truth
5. The church is the foundation of the truth

1. The church is a spiritual household – a family of those called to be saints (1 Cor 1:2)

In the text the metaphor of a house *(oikos)* is used, but this is not a physical fabric. It is not a building of brick or wood. The fact that it is the place where the living God dwells points to the reality of family members. The nature of these family members is well described in 1 Corinthians 1:2. Note what Paul says there. He addresses a local church which is at Corinth. The word church *(ekklesia)* means those called out of the world. This calling is specific. It is a call to be holy which means separate from the world and pure in life and conduct. Paul declares furthermore that this separation is into union in Christ: 'sanctified in Christ Jesus'. While church membership is visible, inasmuch as we are in unity with a local church, it is also universal because Paul reminds the Corinthian believers that they are also one 'with all those everywhere who call on the name of our Lord Jesus Christ'.

We can stretch our minds to think even more widely than unity with all true Christians on the face of the earth. In fact we are one with all the universal Church as described in Hebrews 12:22-24. We are united with all those who have died in Christ and whose perfected spirits are now in heaven. We are one with all God's people from the beginning to the end of time. We await the great day of resurrection when the completed number of believers of all generations will make up the bride of Christ, the new Jerusalem (Rev 21:2).

Until that time we operate in a tangible way as we join with and work together with God's family in a local church. In doing so we must always remember that the local church is the place of highest privilege. We are a family of brothers and sisters. We are the sons and daughters of God. We are the family of love. God is love. The three Persons, Father, Son and Holy Spirit are a family of love. We are called into that family. Hence the baptismal formula of the Trinity. The Triune God is a Trinity of love. That is why there is the great stress on loving one another. Jesus elevates this requirement of loving each other to an abiding ever-present commandment (John 13:34). The apostle John confirms this imperative of love in his first letter and suggests that in this way we can be assured that we are true believers. 'We know that we have passed from death to life, because we love our brothers' (1 John 3:14).

Luke describes the behaviour of the first members of the church following the day of Pentecost. He says, 'They devoted themselves to the apostles' teaching, and to the fellowship, to the breaking of bread, and to prayer' (Acts 2:42). When Christians meet they bond by way of sharing. They will meet too for the Lord's Supper and they will gather for prayer meetings.

There is a closeness in all this which is described in different ways. For instance: 'We who are many form one body, and each member belongs to all the others' (Rom 12:5). 'In him the whole building is joined together and rises to become a holy temple in the Lord. And in him you too are being built together to become a dwelling in which God lives by his Spirit' (Eph 2:21,22).

The words translated 'joined together' (Eph 2:21) are a feeble translation of the text which asserts that believers are closely knit together. In order to describe this closeness Paul makes up his own Greek word used nowhere else, namely *sunarmologoumene* which means 'closely integrated together'.

The importance of every member working together for the advantage of all the others is well illustrated by an event in 1630 when John Winthrop (1588-1649), later to become governor of the Massachusetts Bay Company, led a small group of colonists to the shores of North America. As his ship, the *Arabella*, sailed across the Atlantic, Winthrop stood on the deck and charged his followers to establish a new kind of Christian community. This was his appeal:

> 'We must knit together in this work as one man, we must entertain each other in brotherly affection – we must uphold a familiar commerce together in all meekness, gentleness, patience and liberality, we must delight in each other, make others' condition our own, rejoice together, mourn together, labour and suffer together, always having before our eyes our commission in the work, our community as members of the same body; so shall we keep the unity of the Spirit in the bond of peace, the Lord will be our God and delight to dwell among us.'[2]

Now it is all very well to be closely compacted together but what about considerable differences of race and culture and of social status? Paul reminds us that we are now all one in Christ. He declares, 'There is neither Jew nor Greek, slave nor free, male nor female, for you are all one in Christ Jesus' (Gal 3:28). This diversity is confirmed by the vision of the great assembly of the saved recorded in Revelation 5:9, 'With your blood you purchased men for God from every tribe and language and people and nation.'

Internationalism is an increasing phenomenon in Christian churches. In London, England, in Jakarta, Indonesia, and in many other great cities there are churches in which many nationalities are represented. These differences in character form a diversity which reflects the glory of Christ. While different peoples war and fight each other and often despise each other, Christ unites different peoples in a unity of love. Jesus said, 'All men will know that you are my disciples if you love one another' (John 13:35). And Jesus prayed, 'May they be brought to complete unity to let the world know that you sent me' (John 17:23).

I will look in more detail at differences as follows: diversity of personal character, diversity of spiritual development and growth, and diversity of spiritual gifts.

(i) Diversity of personal character

Increasingly across the world churches consist of all kinds of people drawn from different races and different cultural backgrounds. God puts us together with a variety of people. He puts us with people we like and people to whom we may find it very difficult to relate. He puts us together with people who fit our comfort zone and people who do not. There are many reasons for this. One just referred to is that the unity of Christ's Church is displayed. Churches consisting of a variety of nationalities and ethnic origins are increasing.

(ii) Diversity of spiritual development and growth

The Church not only consists of diverse peoples but individuals who differ greatly. Some are weak believers and others are strong. Some may be physically handicapped. Some may suffer from an impoverished under-privileged background. Some may have the advantage of university while others have hardly any education at all. Lack of education does not mean lack of spiritual discernment. Sometimes those with little academic training have a sharper and better grasp of Christian doctrine. Our Lord chose fishermen to be his apostles. Academia can be an advantage and it was so with the apostle Paul. Members of an average church represent all phases of spiritual growth. Some are babes in Christ while others may have many years of experience and are full of spiritual maturity. Some may have sinful tendencies which cause pain to the members. There are sins like the sin of pride that takes time to mortify. We must always remember that the Church is the arena of progressive sanctification. 'If one part suffers, every part suffers with it; if one part is honoured, every part rejoices with it' (1 Cor 12:26). If a member of a church backslides that causes tremendous concern to the strong members.

The graces of faith, love, humility, gentleness and so on, are learned. Also we are put together with others of holy character so that our sinful propensities can be challenged and mortified. In every church we have to discourage little groupings: students in one little group, mothers in another, the elderly in another. The diversity of a church is part of her glory. We must not choose to associate only with those we like and avoid others whom we do not like or with whom we may have less in common. We who are united to Christ have Jesus in common and that is like saying we have eternal life in common because he is eternal life (1 John 1:2). The 'little clique' mentality must be discouraged in the local church. Do you go out of your way to talk to those in the church who are opposite to you in nationality and background?

J David Hoke of New Horizons Community Church, New Jersey, is on the mark when on his website he wrote as follows:

> 'Our behaviour impacts every other believer in the household. We need each other. I need you and you need me. You need what I have in God and I need what you have in God. When we hold one another at arm's length then the whole church suffers – when we open up to one another, become involved even when it is uncomfortable, and share our lives with each other, then the whole church is built up. Unless we see the church as *the household of God* and ourselves as related to every other believer, we are not seeing the church biblically. But when we do, and when we surrender to that way of life, then we will begin to experience life on a new level. Jesus called it abundant life. Abundant life is not abundant unless it can be shared.'

Pastor Hoke continues:

> 'I am not talking about having close friends, but about becoming exclusive, about not sharing your life with others. Who do you think you are that you have a right to hold your brothers and sisters at arm's length? Don't you realise that God has composed the church so that each member needs every other member? What makes you so special that you can both deprive yourself and others of this needed interaction? You may mistakenly think that you don't need it, but what about others who need you?'

(iii) Diversity of spiritual gifts

Romans 12:3-8 describes a variety of gifts as does 1 Corinthians 12:4-11.

1 Timothy 3 describes the qualifications of elders and deacons and that in itself is a reminder that there are different gifts in a church. In several places in the New Testament a wide diversity of spiritual gifts is described. These have to be recognised. Most of them function naturally but they need to be recognised and encouraged. One of the responsibilities of teachers and preachers is to 'prepare God's people for works of service, so that the body of Christ may be built up' (Eph 4:11,12).

2. The church is an ordered household with elders and deacons – see context 1 Timothy 3

Jesus appointed apostles who in turn left the Church with the permanent order described in the Pastoral Letters, namely elders and deacons. In the ideal church these leaders set the pace spiritually and practically. The elders are concerned for the spiritual growth (progressive sanctification) of the members and the deacons set the pace in the administration of the practical affairs of the church. Paul says that the head of the Church has given some to be pastors and teachers to prepare God's people for works of service (Eph 4:11).[3]

The context in which we find the text 1 Timothy 3:15 is one in which Paul specifies how the leaders are to be recognised. He describes the qualifications essential for elders and deacons. The local church is the only organisation on earth that has spiritual leaders in these two categories, one to teach and shepherd and the other to minister to the practical needs of the church. The recognition of elders and deacons can only come about as a consequence of spiritual family life in the assembly of the living God. As believers grow in grace and knowledge together so the gifts given by the Holy Spirit to individuals develop and function increasingly and so are to be recognised. Those who are called and qualified and recognised by the membership are set aside for office.

Every organisation on earth has an order. An army has generals and officers in different ranks. Professional sporting teams have managers, coaches and captains. Businesses have boards of directors and managers. The local church is unique inasmuch as it has elders and deacons. Different spiritual gifts are given to all the members as is suggested in Romans 12:3ff.

Flexibility is important in large churches where there may be several full-time elders/pastors and perhaps a dozen or more part-time elders. Ideally all the gifts should be used to the best advantage of the church. Likewise in a diaconate responsibilities must be delegated and the diaconate must work in unity as a team.

3. The church is the house of the living God

The local church is the place of expository preaching, the place where God imparts life to the unregenerate. We know that sinners can be brought to life anywhere (Rom 10:5-13) but in the majority of cases it is under the preaching and application of the Word that sinners are brought to life (James 1:18). 'God was pleased through the foolishness of what was preached to save those who believe' (1 Cor 1:21). The church is the place where the Holy Spirit accomplishes his work of regenerating souls and building them up, preparing them for the world to come. The church is where souls are fed and nurtured. It is the place of spiritual renewal. It is where we meet with the living God. In this way the church is the arena in which the work of sanctification is advanced.

The expression 'living God' points us to the reality of spiritual life. Progressive sanctification is advanced in the arena of a living church. This reality is illustrated during the time of the exodus of the children of Israel out of Egypt. If during the time of the exodus a seeker had asked, Where can I find the living God, the Creator of the heavens and the earth? – that enquirer could have been pointed to the camp of the Israelites. There in the middle of the camp of the twelve tribes was the tabernacle. Over the tabernacle was the pillar of cloud and of fire signifying the presence of the living God. All other gods were dead idols. The surrounding pagan peoples worshipped graven images that were dead. These images could not see, or hear, or speak. In contrast to dead idols Jehovah was described as the living God. He is alive to hear our prayers. He is alive to save us from our sins. He gives new birth to dead sinners. He sustains his people with spiritual life. Hence he is called 'the spring of living water' (Jer 2: 13).

The marks of a true church are faithful preaching of the Bible, godly worship, discipline in the membership and the ordinances of baptism and the Lord's table. But these marks must be living. In other words they should be full of spiritual vitality. We worship God in spirit and in truth. If the living God is not present, worship becomes formal and dead, an empty ritual.

When we come together for worship, fellowship or prayer we sense the presence of God. The Triune God is alive among us. The concluding verse of the prophet Ezekiel is in the form of a signpost pointing to the New Jerusalem. The sign says, THE LORD IS THERE.

The presence of the living God among his people is predicted by the prophet Zechariah.

> 'Shout and be glad, O Daughter of Zion. For I am coming, and I will live among you,' declares the LORD. 'Many nations will be joined with the LORD in that day and will become my

people. I will live among you and you will know that the LORD Almighty has sent me to you' (Zech 2:10,11).

'For we are the temple of the living God. As God has said: "I will live with them and walk among them, and I will be their God, and they will be my people"' (2 Cor 6: 16).

4. The church is the pillar of the truth

Jachin and Boaz were the names given to the two freestanding pillars in the forecourt of the temple. They were placed there for beauty as a reminder to all architects of the importance of aesthetic beauty, but we are reminded of that text in Romans 10:15, 'How beautiful are the feet of those who bring good news.' Magnificent is the gospel of good news, which brings salvation. It is the privilege and responsibility of every local church to hold high the saving gospel of Christ. The local church is to propagate the gospel by holding high the only truth that can save. In this way the church is the pillar of truth.

This is all new to those converted from the world. How to witness and share the gospel with others especially relatives and friends who have seen the change is important. This is beautifully illustrated by the experience of Brownlow North. He was a man of wealthy aristocratic background and very worldly. Brownlow North came under deep conviction of sin and spiritual agonies which led to his conversion. He then felt that he must make good the harm he had done by his former godless life and one way to do that was to give out tracts. That sounds easy but it is not when you have no experience in witnessing to the faith. It was a struggle but he pursued this method of bearing testimony to his new found faith. Brownlow North then felt convicted of his need to align himself with Christians in public. Opportunity came when a young man, himself newly converted, invited Brownlow North to join him in street preaching near Kings Cross, London. The young man annoyed the crowd some of whom hurled abuse at the preacher which was the worst blasphemy that Brownlow North had ever heard. He began to doubt the wisdom of casting gospel pearls before these swine when several voices were heard calling upon him to speak, 'We'll hear that stout man with the dark eyes.' From the moment Brownlow North began to preach every eye was fixed on him.[4] He riveted the attention of them all and carried the bulk of the audience with him. This was a remarkable event because in it was the first evidence of a God-given gift to Brownlow North of evangelistic preaching. Very soon he went on to become a foremost preacher and evangelist in the great spiritual awakening which began in America in 1857 and spread with great power to Ulster in 1859 and Scotland in 1859-60. In Scotland and Ulster Brownlow North preached to large crowds of 4,000 and sometimes 7,000 souls.

5. The church is the foundation of the truth

There is a vital connection between the pillar of the truth and the foundation of the truth. The good news of the gospel is to be held high on the pillar but that can only be a reality when there is a foundation upon which the pillar stands. We need the whole Bible. That is our foundation. As Jesus said, 'If you abide in my word, you are truly my disciples' (John 8:31 ESV).

By calling the church the foundation *(hedraioma)* of the truth Paul is declaring that the Bible is entrusted to the Church. The Bible is the basis of the truth. The Bible is different from all other writings because it is inspired by the Holy Spirit. In 2 Timothy 3:16 we read that all Scripture is Godbreathed. How did the early Church recognise which books were inspired and infallible and which not? The answer to that is that the Scriptures are self-authenticating. They bear the marks of perfection and when put together complement each other. The word we use to describe the inclusion of 66 books into one book is 'canon'.

The canon of Scripture has been entrusted to the Church in the sense that it is the Church which is to preserve and defend the Scriptures. The manner in which this is facilitated is by a Confession of Faith. The Confession defines the nature and sufficiency of Scripture. The Confession of Faith is not infallible like the Bible. Rather it is a help which defines the major doctrines of the Faith and when rightly used it protects the Church from unfaithful ministers. If an elder denies the Bible or teaches contrary to the truths as outlined in the Confession then he must resign his office. Instances have been known of churches losing their way in doctrine and then members discovered that their church was committed to a Confession of Faith. That assisted them to get the church back on track.

'The church is the foundation of the truth' is a short statement with a massive meaning. Every church based on the Bible needs to have a Reformed Confession of Faith which spells out the main truths of Scripture. This is necessary because there are cults like the Jehovah's Witnesses and Mormons which claim to be based on the Bible but these either distort essential truth or add to it in such a way as to nullify it. In the 21st century a church should hold to and defend a Reformed Confession of Faith because that Confession represents the whole history of the Christian Church from its inception at Pentecost. The Confession spells out the principal doctrines of the Faith. We can say to those who challenge us, We are founded on the Bible and if you want to know the meaning of the Bible here is a fifty page document explaining what that means. The reason why it is called 'a Reformed Confession' is because in the 16th century the Christian Church came almost to its demise because of accumulated human tradition. Recovery came through a great Reformation, – hence the term 'reformed'.[5]

This foundation of truth is vital for sanctification as it provides an authoritative basis for faith to grow. As believers we are not oddities who have popped up 2000 years after Christ's ascension. We belong to a body of believers who can be traced back through the centuries. We benefit from those who have survived enormous testings. Through many trials Bible truth has been clarified. An example is the all-important subject of the person of Christ who is both God and man without confusion. This is a complex subject. It took several centuries to achieve clear doctrinal statements so that we do not have to build those foundations again. We need to know them well but do not have to rewrite them. .

To grow in understanding of an integrated powerful body of truth and of Church history is an important part of sanctification. To be ignorant is to be weak and vulnerable.

The trust to maintain, defend and teach the Bible belongs to the local church and not to any other organisation. At times in Church history Bible seminaries have become heretical. Damage of the most destructive kind has been done when men have submitted themselves to unbelieving academics who have systematically undermined their faith in the Bible. These men whose faith has been destroyed have gone out with anti-evangelical teaching and undermined the faith of others. Jude and 2 Peter 2 anticipate the entrance into the Church of those who deny the basic doctrines of the faith.

What has this to do with sanctification? All believers are required so to grow in their understanding so that they are able to contend for the faith that was once for all entrusted to the saints (Jude 3).

---

1   John Murray, *Collected Writings*, vol 2, page 299.
2   Quoted in Perry Miller and Thomas H Johnson, *The Puritans,* two volumes, New York: Harper, 1963, 1:197-198.
3   'Pastors' is the term mostly used for full-time ministers of the gospel while elders is the term used for those who are part-time. 1 Timothy 5:17 describes those who direct the affairs of the church well of being worthy to have double honour, especially those whose work is preaching and teaching. There seems to be flexibility here in recognising the work of elders.
4   K Moody Stuart, *Brownlow North – His Life and Work*, Banner of Truth, 1961, page 38.
5   There is a gulf between the Roman Catholic Church and Bible-believing churches because the RC Church teaches that all authority for life and practice rests on the Bible plus tradition. Many traditions which have no basis whatever from Scripture have been added. Human tradition makes void the Word of God (Matt 23). These traditions in the Church of Rome impede the return to the principle of *sola scriptura*.

Helpful books

Wayne Mack and David Swavely. *Life in the Father's House,* 210 page paperback, P and R. Highly commended.

Philip Ryken. *The Communion of the Saints – Living in Fellowship with the People of God.* 230 page paperback, P and R. A practical and helpful book. The author slips in infant baptism as presumptive regeneration which is a serious error (page 37).

Eric Wright. *The Church – No Spectator Sport.* Evangelical Press, 424 pages. The storm of controversy surrounding the so-called 'charismatic gifts' obscures less controversial gifts such as faith and mercy, as well as speaking gifts such as encouragement, or serving gifts such as hospitality. The author extracts biblical principles about spiritual gifts so that we can understand them and seeks to show how crucial the non-spectacular gifts are in local church life and encourages us to make fuller use of them.

Sola Scriptura. The Protestant Position on the Bible. Soli Deo Gloria. 280 pp, paperback. This is a symposium of seven very useful expositions some of which explain the relationship of the Bible to the Church. The chapter by John MacArthur refutes the false claims of the Roman Catholic Church which adds tradition to the authority of the Bible.

Transformation

Oliver Heywood (1629-1702) was a gifted English Puritan. He was one of the pastors ejected in 1662 and suffered persecution and imprisonment often for his preaching. In his book *Heart Treasure* (Soli Deo Gloria, 400 pages), Heywood expounds Matthew 12:35, 'A good man, out of the good treasure of the heart, bringeth forth good things.'

In the course of his teaching Heywod describes the moral transformation going on in a regenerate soul as 'a greater work, and of more value, than the whole material universe. A renewed soul is the epitome of the creation, the clearest likeness of the Divinity on earth, the true portraiture of God in man, and a blessed treasury of spiritual perfections. The soul is the glory of man, and grace is the glory of the soul. Every man is so far excellent as he is religious.'

'A Christian's greatest ornament and dignity consist in what he is with respect to God. Gracious souls are truly precious, and such as are precious in God's account are honourable, and of more worth than the richest princes and largest kingdoms. Well may they be the Lord's jewels, who have a treasure of jewels locked up in their breasts. These precious sons of Zion are comparable to fine gold, though men esteem them as earthen pitchers. As it was with their Divine Redeemer and Exemplar, of whom his despisers said, "He hath no form nor comeliness, and when we see him there is no beauty that we should desire him," so the saints may appear mean and sordid to external view, but could you penetrate their hidden being, you would find them all glorious within.'

❧ Chapter 18 ❧
Holiness and the
Problem of Worldliness

When I was converted in 1953 I was baptised and brought into fellowship with the Central Baptist Church, Pretoria. It was all a marvellous experience. I was immediately taught to be totally dedicated and never miss the weekly prayer meeting. I was also well and truly taught to give the whole of the Lord's Day to worship and good works. A most important factor was public testimony to show that we believers are not ashamed of Jesus and are ready to testify in public. Attendance at and participation in open-air meetings followed immediately after baptism. Tithing was taught to all new members. Coming from a non-evangelical background I was exhorted to shun worldliness and instructed in the taboos of what to avoid. I will return to that presently with regard to fundamentalism. As I look back on that time I realise that my conversion came about during a time of spiritual visitation, a mini-revival. All the converts of that time went on strongly and thrived spiritually. As far as I know not one of them left their first love.

The Western world has subsequently moved into a new era of postmodernism.[1] The effects of that have been profound. It would be difficult to find a more accurate description of the influences on the churches than that given by J I Packer who wrote as follows:

'Flooding Christian communities today is the anarchic worldliness of the post-Christian West. The gigantic corporate immoralism called "permissiveness" has broken over us like a tidal wave. Churches most closely in touch with their heritage have bailed out more of the invading tide than others have been able to do, but none have been very successful here, certainly not among their younger members. Christian moral standards on the sexual, family, social, financial, commercial, and personal fronts have spectacularly broken down, and "new moralities" currently offered prove to be the old pagan immorality, travelling under various assumed names. "The place for the ship is the sea," said D L Moody, "but God help the ship if the sea gets into it." That is an uncomfortable word to hear, for the waves of worldliness have got into the contemporary church and waterlogged it to a very damaging degree.'[2]

Worldliness is an enemy of holiness. For that reason we need to understand what worldliness means. Evaluations of what it is to be worldly vary considerably among Evangelicals. I will survey the principal texts of Scripture, view the example of Moses, and conclude by an examination of how fundamentalists handle the subject of worldliness.

1. What the Scriptures teach

Dealing with the subject of immorality and separation from it Paul writes, 'I have written to you in my letter not to associate with sexually immoral people – not at all meaning the people of this world who are immoral, or the greedy, and swindlers, or idolaters. In that case you would have to leave this world. But now I am writing you that you must not associate with anyone who calls himself a brother but is sexually immoral or greedy, an idolater or a slanderer, a drunkard, or a swindler. With such a person do not even eat' (1 Cor 5:9-11).

In a letter that has not survived Paul addressed the scandal of the incestuous man. In that context Paul shows zero tolerance. There must be a clear line of demarcation between the church and evil behaviour. The church cannot tolerate scandalous sin. The discipline of the incestuous man was essential. All the members at Corinth were required to shun the unrepentant member.

However Paul was careful to affirm that common sense must prevail. Shunning in this case was applied to a church member. It is no solution for Christians to escape the world altogether by living in ghettos or monasteries. The well-known saying, 'We are in the world but not of the world,' is derived from this passage of Scripture.

In 2 Corinthians Paul forbids alliances or partnerships with the world: 'Do not be yoked together with unbelievers. For what do righteousness and wickedness have in common? Or what fellowship can light have with darkness? What harmony is there between Christ and Belial? What does a believer have in common with an unbeliever? What does a believer have in common with an unbeliever? What agreement is there between the temple of God and idols? For we are the temple of the living God. As God has said: "I will live with them and walk among them, and I will be their God, and they will be my people. Therefore come out from them and be separate, says the Lord. Touch no unclean thing, and I will receive you." "I will be a Father to you, and you will be my sons and daughters, says the Lord Almighty"' (2 Cor 6:14-18).

Unequal partnerships of believers with unbelievers are addressed in the form of five rhetorical questions. These challenging questions highlight the incompatibility of spheres in which values and commitments are diametrically opposed. Where the structures of society espouse moral wickedness or religious darkness we must draw lines of absolute separation. Binge-drinking among young people, which has become a plague in the UK, is an example. That is a no-go area. Gambling is another danger in society which must be avoided. Freemasonry with its false religious rites is incompatible with the gospel. Church membership should be barred to those who belong to Masonic orders or to secret societies.

2 Corinthians 6:14-18 makes it abundantly clear that for a believer to marry an unbeliever is unbiblical because interests are diametrically opposed.

It is of the utmost importance to observe how 2 Corinthians 6:14-18 concludes with a call to share the rights and privileges of adoption. 'I will be a Father to you, and you will be my sons and daughters, says the Lord Almighty.' Separation is not a negative exercise. It is positive. We turn our backs on one sphere to belong to another. The passage concludes not at the end of chapter six but with 2 Corinthians 7:1 which is a cogent call to perfect holiness out of reverence for God. Separation is from the world to a new world of holiness. It is positive. We have a new world to look forward to, a new world to prepare for. We anticipate the glory of the New Jerusalem. Without holiness no one will partake of that. The Christian life is packed with good works and enterprises. The lost world should never see sourness in Christians as though they are hard done by. Rather they should see joy that believers have eternal life and are active participants in God's eternal kingdom.

That separation from the world is positive and constructive can hardly be exaggerated. For instance the exodus of the Israelites out of Egypt is treated in the whole Bible as *the* major biblical paradigm for holiness. 'Now if you obey me fully and keep my covenant, then out of all nations you will be my treasured possession. Although the whole earth is mine you will be for me a kingdom of priests and a holy nation' (Ex 19:5,6). The Lord separated Israel from Egypt to make them a holy people. They were to become the vehicle for his truth in the world and a people from whom the Saviour of the world would eventually come (Deut 18:15).

It must be stressed that all separation from impurity to holiness must be based on grace. By grace we have been saved and having been saved we now live by grace and not by works. Our works are essential not in order to be justified but because we have been justified and now need to live consistently with that (Rom 6). Separation from the worldly life and values is never to vaunt our superiority over unbelievers. We hate pharisaism and must avoid it. At the same time the Scriptures warn that there will be persecution and mockery (Matt 5:11,12). All we do as Christians is never to earn favour with God. We do not have to earn anything since we are already in the family by adoption. Our status and privilege cannot increase. We must live holy and pure lives to be consistent with our calling into God's family.

So far we have examined the stark difference between believers and outright profligate sinners like drunkards or swindlers. A Christian can avoid scandalous people and yet be thoroughly worldly-minded. Therefore we must examine more Scripture to get to the heart of worldliness.

John's warning about worldliness is well known: 'Do not love the world or anything in the world. If anyone loves the world, the love of the Father is not in. For everything in the world – the cravings of sinful man, the lust of his eyes and the boasting of what he has and does – comes not from the Father but from the world. The world and its desires pass away, but the man who does the will of God lives forever' (1 John 2:15-17).

The word 'world' (*cosmos*) is used frequently in the New Testament in different ways. For instance, 'He was in the world, and though the world was made through him, the world did not recognise him' (John 1:10). Here we have the world understood in terms of geography. The whole cosmos is created by God. However, the world (people created by God) did not recognise the Saviour the Father sent. And it is these people who are lost that God loves as we read in John 3:16: 'For God so loved the world that he gave his one and only Son, that whoever believes in him shall not perish but have eternal life.'

Referring to the world of lost people John says, 'The whole world is under the control of the evil one' (1 John 5:19). We can define the lost world as mankind living in the kingdom of darkness and under the dominion of Satan. This sinful, rebellious, lost world is in opposition to Christ and his kingdom. The lost world expresses itself in independence from God and his Christ and lives for its own values. Jeremiah states the matter simply, 'My people have committed two sins: They have forsaken me, the spring of living water, and have dug their own cisterns, broken cisterns that cannot hold water' (Jer 2:13). This sinful world is characterised by people who are determined to create their own pleasures and at the same time shut God out. In spite of this we are to love the lost people of this world and seek to bring them the good news of salvation in Christ. At the same time we are to be careful not to love the worldly values for which they live and which they serve.

Worldliness can be defined as 'mankind living in the kingdom of darkness and under the dominion of Satan'. With that in mind we consider James who declares: 'You adulterous people, don't you know that friendship with the world is hatred toward God? Anyone who chooses to be a friend of the world becomes an enemy of God' (James 4:4). James implies that the world is adulterous and to become engrossed in that sphere is to become an enemy of God. Many of those who drive the modern media are besotted with adulterous ways and reflect the lost world. In the political realm if a politician steals another man's wife he will probably get away with it, but if he is found guilty of theft he will be compelled to resign. The world is pragmatic. God's commandments 'Do not murder' and 'Do not steal' stand because worldly security is seriously undermined if these commandments are abandoned. Society will fall into a chaotic state if murder is not punished and justice maintained. But the adultery commandment is inconvenient in our secular pagan world. It becomes a subject for frivolity and joking. Sadly at the same time everyone knows that extreme and deep personal pain and family damage follow infidelity. James is saying that if a professing believer accords with these adulterous values of the unbelieving world he denies the faith and is in fact an enemy of God.

John opens up this subject in his first letter. He declares that 'the cravings of sinful man, the lust of his eyes and the boasting of what he has and does – comes not from the Father but from the world' (1 John 2:15-17). This is an accurate description of how the world operates. The cravings of sinful man refer to the panderings to physical appetites. Basically these appetites are not evil but when they get out of control they are sinful and ultimately disastrous. The most common examples today are drug addiction and alcoholism. Experimentation with drugs leads to addiction and addiction leads to early death. Alcoholism begins with extra drinks that are not necessary. This leads to addiction and when addiction takes control the end is the destruction of soul and body.

John speaks of the lust of the eyes. The world is characterised by the desire to see things for the sake of sinful pleasure. David Jackman in his commentary on 1 John hits the mark when he writes, 'In our society with its increased technological capabilities this now reaches alarming proportions, as pornography begins to invade the homes and lives of many children.' Pornography is available freely on the internet and pornography on TV channels is out of control.

When John speaks of 'boasting of what he has and does' this finds its expression especially in boasting about material possessions and wealth. The reference to 'what he does' refers to boasting about worldly status and achievement. Attaining wealth and status is a major characteristic of Western society. When economic conditions improved in Spain in the 1960s and 1970s and freedom of religion replaced the stranglehold of the Roman Catholic Church many believers hoped that this would herald a revival of evangelical Christianity. However that did not happen. The vast majority in Spain fell in love with materialism and better standards of living rather than spiritual values. The same tragic outcome could happen in China when freedom eventually comes to that huge nation. The people there who have suffered poverty can easily fall in love with materialism and use their greater freedom to pursue wealth rather than Christ.

Jesus' teaching on this theme is clear. 'Do not store up for yourselves treasures on earth, where moth and rust destroy and where thieves break in and steal. But store up for yourselves treasure in heaven where moth and rust do not destroy and where thieves do not break in and steal. For where your treasure is, there your heart will be also.' 'No-one can serve two masters. Either he will hate the one and love the other, or he will be devoted to the one and despise the other. You cannot serve both God and Money' (Matt 6:24)

This subject of money and status reminds us of Moses who forsook both for the sake of God and his people.

2. The example of Moses

Moses stands out as one who resisted the attractions of the world. It is fairly argued that he was not typical on account of his prestigious position in Egypt. However all Christians have their own sphere in which to battle and the principles are the same.

J C Ryle in his book *Holiness* comments: 'The men of God who are named in the former part of chapter eleven of Hebrews are all examples for us beyond question. But we cannot do what most of them did, however much we may drink into their spirit. We are not called upon to offer a literal sacrifice like Abel, or to build a literal ark like Noah, or to leave our country literally, and dwell in tents, and offer up our Isaac like Abraham. But the faith of Moses comes nearer to us. It seems to operate in a way more familiar to our own experience. It made him take up a line of conduct such as we must sometimes take up ourselves in the present day, each in our own walk of life, if we would be consistent Christians' (page 132).

The author of Hebrews was inspired to depict the experience of Moses in a way which highlights the crisis in Moses' life. The text runs like this:

'By faith Moses, when he had grown up, refused to be known as the son of Pharaoh's daughter. He chose to be ill-treated along with the people of God rather than to enjoy the pleasures of sin for a short time. He regarded disgrace for the sake of Christ as of greater value than the treasures of Egypt, because he was looking ahead to his reward. By faith he left Egypt, not fearing the king's anger; he persevered because he saw him who is invisible. By faith he kept the Passover and the sprinkling of blood, so that the destroyer of the firstborn would not touch the firstborn of Israel' (Heb 11:24-28).

It is noteworthy that these attractions of Egypt were lawful. It would not be sinful if Moses like Joseph before him were to become prime minister or occupy a very high office in government. Riches in themselves need not be sinful. Abraham and Job were very rich. The pressure came for Moses inasmuch as he was called to ally himself with his own people suffering as slaves in Egypt. Even though we occupy humble circumstances compared with Moses in Egypt we are called to ally ourselves with God's people. That is costly. It is even more costly when individuals are called into the ministry. For instance Dr Martyn Lloyd-Jones aged 27 turned away from a wonderful career as a cardiologist, a career for which he had been well trained.

What was it that Moses gave up and refused?

Firstly Moses gave up rank and honour. He refused to be known as the son of Pharaoh's daughter. It seems like ingratitude in Moses to turn away from Pharaoh's daughter. After all, she had rescued him as an infant, adopted him and provided him with all the advantages of the best education in Egypt. Our sympathy is aroused for Pharaoh's daughter. However is it Moses' personal relationship with Pharaoh's daughter that is in view? I think not. Rather the text refers to Moses' reputation and to the extraordinary opportunities that belonged to him. Rank, prestige and power had come to him and were his by right to maintain and increase. In our British media we follow the careers of prime ministers and those who hold cabinet portfolios. If for instance the Chancellor of the Exchequer announced his resignation because he was going to study to enter the Christian ministry it would be sensational. Such a thing is unprecedented. It was a major move for Moses to leave a position of power and honour and identify himself with a slave people.

Secondly Moses chose to turn his back on the pleasures of sin. Doubtless there were all kinds of pleasures which wealth could afford in Egypt. Many pleasures we think of today are lawful pleasures such as musical concerts or sporting events. The problem is that very soon they can become all-absorbing and idolatrous. For instance I know of an opera singer who has sung in most of the famous opera houses of the world. Eventually he turned his back on that career. He said it was impossible for him to live a disciplined Christian life and maintain an uncompromised Christian testimony in the world of opera. Some Christians may succeed but it is very difficult.

A high percentage of people live for pleasure. It is their religion. To enjoy themselves is for them the reason for living. If there is unlimited money there is no end to lawful pleasures such as ocean cruises and holidays abroad. But is that the way we are intended to live? Moses would have had the means to enjoy every kind of privilege and pleasure. But how can a Christian live for holidays abroad and for ocean cruises and spend weeks of their lives at major sporting events like the Olympic Games when he or she belongs to a worldwide family of believers suffering persecution and often suffering poverty and the lack of basic needs in life? This was the tension for Moses. All the pleasures available to him would become sinful if at the same time he ignored his own people and failed to make himself one with them.

Thirdly Moses gave up riches. The text says that Moses gave up the treasures of Egypt for the sake of Christ whom he esteemed of greater value. We know from the historical records that Egypt was fabulously wealthy. Much of this wealth came as a result of cheap slave labour as is seen in the example of the Hebrew slaves. Wealth is a very powerful attraction. One of the reasons for this is that wealth is a form of security. Political leaders often amass fortunes for themselves and store them away in Swiss banks for the time when they may be deposed. It is no small thing to turn away from wealth which provides security for the future. How is it possible to give up security for insecurity? That is a step of great magnitude. From having the security of great wealth Moses identified with his Israelite brothers who were slaves. That is momentous. It is like our Lord Jesus Christ who although he was rich, the whole universe belonging to him, nevertheless for our sake became poor (2 Cor 8:9).

Acts 7:22-29 tells us, 'Moses was educated in all the wisdom of the Egyptians, and was powerful in speech and action. When Moses was forty years old, he decided to visit his fellow Israelites. He saw one

of them being ill-treated by an Egyptian, so he went to his defence
and avenged him by killing the Egyptian. Moses thought that his
own people would realise that God was using him to rescue them,
but they did not. The next day Moses came upon two Israelites who
were fighting. He tried to reconcile them by saying, "Men, you are
my brothers; why do you want to hurt each other?" But the man who
was ill-treating the other pushed Moses aside and said, "Who made
you ruler and judge over us? Do you want to kill me as you killed
the Egyptian yesterday?" When Moses heard this, he fled to Midian,
where he settled as a foreigner and had two sons.'

This account derived from Exodus chapter two suggests that
Moses brought about his own demise from power and prestige in
Egypt through an impetuous action rather than a virtuous love for
his people. However if we look carefully at the record we can see
that Moses had indeed already determined that he was going to try
and rescue his fellow Israelites. He did not know how that could
be achieved but he had decided in his heart that he would align
himself with the Israelite slaves.

3. How fundamentalism solves the problem of worldliness

Fundamentalism as a movement became widespread within
evangelicalism during the 1920s. This movement was largely a
reaction against modernism. While the movement is not as strong
as it used to be there are still many fundamentalist churches
around the world. Some Reformed Baptist churches today adopt
fundamentalist principles. I was converted in a fundamentalist
Baptist church and so am familiar with the fundamentalist
approach to worldliness. That approach is to name, shame and
forbid specific practices. In my experience these were smoking,
drinking alcohol, attending cinema, dancing and, for ladies,
wearing make-up. These rules were not actually written in
the church constitution and were not mandatory for church
membership. But anyone involved in these worldly practices
would hardly be passed for baptism and church membership.
They were frowned on so that no self-respecting church member
would indulge in these practices.

Each of the above needs evaluation. The easiest is smoking. The tide has turned to such a degree that even the world discourages smoking and forbids it to take place in designated areas. Drinking alcohol is not forbidden in Scripture and the wine of the communion table is real wine. The Scriptures forbid all excess. 'Wine is a mocker and beer a brawler' (Prov 20:1, see also 1 Peter 4:3 and Isa 5:11). A major problem arises when those battling with alcoholism enter church circles. When that occurs offence must be avoided at all costs. 'It is better not to eat meat or drink wine or to do anything else that will cause your brother to fall' (Rom 14:21). Total abstinence is appropriate under those circumstances. The question of attending cinema has been overtaken by TV. Movies are watched at home. Most Christian households have TV but strict control has to be exercised since there is so much which is vile. The text of Philippians 4:8 needs to be placed over every TV set. Some households ban TV and are probably better off for it since much time is saved for better pursuits. There are different kinds of dancing. Some is lascivious and on that account is out of bounds for believers. With regard to make-up Paul provides this principle to go by, 'I want women to dress modestly' (1Tim 2:9). This does not ban make-up. For us today the problem is immodest dress. How many pastors have the courage to address that problem?

The Bob Jones University in America is well known as fundamentalist. There are strict rules even about dress and short hair cuts for men. The line is not always easily drawn. For instance in gambling there is a difference between the evil of compulsive gambling and raffle tickets for charity. Also it would be difficult to make a ruling about the stock markets. Investment is not regarded as gambling but investment can become gambling in the high-risk sectors of the stock market. Fundamentalism has often made pre-millennialism mandatory. The precious unity of Bible-believing Christians is damaged when fundamentalists are ultra-separatist, proud and censorious.

While it is important to encourage a pure God-honouring way of life there is always a danger of legalism. Smaller issues are sometimes used in a derogatory and unwise way. For instance we cannot dismiss fellow believers because they differ with us on these issues. One can say a donkey does not smoke or wear-make up but that does not make a holy donkey! Another danger is pharisaism. The Pharisees made up many rules about the Sabbath which were unwise and which made them judgmental of others. Another danger is to give the impression that Christianity is mostly about rules. That can invite satire like the verse:

> There are three things I must not do –
> I must not gamble, smoke or chew.
> There's one thing more I must not do –
> *I must not stand in a cinema queue.*

When abstinence is associated with dedication, namely, the idea that I avoid worldly activities because I am totally devoted to the cause of Christ, that is advantageous. When I was converted through the lives of evangelical students at university it was their joyful dedication and holiness of life that was compellingly attractive to me. I was impressed by their outright, unashamed confession of Christ and by the fact that the believers were separate from the world. There is often more zeal for evangelism and more dedication to serve among those of fundamentalist persuasion than those who are indifferent about worldliness and who seem to be afraid to be out of step with worldly behaviour.

The mistake frequently made today is to lack diligence in instructing new converts early while they are filled with wonder at the grace of God in their salvation. That is the ideal time to teach them the responsibilities of church membership, of tithing, the responsibilities of the Lord's Day, of attendance at and participation in the prayer meetings, and of the dangers of worldly standards especially with regard to purity and sexual morals. The devil soon makes his counter-attack and new converts need to be well equipped. I have noted too that it is important to elevate the importance of baptism and the Lord's Table. The way to the Lord's Table is through baptism and church membership.

Every generation will have its own judgements of what constitutes worldly behaviour. We must take the principles in Scripture and evaluate what is inappropriate for us as believers. In everything courage must be combined with humility. We are sinners saved by grace.

---

1   One of the best books describing postmodernism is by Gene Edward Veith, Jr. *Postmodern Times, A Christian Guide to Contemporary Thought and Culture*, Crossway Books, 216 pages, 1994. The principal elements making up postmodernism, namely deconstruction, moral relativism, pluralism and existentialism are described in a 28 page booklet by Erroll Hulse obtainable freely from Chapel Library, 2603 W. Wright Street, Pensacola, FL 32505, USA.

2   J I Packer, *Keep in Step with the Spirit*, IVP, 1984, page 102.

Christians must relate to the world

Worldliness about which we are warned in the Bible concerns the worship of people, of hobbies, of sport and of activities where God is excluded.

Unbelievers attribute the glory of 'nature' to blind chance. Christians glorify our Triune God for the creation of the heavens and the earth. 'The heavens declare God's glory, their grandeur tells his worth' (Ps 19:1). Believers admire and enjoy mountain ranges, forests, rivers and valleys, the starry skies, myriads of species, all perfect in their kinds, which God has created (Ps 104). Through high-tech photography the glories of creation are displayed in the oceans and along the coral reefs. Intelligent design is highlighted in extraordinary detail. Millions of years are claimed in order to accommodate evolution as an explanation. Creation is the explanation.

Christians should relate to science and culture. It is the doctrine of common grace that enables them to understand this. Common grace is God's benevolence to all mankind. He restrains sin. He has created all the sciences: mathematics, physics, medicine and biology etc. The vastness of God's benevolence is seen in architecture, schools, libraries, universities, scientific research and charitable organisations that abound to relieve the sufferings caused by earthquakes, floods and other disasters.

The Scriptures highlight the early development in animal breeding, metallurgy and music (Gen 4:20-21). For a full treatment of the subject of common grace see Cornelius van Til, *Common Grace and the Gospel* (P and R, 1972).

Christians must not be intimidated by evolutionary humanism. This is God's world and he is not to be driven out of it. He created it and it belongs to him. Eventually it will be completely renewed in the new heavens and the new earth (Rev 21:1-4).

❧ Chapter 19 ❧

When Holiness Invades Society

In this title holiness is personified. When a Christian who practises personal holiness goes out to work it will not be long before conversations will be about current affairs. A whole range of subjects can be brought up and in all of them holiness of life will have relevance. Likewise when his believing wife takes the children to school and meets teachers and other mums who are not Christians, all kinds of topics will be the subject of conversation. Francis Schaeffer's book *The God Who is There* made a major impact among Evangelicals.[1] Schaeffer urged Bible believers to understand the current philosophy and its road to despair. He encouraged us to comprehend the subjects of art, music, culture and cinema. In his application Schaeffer wrote, 'The world has a right to look upon us and make a judgment. We are told by Jesus that as we love one another the world will judge, not only whether we are his disciples, but whether the Father sent the Son.'[2] That is another way of saying that holiness is the test. Holiness is not to be locked up. It is to be seen corporately. Believers need to invade society which is clearly affirmed by our Lord when he said: 'You are the light of the world. A city on a hill cannot be hidden. Neither do people light a lamp and put it under a bowl. Instead they put it on its stand, and it gives light to everyone in the house. In the same way, let your light shine before men, that they may see your good deeds and praise your Father in heaven' (Matt 5:14-16).

The prevailing climate for that generation up to 1968 when Schaeffer's book was published was for Evangelicals to avoid the above named subjects as worldly and certainly to avoid politics. Social action was regarded as the stock of liberal non-gospel churches. My early experience began while living in South Africa during the apartheid era. The prevailing opinion of evangelical churches for the most part was mild disapproval of apartheid. In contrast to that liberal churches were militantly opposed to that dreadful system and actively and courageously campaigned against it. Among Evangelicals the opinion was that our business was personal salvation and that it was best to leave politics to the politicians. In 1994 I had occasion to meet and have time with Nelson Mandela. He told me that the churches played a significant role in the liberation of the black people.

Here I will set out to show that the Bible calls loudly and clearly for social action by the godly. Holiness is not to be kept confined to Christian homes and church meetings. Holiness must invade society.

Does the Bible teach this? It calls for justice so clearly as to remind us of the trumpets and high-sounding cymbals mentioned in Psalm 150. The Lord declares that he is revolted by the hypocrisy of those who make a pompous show of their religion and at the same time have hands full of blood and neglect the fatherless and the widows. This inconsistency is repugnant. Blood here may not mean first degree murder but rather withholding the essential means of life for the poor.

> 'Stop bringing meaningless offerings! Your incense is detestable to me. New Moons, Sabbaths and convocations — I cannot bear your evil assemblies. Your New Moon festivals and your appointed feasts my soul hates. They have become a burden to me; I am weary of bearing them. When you spread out your hands in prayer, I will hide my eyes from you; even if you offer many prayers, I will not listen. Your hands are full of blood; wash and make yourselves clean. Take your evil deeds out of my sight! Stop doing wrong, learn to do right! Seek justice, encourage the oppressed. Defend the cause of the fatherless,

plead the case of the widow. "Come now, let us reason together," says the LORD. "Though your sins are like scarlet, they shall be as white as snow; though they are red as crimson, they shall be like wool"' (Isa 1:13-18).

The concluding call is to repent of these most grievous sins of omission: justice neglected, the oppressed ignored, the orphans left defenceless, the widows sidelined.

Isaiah takes up this theme in chapter 58. The people fasted but it was not spiritual as it ended in irritability, in quarrels so atrocious that some meetings ended in fisticuffs. Lest you think such a thing belongs to the past remember that in some churches the general business meeting is the most feared of meetings because it is known to be the place where it is likely for dishonourable divisions and quarrels to be expressed.

Again all is not lost. The most wonderful promise of revival is proclaimed on condition of repentance and positive action.

'Is not this the kind of fasting I have chosen: to loose the chains of injustice and untie the cords of the yoke, to set the oppressed free and break every yoke? Is it not to share your food with the hungry and to provide the poor wanderer with shelter — when you see the naked, to clothe him, and not to turn away from your own flesh and blood? Then your light will break forth like the dawn, and your healing will quickly appear; then your righteousness will go before you, and the glory of the LORD will be your rear guard. Then you will call, and the LORD will answer; you will cry for help, and he will say: Here am I. If you do away with the yoke of oppression, with the pointing finger and malicious talk, and if you spend yourselves on behalf of the hungry and satisfy the needs of the oppressed, then your light will rise in the darkness, and your night will become like the noonday. The LORD will guide you always; he will satisfy your needs in a sun-scorched land and will strengthen your frame. You will be like a well-watered garden, like a spring whose waters never fail' (Isa 58:6-11).

The LORD loves righteousness and justice (Ps 33:5; Heb 1:9). Justice (mišpāt) is expressed three times in the first Servant Song (Isa 42:1-4). Its meaning is versatile and is made clear by the contexts in which it is employed. It has to do with establishing the truth and righting wrongs. The promise is that Yahweh's Servant will bring justice to the nations. He will not falter or be discouraged till he establishes justice on earth (Isa 42:4). The Servant's ministry is to the bruised reed and the smouldering wick. These images convey the idea of brokenness and weakness. This can refer to those struggling to survive spiritually but also to orphans, the disabled, the frail, the persecuted and the imprisoned. With regard to the latter in countries like North Korea, Iran and Eritrea thousands are imprisoned in barbaric conditions for no other reason than being Christians. Isaiah 61:1-3, cited in Luke 4:18,19, enlarges on the Servant's ministry. It is to all but expressly to the poor, the broken-hearted, those in captivity and to prisoners. His ministry will also include the day of vengeance of our God.

When Christ revives his churches there is an outgoing and ongoing impact of righteousness in society. Corruption is repudiated. Honesty is established. I remember being stopped by police in Cameroon for no other reason than bribery – give us money and you can move on! The pastor/driver delivered a stinging rebuke and a mini-sermon to the officers who became ashamed and confused. We drove on without any further interference. Just administration exists in many countries but has still to reach many nations where corruption and misrule are the order of the day. Zimbabwe is notorious. But 'he will not falter or be discouraged till he establishes justice on earth' (Isa 42:4). This justice will eventually be universal (Ps 72:8; Zech 8:20; 9:10).

Isaiah's emphasis on the necessity of social justice was stressed by other prophets as we see in Jeremiah 7:4-11; Psalm 50:8-15; 72:12-14; Hosea 6:6 and Amos 4:4; 5:21-25. Micah who was contemporary with Isaiah in Judah, is eloquent on this theme: 'He has showed you, O man, what is good. And what does the LORD require of you? To act justly and to love mercy and to walk humbly with your God' (Micah 6:8).

This emphasis on social care is continued in the New Testament. Remember the ministry of Jesus: You know how 'God anointed Jesus of Nazareth with the Holy Spirit and power, and how he went around doing good and healing all who were under the power of the devil, because God was with him' (Acts 10:38).

In his letter James tells us, 'Religion that God our Father accepts as pure and faultless is this: to look after orphans and widows in their distress and to keep oneself from being polluted by the world' (James 1:27). James was the kind of preacher who would not be allowed within ten miles of today's media. His burning rebuke of exploitation by the rich runs like this: 'Your gold and silver are corroded. Their corrosion will testify against you and eat your flesh like fire. You have hoarded wealth in the last days. Look! The wages you failed to pay the workmen who mowed your fields are crying out against you. The cries of the harvesters have reached the ears of the Lord Almighty. You have lived on earth in luxury and self-indulgence. You have fattened yourselves in the day of slaughter. You have condemned and murdered innocent men, who were not opposing you' (James 5:3-6).

In the great day of judgement assessment will be made according to good works. The reason for this is that good works are an essential evidence of holiness and vindicate the quality of the work of the Holy Spirit in the lives of believers who are justified on account of imputed righteousness. This is how the righteous are described by Jesus: 'Then the King will say to those on his right, "Come, you who are blessed by my Father; take your inheritance, the kingdom prepared for you since the creation of the world. For I was hungry and you gave me something to eat, I was thirsty and you gave me something to drink, I was a stranger and you invited me in, I needed clothes and you clothed me, I was sick and you looked after me, I was in prison and you came to visit me"' (Matt 25:34-36).

Social care has always been characteristic of Bible believers. In the age of monasteries these often became the source of care for the poor and sick and frail. Such was the case here in Leeds in the twelfth century at Kirkstall Abbey which was an extensive Cistercian monastery.

During the revival of the 18th century that swept through Britain under the preaching of men like George Whitefield, John Wesley, Howell Harris and Daniel Rowland, thousands were converted. In turn these converted Christians reformed prisons, infused clemency into penal laws, abolished the slave trade and gave leadership to nationwide education of children.[3]

It can be argued that the lack of a spiritual awakening led to the horrors of the French Revolution when the government was taken over by mob rule. Great numbers went to the guillotine without justice.

The biblical teaching that we are created in the image of God was replaced by evolutionary humanism with its principle of the survival of the fittest. This made way for the view that the weak, the unfit and the undesirable can be exterminated. When Adolf Hitler rose to power in Germany there were several brave pastors who opposed Nazism. They paid for it with their lives. Dietrich Bonhoeffer was one but there were lesser known men such as Paul Schneider.[4] At the time of the rise of Hitler Cardinal Pacelli (who later became Pope Pius XII) was the Roman Catholic leader in Germany from 1933 to 1939. In exchange for Catholic withdrawal from social and political life Pacelli negotiated religious and educational advantages for the Catholic Church. Pacelli's scandalous wartime silence when the Jews were under persecution is still the subject of fierce debate.[5] It is a sad commentary that light was extinguished in pre-war Germany.

There is an army of forgotten heroes who accomplished extensive social care. Andrew Reed (1787-1862) was one such. He was a pastor who from a small beginning built up a congregation of 2000 in Stepney, London. He established three orphanages, two homes for those with learning difficulties and a hospice for those with severe physical disabilities.[6]

A remarkable book by Kathleen Heasman documents the extent of social enterprise by Evangelicals in England and in London in particular during the 19th century.[7] Any study of that period must take into consideration the large drift from the country to the cities, a rapidly increasing population, and neglect by the State to deal with squalid conditions and appalling poverty in the slum areas. The proportion of Evangelicals was so large that compared with today it is hardly credible. For instance Heasman suggests that just under fifty percent of the people of London attended church or chapel regularly and three quarters of the attendees were Evangelicals. The proportion of Evangelicals might be optimistic and present day research puts the figure of church attendance in London during the 19th century at 24 percent compared with 4.5 percent in 2010.[8] Philanthropic enterprises of every kind were established. Most of these sprang from the Evangelicals. The work achieved by Evangelicals was out of all proportion to their size. For instance most of the children's homes were controlled by Evangelicals. The way of life for children was directed by biblical principles. A Baptist minister, Dr Thomas Barnardo, with his wife, established homes for orphaned children. By 1904 the number cared for was over 7000. Barnardo was brilliant at preparing the children for employment.[9] The different needs of boys and girls were studied and different congenial régimes established for them. All over England enterprises inspired by evangelical faith were set on foot to minister to and provide for the destitute, for the homeless and for prostitutes. Practical efforts were made to reform those released from prison. Ministries were created to meet the needs of the blind and the deaf, the unsound of mind and body, the sick and the aged. Ministries were organised for sailors and soldiers.

Note should be taken of Charles Haddon Spurgeon. While most of his time was taken up with preaching three times a week and devoting one day a week to the students in Spurgeon's College he was involved in extensive social work in which he was assisted by his church officers and members. Spurgeon asserted: 'Every member who joins my church is expected to do something for his fellow creatures.'[10] Arnold Dallimore in his gripping biography tells the story of Spurgeon's industry in two chapters. One is titled 'The Growth of the Spurgeonic Enterprises' and the other 'Almshouses and Orphanage'.[11] One of the many organisations was the Colporteur Association. By 1878 94 colporteurs made 926,290 visits in cities and in rural areas selling Bibles and Christian books and preaching the gospel wherever openings were given.

The establishment of a large orphanage at Stockwell was a major undertaking described in a thrilling way by Arnold Dallimore. Another sphere of care was for widows. From Spurgeon's predecessor John Rippon the church at New Park Street inherited homes for widows. Spurgeon made it his business to keep these well supplied with their needs. He also had a school constructed adjoining the Widows' Almshouses accommodating 400 children.[12]

These last few paragraphs have focused on the 19th century. Needed is a researcher to see if evangelical social enterprise continued through the 20th century. We know that much was achieved but the decline of all religions including evangelical religion has been alarming. The contrast today in a secular society with previous times of revival is stark.

It is noteworthy that in South Africa it is Evangelicals who have risen to the challenge of building orphanages for children afflicted with AIDS. An example is a couple I know who took early retirement in order to establish a home for little children infected with AIDS which has proved a very demanding but also a very rewarding work.

I have been a member and associate pastor of Leeds Reformed Baptist Church for 24 years. For 20 of these I was an elder alongside Peter Parkinson the founder and leading pastor of the church. In 1987 he began a work of caring for homeless young men. This turned into a charitable work called *Caring For Life*.[13] CFL has grown to include several spheres of care for people with special needs including refugees. There is a full-time staff of 42 and a further 40 weekly volunteers and in addition six full-time 'Time for Jesus' volunteers. Since 1987 CFL has housed over 3,000 people, over 500 of whom were considered to be extremely difficult to house and whose housing placements had continually broken down. The success rate for all those housed has consistently averaged at over 97% every year. That means that the placements have not broken down. The residents have kept their housing in good order with no complaints from neighbours or landlords. Over 700 of these referrals had a criminal record with a further

1,400 having had some encounters with the police. After coming to *Caring For Life* 87% never committed any further crimes! *Caring For Life* attributes these exceptional achievements to their underlying theological foundation with a biblical view of man and his relationship to his Maker and Saviour. This work grew out of the soil of a local church of modest size. It is an example of what is involved in going out into the highways and byways and meeting face to face those whose need is extreme. Most who have known only poverty, abuse and rejection do not have the remotest idea of what holiness is until they actually see Christian love in practice.

CFL has also given an opportunity to voluntary helpers who find fulfilment and development of their gifts in caring for those with disabilities or with learning difficulties. Churches have been given an example of what can be done in society where many fall through the cracks of the social system into meaninglessness and despair. Missionary needs have been kept in focus and in the course of its short history CFL has established two orphanages in Romania. Is CFL exceptional? Very few have the necessary gifts to grow such a work which depends on the support of many churches. There are similar organisations in the UK.[14]

Holiness and Politics

Politics is the art or science of government. It concerns forming and implementing laws. Politics includes just about the whole of human life: marriage, property, tax, education, medicine, travel, police and army, conservation and even where we may or may not bury our dead. Of course there is a difference between practical hands-on work involved in social care and in promoting political policies. This is illustrated again by the example of Spurgeon who as I have shown devoted much energy to social enterprises but in addition to that a small fraction of his time was given to politics. This he did mostly by correspondence. Like John Calvin before him his reputation carried weight and therefore he could write to leaders expressing the biblical position on a variety of subjects. He was well known for his protests at the belligerent imperialistic foreign policy of the Tory government. His views were given wide publicity in the European press.[15] He always opposed the Anglican Establishment which promoted legislation restricting the rights of nonconformists. For instance they were barred from Oxford and Cambridge Universities.

Over the past forty or so years the philosophy of Western Europe has changed from modernism to postmodernism. Old moral values have eroded away. Evolutionary humanism dominates the media. Moral absolutes have been undermined. In the UK lack of moral leadership has led to much anti-Christian government legislation. Whereas believers used to think it safe to leave politics to the politicians this is no longer the case. We have to mobilise and unite to fight every inch of the way if society is to recover in such spheres as the sanctity of life, of marriage and the family.

Should Christians engage in politics? Should Christian pastors preach politics? In the UK it is well understood that pastors should not engage in party politics. However when it comes to moral issues such as abortion, euthanasia and marriage it is different. During June 2010 Wayne Grudem the famous author of *Systematic Theology* [16] made a ten-day tour of the UK. His subject was The Christian and Politics. On the 26 June 2010 I attended one of these meetings, organised by The Christian Institute, at Christ Church, Fulwood, Sheffield. About 200 attended two lectures by Grudem followed by a question and answer time. A book, *The Christian and Politics,* by Wayne is scheduled for September 2010.

On the theme The Christian and Politics Wayne listed five negatives in order to arrive at a positive and balanced conclusion. The first wrong view of politics is that of compulsion by which the government compels and enforces religion. After an appalling record by Roman Catholics and Anglicans the practice of enforcing absolute conformity in religion has been abandoned. Islamic nations enforce Islamic religion on all those born into Islam. To become a Christian is regarded as apostasy and is subject to the death penalty. Author Patrick Sookhdeo documents alarming instances of how the apostasy law is applied in Muslim régimes today.[17] The Christian doctrine is one of freedom of individual conscience and freedom of religious practice for all. The stress is on *all*.

The second wrong view excludes religion from the public square which is the position actively followed by secularists in the USA and the UK. This position opposes all reading of the Bible or of prayers in public meetings outside churches or exposure to texts like the Ten Commandments in public places. Joseph and Moses in Egypt, Daniel in Babylon, Jonah in Nineveh, John the Baptist's reproof of Herod, Jesus and the Sanhedrin and Paul before Felix and Agrippa are examples of men who boldly carried the Word of God into the public arena. God's message must invade the public square.

The third wrong view is expressed by Greg Boyd in the USA which is that all governments are satanic. Boyd, an ardent pacifist, advocates withdrawal from the satanic realm of politics. This view (see Romans 13:1-4) is so shallow that I was surprised that Wayne should devote time to it.

The fourth wrong view is that we should do evangelism and not politics. No! It is not one or the other. 'The reason the Son of God appeared was to destroy the devil's work' (1 John 3:8). God calls believers to be salt and light in education, school, college, university, commerce, law, army, police services, medicine, science, social care, prison services and sometimes in civil government.

The fifth wrong view is that we should do politics and not evangelism. Certainly we do not want pastors to be second-rate politicians or politicians to be second-rate gospel preachers. Each sphere has its place. Church and State are separate. The one informs the other. We do need our pastors to be clear on the principles that undergird political legislation. The prophets Isaiah, Jeremiah, Jonah and Amos preached messages of repentance to foreign nations.

In some developing countries Christians pay a heavy price for opposing corruption. For instance many lives have been lost in seeking to arrest corruption and drug trafficking in Columbia, a country notorious for lawlessness. A whole sector of the nation is run by a Mafia of drug barons. A civil war is in progress in the attempt to combat the drug trade.

Corruption is endemic in the national life of many African countries. Christians are faced with a massive problem of combating this evil. To blow the whistle on dishonesty can cost you your job and even your life as the following description from the World Cup shows.

Corruption prevailed in the construction of the new stadium for the World Cup in Nelspruit. The Mbombela stadium stands proud against the Mpumalanga sky supported by orange pylons that resemble giraffes. It was built on farmland just outside Nelspruit at a cost of R1.3 billion – way over the R875 million budgeted. But in the background was scandal, malpractice and murder. Bongani Bingwa (Carte Blanche presenter): 'There's a hive of activity here as workers put the finishing touches to this magnificent stadium. Its unique design is thought to dazzle soccer fans as part of the World Cup extravaganza. But behind the scenes is an intricate web of deceit, corruption, political assassination and unfulfilled promises.'

Jimmy Mohlala, speaker of the Mbombela Council, which governs Nelspruit, was the first to blow the whistle on corruption. It cost him his life. An unknown gunman shot him dead outside his home last year. Jimmy had been instrumental in exposing financial irregularities connected to constructing the stadium. Among the crowd at his funeral was Lassy Chiwayo, Mbombela's Executive Mayor. Bongani: 'Was he assassinated?' Lassy Chiwayo: 'Look, the incident, you know, that happened on that fateful day in his own home... to me it's nothing but an execution, owing to the stance he took, especially around the investigation of 2010-related tenders. So, my belief to date has been that he was assassinated.'

Conclusion

In this chapter I have described the subject of social care. It simply is not realistic to leave this realm to the government, not if we believe that we are to love our neighbours as ourselves.

I have also shown that we must contend for truth wherever that impinges on the way we live. That is political. For instance if you were living in India prior to 1829 and your Hindu neighbour died what would your attitude be when you were invited to attend the burning alive of his widow on a funeral pyre? Would you not be horrified at the thought of your neighbour suffering so cruel a death? The only way that such a practice came to an end was by political action. Legislation forbidding the burning of widows on funeral pyres was passed in 1829. That political action required leadership and leaders required supporters. It was the light of Christianity that brought that horrendous practice to an end.

That may be an unusual example. But challenges are coming thick and fast. Do you want your children at school to be taught that homosexuality is a legitimate alternative lifestyle to man/woman marriage? Are you happy about your children being taught that evolution explains the universe? Are you agreeable to the idea that teaching creationism must be banned in our schools? There is no way that Evangelicals can escape the necessity of contending for biblical principles in the public domain. When we do this it is important to maximise Christian unity and stand together wherever this does not seriously compromise truth.

---

1   Francis Schaeffer, *The God Who is There*, Hodder and Stoughton, 190 pages, 1968.
    Recently Ranald Macaulay wrote on the relevance of Schaeffer's ministry to the challenges of the 21st century. Schaeffer ministered with a prophetic voice in predicting Western culture's intellectual and moral bankruptcy. He anticipated the effects of various trends within Evangelicalism. Whilst viewing the Church as having a vital role in redeeming culture he observed the ineptitude and powerlessness of retreating from culture (the 'pietist hangover'). *Francis Schaeffer: A Mind and Heart for God.* Editor Bruce A Little, 108 pages paperback, P and R Publishing, 2010.
2   *Ibid*, page 152.
3   Derek Thomas, *Isaiah*, EP, page 29.
4   Paul Schneider, *20th-century German Pastor and Martyr,* Victor Budgen. Reformation Today, issue 54.
5   John Cornwell, *Hitler's Pope, The Secret History of Pius XII*, Viking, 430 pages, 1999.
6   Ian J Shaw, *A Biography of Andrew Reed, The Greatest is Charity*, EP, 430 pages, 2005.

7   Kathleen Heasman, *Evangelicals in Action, An Appraisal of their Social Work*, 310 pages, Geoffrey Bles, London, 1962.
8   The Christian Research Organisation. Information can be obtained on the internet.
9   Gladys Williams, *Barnardo the Extraordinary Doctor*, Macmillan 1966. Other fine biographies of Thomas Barnardo are by J H Batt, 1904, and A E Williams, George Allen and Unwin, 1943.
10 David Kingdon, *Spurgeon and his Social Concern*, Reformation Today, issue 126, page 17.
11 Arnold Dallimore, *Spurgeon*, Banner of Truth, 252 pages, 1985.
12 Lewis Drummond, *Spurgeon Prince of Preachers*, see chapter eight, Spurgeon's Social, Educational and Outreach Ministries, Kregel, 882 pages, 1992.
13 Juliet Barker, *The Deafening Sound of Silent Tears*, Canterbury Press, 176 pages, 200. This moving account will bring tears to your eyes as you learn of those who have been rescued from desperate circumstances and also how extraordinary financial needs have been met.
14 This can be verified by searching the internet. *Care* is one example and *Tear Fund* another.
15 Patricia Stallings Kruppa, *Spurgeon – A Preacher's Progress*, Garland Publications, New York and London, 1982. The authoress devotes 80 pages to Spurgeon's political activity.
16 Wayne Grudem, *Systematic Theology*, IVP, 1264 pages, 1994.
17 Patrick Sookhdeo, *Freedom to believe – challenging Islam's apostasy law*. Isaac Publishing, 180 pages, 2010.

Holiness and Roman Catholics

When the Philippian jailer cried out, 'What must I do to be saved?' Paul answered, 'Believe on the Lord Jesus and you will be saved' (Acts 16:31). If the same question is put to priests of the Roman Catholic Church, 'What must I do to be saved?' most of them will answer according to their catechism: 'Holy baptism is the basis of the whole Christian life. Through baptism we are freed from sin and reborn as sons of God' [*Catechism of the Catholic Church*, Geoffrey Chapman, 1994, page 276]. However we note that multitudes are baptised as infants in the Roman Catholic Church and thereafter show no signs whatsoever of regeneration. Water whether sprinkled in a few drops or used in immersion does not regenerate.

In Scripture repentance and faith are the evidence of the new birth. In every instance in the book of Acts baptism followed repentance and faith (for examples see Acts 2:41; 8:12; 10:47,48; 16:15 and 33; 18:8; 22:16).

In Roman Catholicism justification and sanctification are not kept as separate entities as explained in Romans chapter six, but are confused as we read in their catechism, 'Justification includes the remission of sins, sanctification and the renewal of the inner man.' [*Ibid*, page 439].

Roman Catholics are taught to observe the sacraments and trust that by their good works they might find salvation. This is tragic because the Word is clear: 'Therefore no-one will be declared righteous in his sight by observing the law; rather, through the law we become conscious of sin' (Rom 3:20).

Notable is the fact that in the subject index of the 690 page Roman Catholic catechism referred to above there is no mention of 'assurance'. How can there be assurance when we know that our good works always fall short of perfection?

Does this mean that no one is saved in the Roman Catholic Church? Happily God does save muddle-headed believers. To be joined to Christ by faith is to have salvation even though there may be confusion about doctrine. Souls find Christ by searching for him in Holy Scripture. The Protestant Reformers of the 16th century were Roman Catholics before they embraced the doctrine of justification by faith alone.

✿ Chapter 20 ✿

Holiness and God's Gymnasium

Paul's exhortation to his son Timothy, 'Train yourself to be godly' (1 Tim 4:17), is made in the context of physical training. Literally translated the text could read, '*Gymnase* yourself to be godly.' suggesting gymnastics and the rigorous training that is involved in the gymnasium. That there are parallels in discipline between physical and spiritual exercising is suggested by Paul's reference to physical training having some value. He affirms that while bodily exercise has some profit, 'godliness has value for all things, holding promise both for this world and for the life to come'.

In the context, the exhortation to exercise to godliness is preceded by a negative. The apostle urges that no time be wasted on futile matters such as old wives' tales and godless myths. Rather Timothy is to exercise himself to godliness. The temptation today is not old wives' tales but rather the expenditure of too much on lawful and enjoyable pursuits. The harm is done when these squeeze out that time which is essential for the nurture of godliness.

We can get to the heart of 1 Timothy 4:7-8 as follows:

The objective | *Godliness*
The advantage of godliness | *Gain in this world and the next*
How to grow in godliness | *Exercise in God's gymnasium*

The objective: *Godliness*

What is godliness? The word *eusebeia* occurs about ten times in the letters of the New Testament. Its meaning can be derived from its usage. The most telling place is where Paul declares, 'Beyond all question, the mystery of godliness is great:

> 'He appeared in a body,
> was vindicated by the Spirit,
> was seen by angels,
> was preached among the nations,
> was believed on in the world,
> was taken up in glory' (1 Tim 3:16).

The incarnation of our Lord was the advent into this world of pure and perfect godliness or God-likeness. The incarnation is unique. Any God- likeness that we attain is by virtue of our union with the Son of God. That godliness or God-likeness is the result of conformity to him through the work of the Holy Spirit. 'And we, who with unveiled faces all reflect the Lord's glory, are being transformed into his likeness with ever- increasing glory, which comes from the Lord, who is the Spirit' (2 Cor 3:18).

Godliness (*eusebeia*) is cousin in meaning to holiness. God-likeness is the objective or aim of growing in holiness or advancing in sanctification. It is a progressive work. It involves as we have seen a transformation through the exercise of renewing of our minds (Rom 12:1,2). Godliness or holiness is the supreme purpose of our lives here on earth and the pursuit of godliness involves us all the time. It is comprehensive inasmuch as all our faculties are involved in the exercise, which is to godliness. It involves the way we think and speak and act.

German piety

The Greek word *eusebeia* translated 'godliness' refers not only to the end result of godliness (God-likeness) but the actual practice of godliness that leads to the result. In evangelical history the word piety has been used to describe the practice of godliness. A Pietist movement began in 1675 when a German pastor of the Lutheran Church, Philip Spener (1635-1705), published a treatise with the title *Pia desiderata* which instantly became a best seller. The book consisted of a passionate appeal for the practice of personal devotion (Bible reading, devotion, prayer), but also called for the practical outworking of godliness by way of social care, philanthropy, caring for orphans and the poor. Unfortunately, in its later development, an unnecessary division developed between the intellectual and the devotional emphases. This proved fatal during the latter part of the twentieth century when it was essential to resist modernism along the lines of a well thought out biblical basis. It was fatally inadequate to think that the maintenance of the devotional life would be an adequate protection of the Church. Devotion is indeed essential but the Faith has to be earnestly defended (Jude 3).

English piety

The English Puritans were the supreme devotees of practical piety. They did not make the mistake of allowing an unnecessary division between the mind and the heart. Richard Rogers (1550-1620), Puritan preacher of Wethersfield, Essex, had his book *Seven Treatises* published in 1603. This work was a daily rule of life in which Rogers sought to apply the teaching of Scripture to every human activity and to deal particularly with the use of time for every hour of each day. His close friend and neighbour Ezekiel Culverwell expressed the wish that readers of the *Seven Treatises* could have seen with their own eyes and heard the doctrine with their own ears. Here we observe the very essence of godliness. Rogers kept a diary and from it can be seen a man walking as closely as possible with God.

Later Richard Baxter (1615-1691) after the Great Ejection of 1662 gave himself full-time to writing *A Christian Directory*. In this Baxter expounded the godly life for personal living, family duties, church duties and duties to our neighbours and rulers. If printed out at the average size page today this work would come to about 1,600 pages.

Exercise – fervent, constant and intelligent

If training must be fervent to succeed, then it also needs to be constant. Athletes motivated to win honour for themselves or their team stick by firm rules of constant and vigorous training habits. It is virtually impossible to succeed without constancy of exercise and practice. Training habits and rules have to be built into the lives of the athletes. The same principle of discipline applies in the spiritual realm. It is only by the exercise *of doing* that progress can be made. We must make rules for ourselves to keep. There are those who will protest that this is legalism! It would be futile to object to legalism in the gym or on the athletic track where coaches set the disciplines, or in the classroom where the standards are set for academic exams. Either you do the work or you fail. By all means set your own rules or habits but if you remain undecided about discipline you will never attain anything worthwhile. The leader of a family must measure the state and stamina of the members of his family and make wise decisions about the lifestyle of his family. Likewise those who lead a church must decide with the co-operation of the members on the times and extent of worship and service. Deciding and doing there must be.

We need to build into our way of life attitudes of consistency and reliability in assembling ourselves together for worship and the set times of corporate prayer. These events should go down in our diaries and all other matters be regarded as secondary to these primary practices.

To follow the illustration of athletics or gymnastics further, training must be intelligent to be of any use. The athlete or gymnast thinks carefully about what he is to do, exactly how to do it, and precisely what skill is involved. The spiritual equivalent of this is meditation.

Meditation a necessity

Meditation involves the action of all the powers of the soul. This is more than simple reflection of the mind about the truth of God. Meditation is thinking through to practice. First we think an issue through and then transpose thought into action, as we see in the command given to Joshua, 'Do not let this Book of the Law depart from your mouth; meditate on it day and night, so *that you may be careful to do everything written in it*' (Josh 1:8).

Thomas Manton suggests that there are three sorts of meditation, 1. When a man compares the Word and providence, 2. When a man searches into the meaning of the Word to find out the mind and will of God, and 3. When a man considers how he may act upon the Word and make it fit for use and practice.[1] It is this last form which is especially relevant for our subject.

Meditation is preparatory to prayer and to worship and to the Lord's Table, but especially is meditation preparatory to spiritual exercises, the various practical areas of which we will now attend to.

Exercising to godliness for the whole of life

Where should we begin? The first priority is the use of time and that in order to safeguard our spiritual fitness and vitality. If we start with our religious exercises we shall thereby safeguard and protect the pearl of great price, that which is most precious. The chapel occupies the central place in the ancient colleges at Oxford and Cambridge. All other faculties or departments are built around that centre. Our Creator will enable us to apply ourselves to all the subjects he has created with true devotion, appreciation and wisdom when he is put first. It is a basic principle that if we honour him he will honour us.

Exercising ourselves with regard to the use of time.

Our time in this world compared to eternity is exceedingly short. We must be wise therefore in making the best use of time. Paul uses the strong word, *redeeming*. 'See then that you walk circumspectly, not as fools but as wise, redeeming the time, because the days are evil' (Eph 5:16 NKJV). We live in a culture in which there are many lawful pleasures and entertainments: sport, music, wild life TV programs, world affairs and so on. If we do not think about the need to redeem time in order to devote ourselves to spiritual activities we can easily find that our time has been squandered in such a way that we have nothing to show for it. We must seize our opportunities. Time lost cannot be regained. A person who throws bank notes into the fire would be regarded as crazy. Yet time is more precious than money. We must exercise ourselves to godliness by thinking carefully about the best use of time. Every day should begin with this particular exercise. To that should be added a long-term view of our use of time which leads directly to the Lord's Day.

Exercising ourselves to godliness on the Lord's Day

In the New Testament the principal teaching on the Sabbath is from the Lord himself. He said that the Sabbath was made for our benefit. He being the Lord of that Day had the right to change it to the first day of the week. He rose on that Day and the Holy Spirit was given on that Day. It is Christ's own Day over which he rules, literally 'I was in the Spirit on the Lordly Day'.[2] That day is given and organised so that believers might receive maximum profit by it. Therefore it requires preparation by way of spiritual exercises. To draw from our illustration once more, as the Olympic athlete prepares his mind especially for the great day of competition, so believers who derive the most benefit from the Lord's Day are those who have prepared themselves for it and who assist the preacher in prayer before it. The Lord's Day being the first day of the week in turn provides the opportunity of spiritual preparation for all the demands and responsibilities of the six days to follow.

A believer who lives to 80 having believed from the age of 10 will have had the equivalent of ten years to devote entirely to spiritual affairs and the fellowship of the church. If he uses the Lord's Day well the spiritual benefits will be immense.

In preparing for the Lord's Day we should be careful about resisting encroachments which will rob us of time that is required for worship, for fellowship, for study and rest and special service. It will also include maximising advantages of the worship services.

The constituent parts of the services should be considered, singing, prayer, preaching. We should reflect on the need to render worship, praise and thanksgiving. We should exercise ourselves to godliness in seeking instruction, direction and correction from the preaching. The object of attending the ordinances is to meet God personally in them. We need to exercise ourselves to godliness with regard to preparing for participation at the Lord's Table. Also we should observe that for many the Lord's Day provides the only time of the week for an extended time of reading and meditation. How important it is therefore to exercise to godliness with regard to the choice of reading matter, which will convey spiritual improvement.

---

1   Thomas Manton, *Works*, vol 8, page 12.
2   *tē kuriakē hēmera*. 'Lordly' is an adjective describing the nature of the day. In the beginning 'God blessed the seventh day and made it holy' (Gen 2:3). To make holy is to set apart. He set that day apart from the other days.

Christ Is the King of glory

For the mighty conqueror there is the call for the gates to be lifted up. Five times the title 'King of glory' is ascribed to the victor (Ps 24:7-10). The title 'Lord of glory' is given to Christ in 1 Corinthians 2:8 and by James who describes Jesus as 'our glorious Lord Jesus Christ' (2:1). He is the Lord 'mighty in battle' (Ps 24:8). Remember the battles he has fought with Satan, with death and with hell. He is victor over our worst enemies, namely the devil and death. He has triumphed over the devil who is the cause of death, over the grave which is the prison of death and over hell which is the domain of the second death. To him rightly is ascribed the title 'The King of glory'.

Psalm 24 is written to be sung in responsive parts. Christopher Idle renders the refrains like this:

A Who is the King, this King of glory?
    Where is the throne he comes to claim?
B Christ is the King, the LORD of glory
    fresh from his victory.

    Lift high your heads, you gates
    and fling wide open your ancient doors, for
    here comes the King of glory
    taking universal power.

A Who is the King, this King of glory?
    What is the power by which he reigns?
B Christ is the King, his cross his glory,
    and by love he rules.

    All glory be to God
    the Father, Son and Holy Spirit;
    from ages past it was,
    is now, and evermore shall be.

✈ Chapter 21 ✈
Holiness and the Full Armour of God

T he whole of the Christian life can be described as a spiritual battle. As believers we constantly engage in spiritual warfare. All the equipment required for the battle is provided for us. Soldiers require training and it is paramount that they have full provision for their needs in every situation.

As we come to this subject, I would like to introduce it by referring to the best known author on this theme, namely, William Gurnall (1616-1679). His ministry of thirty-five years spanned a most stirring and momentous period of English Church history; the civil war, the elevation of Oliver Cromwell to Protector, the virtual abolition of episcopacy, the restoration of the Stuarts to the throne, followed by the act of Uniformity, which led to the Great Ejection of about 2,000 ministers from the Church of England.

During the civil war Gurnall was impressed by the fact that the real war is not a physical one with physical weapons, but a spiritual one with spiritual weapons. For twelve years he preached a series of expositions on Ephesians 6:10-20 and at the same time produced his famous book, *The Christian in Complete Armour*. This work is one of the great Puritan and Christian classics because with tremendous spiritual unction it deals with the spiritual warfare in which we are all engaged. It is as relevant now as at the time it was written.

We can break down this comprehensive subject as follows:

1. We need to know who Satan is.
2. We need to know Satan's methods.
3. We need to know our weapons.
4. We need to know ourselves in relation to the provision made for us in our warfare.

1. Who is Satan?

Jesus said that he saw Satan fall like lightning from heaven (Luke 10:18). Ezekiel describes the fall of the city of Tyre in poetic form. This is expressed in such a way that we can see how Satan fell. *'You were the model of perfection, full of wisdom and perfect in beauty ... You were anointed as a guardian cherub, for so I ordained you. You were on the holy mount of God; you walked among the fiery stones. You were blameless in your ways from the day you were created till wickedness was found in you. ... so I drove you in disgrace from the mount of God, and I expelled you, O guardian cherub ... your heart became proud on account of your beauty... so I threw you to the earth'* (Ez 28:12-17).

A similar description is provided in Revelation chapter 12 where Satan is described as a great red dragon whose tail swept a third of the stars out of the sky and flung them to the earth.

From the names given to Satan we learn about his character. In a similar passage to Ezekiel 28 Isaiah describes Satan as Lucifer which means shining one or light bearer. Satan in his pride attempted to make himself like the Most High. He said, 'I will raise my throne above the stars of God; I will sit enthroned on the mount of assembly' (Isa 14:13,14). Let us ever remember that pride was and is the great sin of Lucifer, and that one third of the angels were proud enough to fall with him. The name devil (*diabolus*) means accuser. He accuses the brethren. Another name is 'that ancient serpent', reminding us of the fall of mankind in Adam through the guile of the devil who came in the form of a serpent. The name 'Satan' tells us a lot because it means hater. Lucifer hates God and his people.

As far as we are concerned we must always be watchful to avoid the traps or pitfalls in which the devils attempt to ensnare us (1 Tim 3:6; 2 Tim 2:26; 2 Cor 2:9-11 and 11:13-14). The evil angels are so cunning that they can even deceive the very elect (Matt 24:24; 2 Thess 2:8-10, 1 Tim 4:1,2).

The wording in Ephesians 6:12 referring to 'rulers', 'authorities' and 'powers', reminds us of order and rank. The fallen angels are united in a highly efficient and organised army. As spirits they are highly intelligent, immortal and not subject to weariness.

Satan leads and organises his well ordered and united forces in persecuting Christ's Church. Part of his malice is to promote systems of deception. He sows errors in churches. He seeks to disfigure and destroy the testimonies of believers. So diabolical is Satan that after he has caused untold harm, mischief, war, bloodshed and suffering through sin, he then suggests the idea that the blame for it all lies with our Creator.

2. We need to know Satan's methods

Since Satan possesses superior intelligence and greater experience, we have to be on our watch. He has his schemes. He uses his cunning to try and destroy the Christian. This he does by repeating what was so successful in the first instance in the fall of our first parents. He succeeded in getting them to doubt God's Word. He then succeeded in getting them to rebel against his rule. Of course there are many other sins besides rebellion. What we need to remember is that ungodliness leads to unrighteousness. Once Satan succeeds in separating people from God, then restraints are removed and the way lies open for all kinds of wickedness.

Thomas Brooks in his book *Precious Remedies against Satan's Devices,* distinguishes different categories of strategy. The first category of devices concerns temptation to sin. If Satan fails to destroy the believer's testimony by getting him to sin, he will then employ strategies to make him a weak and ineffectual Christian.

Brooks also deals with the subject of how Satan exploits weaknesses. Those who are by nature proud or wise in their own eyes make easy work for Satan. He is easily able to exploit the weaknesses of the ignorant or those who have been taught erroneous doctrine.

One of the major specialities of our adversary is his work to divide Christians so that instead of fighting as God's united mighty army they are fighting each other. How can a kingdom divided against itself, stand? The devil is the inventor of sects and cults as well as the corrupter of the true Church. It is inevitable that Christians will be troubled by error within the Church, and time has to be spent on reformation.

Through history Satan has succeeded in corrupting the Church by adding to the Scriptures the traditions of men. It required the 16th-century Reformation to bring the Church back to the Bible. In modern times Satan's greatest conquest has been to destroy many churches and denominations through modernism which is rejection of the authority of Scripture presented in the respectable clothes of scholarship.

Besides that Satan has worked to establish whole religions or systems of philosophy which keep people locked up. He has done this either with false systems, or large cults such as Jehovah's Witnesses and Mormonism, or with Eastern religions in which there is no teaching about the holy character of God, the provision of salvation, the forgiveness of sin and reconciliation through the saving work of Christ. Satan and his angels have masterminded and now control these systems and use them to impede the gospel. In the great day when everything is unveiled we will be amazed to see how Satan and his allies have organised their spiritual forces.

With regard to evangelical Christianity we have seen the centre of gravity move from truth to experience and feelings. The essence of all religion is how people feel. Thus liberals who do not believe in Adam as a real person, or in the deity of Christ or his literal resurrection unite with Roman Catholics in the Ecumenical Movement. Liberalism is worse than Roman Catholicism but we need to remember that

Rome has not changed. Tradition and the centrality of the Mass and Mary are the same. The Ecumenical Movement is a masterpiece of deception because it is unity without truth.

By reviewing the various pieces of armour provided we can be reminded of Satan's powers and devices. His design is to destroy our faith in the truths of God's Word (hence the girdle of truth). He will attempt to destroy our standing of justification by imputed righteousness (hence the breastplate of righteousness); he would try to destroy a Christian's usefulness by crippling his ability to move in the battle (hence the shoes); he will aim to destroy a believer's assurance of salvation, his hope of eternal life, and thereby his peace of mind (hence the helmet of salvation); he will attempt to destroy the Christian's exercise of faith (hence the shield of faith); he certainly will aim to destroy the believer's ability to counter attack and win battles for God's kingdom by means of the Word of God (hence the sword of the Spirit).

3. We need to know our weapons

We can well imagine Paul composing the letter to the Ephesians while actually being able to see Roman soldiers and the formidable instruments of war which were theirs. Our weapons are spiritual. It is important before we look at the weapons one by one that we grasp the wonder of them.

First of all God himself fills the Christian with power as he uses the armour. This is evident in the opening exhortation, 'Be strong in the Lord *and in his mighty power*' (verse 10). There is a supernatural, glorious brightness and power in all the weapons. They all complement each other and constitute a fullness which can make the Christian irresistible. Lack of care or expertise with any one of the weapons or pieces can mar the whole. A soldier who cannot move in battle because his shoes are the wrong size is clumsy and hampered. A soldier who cannot use his sword with agility and power will be beaten. All the weapons harmonise which reminds us that there is a majestic wholeness about the mature Christian.

It is important to remember that the battle is not one of defence only. When our Lord was attacked by Satan, see Matthew 4, he did not only defend himself, he beat Satan back. He defeated the devil with the Word of God.

In this same context I would boldly affirm that the whole armour can be taken in the strongly aggressive sense of evangelism. We have a mandate to conquer the world (Matt 28:18-20). We have been given the necessary equipment. We must train to storm the gates of hell which will not prevail against us. We must attack Satan's fortresses with determination and courage. Our churches must be constantly mobilized and trained for evangelism. Our very best troops must be trained for special service duties in difficult fields abroad. We should look out for modern William Careys and maintain a world vision.

The morale of an army is a matter of the utmost importance in warfare. In dealing with the Christian warfare expositors mostly omit this aspect. No soldier fights on his own, he is part of a body. Ephesians 4:1-6 is just as important as Ephesians 6:10-20. Every Christian should be a member of a local church and be subject to spiritual leadership, instruction and oversight.

Now we examine the armour piece by piece.

The belt of truth

This is first because it formed the anchor or basis of the protecting armour. The truth of God as a whole is a foundation of our faith. Satan belittles Christian doctrine and would try to persuade believers that it is not important. He has always laboured to destroy faith in the Bible. Our Lord said, 'Then you will know the truth, and the truth will set you free' (John 8:32). He is speaking about the whole Bible, the entire written revelation of God. This truth has been given to us as a whole. It is a tremendous possession. It is the source of our knowledge and our authority. How important it is that we should know it well and experience its power and effectiveness. All through history, but particularly during the last

150 years, our adversary has attempted to destroy the Bible as a book to be believed and trusted. The truth must be buckled on. That is, it is all joined together in one unity. We believe it as a whole, and as a whole it forms our defence.

The breastplate of righteousness in place

The word 'righteousness' is one of the great words of the New Testament. The righteousness which is provided by God for our justification, is the righteousness of Christ (PhiI 3:9; Rom 1:16,17 and 3:21). The whole merit of Christ in his life and death, is imputed to us, or credited to us, when we are joined to him by faith. Christ's righteousness is put upon us or wrapped around us with a perfect fit like the armour. On this basis the Father himself justifies us (Rom 8:33). This gives the Christian a strong assurance. The devil's accusations bounce straight off this armour. His tactic is to accuse the believer and discourage him, but if God accepts him, who can condemn him?

Justification by faith is the foremost and foundational truth of the Bible. It is a glorious provision for the believer to possess the Lord as his righteousness (Jer 33:16). This righteousness is perfect and complete and therefore, our justification is perfect and complete. Justification can never be partial. Either a judge acquits or condemns. We are externally perfectly righteous in God's sight. Note it says that the breastplate must be in place. It is a perfect fit because it is a perfect provision.

Christians must understand and appreciate the great importance and relevance of justification by faith. This is vital. This truth must fit them perfectly. They will find it a glorious defence in the battle. Christ's righteousness is impregnable.

Your feet fitted with the readiness that comes from the gospel of peace.

In ancient battle, agility and speed of movement were essential. Often it proved *the* crucial factor. Sportsmen take great care about fitting the right shoes. In many athletic events and competitive exercises, correct footwear is of paramount importance. In hand to hand combat sure footing was essential. The Roman battalion moved forward one, two or three steps, like one man, at the command of their leader. Their shields acted as a solid wall of defence against the enemy. At the same time their swords were used to compel the enemy to retreat.

The way in which the apostle refers to the fitting of the shoes should be noted, together with the fact that they are associated with the gospel of peace. There is the aspect of careful preparation and attention to detail, in order to be ready. Then there is the aspect of purpose. We move forward in battle to conquer for the cause of peace, for our Captain is the Prince of Peace. The similarity of thought with the words of Isaiah 52:7 is compelling,

> How beautiful on the mountains,
> are the feet of those who bring good news,
> who proclaim peace,
> who bring good tidings,
> who proclaim salvation.

Paul cites this passage in Romans 10:15. The Church can be thought of as an army sent out to conquer the entire world for Christ. To achieve that, preparation is needed. Christians should always be meditating in the truth. In this way their minds are always ready to seize opportunities to witness for the truth. This activity will truly involve them in a battle. Yet they must not be afraid, because their mission is one of peace. We come to bring peace. Yet it is inevitable that, in bringing peace, the light we bring will conflict and clash with darkness. All the pieces of our armour shine with the bright light of Christ when we move into the battle for him. Satan will say, 'Don't be a fanatic! Don't be a nuisance to people! Don't upset them! Don't disturb them!' But we must use the Word which says, 'Therefore go and make disciples of all nations' (Matt 28:19).

Bearing a clear and bold testimony for the truth, both individually and corporately, is very important. This fact highlights the importance of sound instruction in a church and the need for pastors to make sure that that teaching is understood and put into practice.

The shield of faith, with which you can extinguish all the flaming arrows of the evil one.

Prominent here is the fact that Satan and his forces are spiritual. They can assault us in our thoughts. This reminds us of the reality of the spiritual world. How can a demon know what we are thinking? A demon is a spirit. That is why he knows.

The flaming arrows are thoughts and temptations, which are evil. We can easily be guilty of originating our own evil thoughts, but these flaming arrows are suggestions that are suddenly shot from outside into our minds. It can be a vicious slander about someone, or a provocation to hatred, or appalling fear, or a violent lust, or a horrible pornographic image, or a deep-seated resentment, or even an awful blasphemy against God! The suddenness and the fiery nature of the arrows indicate that they emanate from demons. With some believers these attacks can be so prolonged and vicious as to cause intense suffering.

The only way to handle this problem is with the shield of faith. The shield measured four feet ten inches by two feet six inches; adequate to protect the whole body, very similar in size to the shields used by riot police today. The arrows fired had burning heads, calculated to wound mortally. The shields were constructed to absorb these arrows and quench their flames. By faith the Christian has to fend off and resist the vile and hurtful evil thoughts that are fired.

The shield is a shield of faith because it is by faith that we vigorously resist these arrows – *all* of them. The word *all* is important. We must extinguish them *all.* For instance, a vicious slander defaming someone may be shot into the mind. That slander must in every respect be destroyed or extinguished by faith.

The fact that two items of armour are mentioned in 1 Thessalonians 5:8 and that in a slightly different way, shows that we must not be rigid in our interpretation of the armour. By faith in what is true, and love for others, we resist that which defames or slanders them.

The helmet of salvation

The helmet was carefully designed to protect the head which is exposed and which is so strategic. Clear vision is essential in any battle. The helmet in 1 Thessalonians 5:8 is called, 'The hope of salvation'. This raises the important subject of assurance. There is nothing uncertain about our hope. We know that there is now no condemnation to those who are in Christ (Rom 8:1). Those who lack assurance of salvation are vulnerable. It is much easier to win a battle with a person, if he or she is not sure.

There are many ways in which our adversary tries to knock off the helmet of salvation. He will, for instance, attempt to undermine our faith in God's Word. His favourite attack is to sow doubt and then to exploit that doubt. 'Has God said?' is a favourite approach of Satan. It may be the theory of evolution presented in a glossy way by *The Geographic Magazine* or some other reputable journal. That theory is based on much imagination and juggling about with a few bones. The general public do not know how spurious the whole theory is and it is easy for a believer to begin to doubt the reliability of Scripture.

The unity of the armour, the body girded with truth, the breastplate of righteousness and the helmet of salvation should be noted. Satan will attempt to strike a mortal blow at our faith in the truth of God and thus remove our helmet of hope. If this does not succeed, he will strike at the breastplate. He will accuse of sin, or attempt to remove assurance by getting the believer to think that his justification is based on his good works. Our works can never justify us. They are necessary as evidence that our faith is genuine, but all our good works do not form the basis of salvation. Christ's righteousness is the basis. We can readily see how important it is to be clear about this if we are to maintain our hope and assurance.

We must always maintain a clear mind about the foundations of our salvation and seek to have a strong, well-grounded assurance that we possess the gift of eternal life. We keep our helmet of salvation always in place when we keep our minds clear, and our understanding of the gospel relative to ourselves, firm.

The sword of the Spirit, which is the Word of God

How can it be that a Christian who is so limited in his spiritual powers can actually put demons to flight? 'Resist the devil, and he will flee from you'? (James 4:7). The answer to that question is that the devils, for all their knowledge, power and experience, hate and dread the Word of God. The words of God include sentences of certain and eternal ruin for the fallen angels. They are doomed to the lake of fire (Rev 20:10).

'The Word of God is living and active.' It is described as being 'sharper than any double-edged sword' (Heb 4:12). We see this illustrated in the way our Lord used Scripture against Satan in the temptation in the wilderness (Matt 4:1-11).

Ultimately it was the sword that gave Caesar's soldiers their power. A thorough and living knowledge of the Word of God can make a Christian into a most effective power, to advance the cause of Christ. However, it is not a knowledge of the Word alone, or even the ability to use that Word in engaging the powers of darkness. There are further factors. There are true Christians who are very knowledgeable, but they are apathetic and lack zeal. Observe that this passage concludes with an exhortation to be constant in prayer. Prayer is the way in which we show our dependence upon God and also the way by which we are empowered by the Holy Spirit. As Ephesians 6:20 suggests, there are all kinds of prayers. We must be proficient in them all, because only in that way will we be powerful in using all the armour of God.

We need to know our weapons. That is one factor. Power in using them is another. That is where prayer is essential.

A good soldier will know the enemy, know his strategies and know his own armour and how to use it. Yet there is a further important factor, which we now consider.

4. We need to know ourselves in relation to the provision made for us in our warfare

It is one thing to know about the weapons and to know about the truth. It is another to have the will to fight. The Roman legion had a will to conquer for Caesar. The question of will-power, morale, vision, determination and energy is of the utmost importance. Hence the prominence of exhortation in Ephesians 6:10-20, '*Be strong* in the Lord and in his mighty power.' '*Put on* the full armour.' '*Stand firm then.*' 'Pray in the Spirit *on all occasions* with all kinds of prayers and requests.'

These commands are essential. We have to be stirred into action. Without effort we will become lethargic and our armour will be neglected. Of all the commands, the one which urges prayer is the most important. By constant prayer we are assured of the vitality of the Holy Spirit, who enables us to be strong and to employ the armour.

Not only are we to be strong in the Lord's mighty power, but we are to stand firm. There are times when we are weary and when we seem to be losing the battle. It is just at that time that we must hold on and not retreat under any circumstances. We may call for fellow believers to come and help us in the battle. It may be the pastor who is needed. However, if all the others are themselves engaged in fierce battle, and cannot help, we have the Captain of our salvation, Christ Jesus, to fight for us. He will never leave us or forsake us (Heb 13:5,6). He always intercedes on our behalf (Heb 7:25).

> Stand, then, in his great might,
> With all his strength endued;
> And take, to arm you for the fight,
> The panoply of God.
> To keep your armour bright,
> Attend with constant care,
> Still serving in your Captain's fight,
> And watching unto prayer.[1]

Concluding questions

Having surveyed our provision for warfare, we should stand back and ask the question, How strong are the Lord's soldiers today? Since prayer is a crucial activity, we should ask about our prayer meetings. Are they well attended and are they characterised by zeal? Also, we should ask about the prayer-lives of believers. Are they strong in prayer?

An outstanding feature of the full armour is that the whole description presupposes an excellent knowledge of Scripture. Every piece of armour points to the need of a living knowledge of the truth. The shoes point to preparation in the gospel. The sword assumes that the Scriptures are well known and can be appropriately used in battle. Satan's purpose is to replace the Word with the traditions of men. During the centuries preceding the Reformation the Church became sacrament-centred, rather than Word-centred. The task of the Reformers was to restore the authority of Scripture. In our generation, Satan has succeeded in making the Church feeling-centred and entertainment-centred. In many churches, the pressure is on to produce warm feelings and to put on a good show. That is not training for war! It is foolishness! The result is that an anti-doctrine attitude is engendered and ignorance prevails.

Instead of vigorous training in the truth congregations are entertained. They learn little and are content with repetitive choruses, sentimental feelings and prayers, which revolve around themselves and their own little circle of interests.

If the trumpet were to sound in your church or Christian Union group, how many would there be who would respond to the discipline of spiritual war, and the effort of mind and will to know the truth and use it in battle? How much stamina would there be? How many would respond by saying that they did not *feel* like fighting? They would prefer to listen to music, and really they are not interested in anything that does not make them *feel* good. What kind of army is that? Little wonder that we do not have recruits for the mission field and for long-term sustained evangelistic endeavour! You cannot be a good soldier of Jesus Christ without the hardship of discipline and training. Let us exercise ourselves in godliness and put on the whole armour of God!

---

1   Christian Hymns, 715

Recommended books

William Gurnall, *The Christian in Complete Armour,* 1,200 pages hardback. This classic has been modernised and published in three paperback volumes by the Banner of Truth. This work is highly commended.

Martyn Lloyd-Jones, *The Christian Warfare,* an exposition of Ephesians 6:10-13, Banner of Truth, 371 pages.

Martyn Lloyd-Jones, *The Christian Soldier,* an exposition of Ephesians 6:10-20, 361 pages, hardback, Banner of Truth.

Thomas Brooks, *Precious Remedies Against Satan's Devices,* 252 page paperback, Banner of Truth

Frederick S Leahy, *Satan Cast Out,* Banner of Truth, 181 page paperback.

James Philip, *Christian Warfare and Armour,* CLC, 126 page paperback.

Peter Jeffery, *Stand Firm,* a young Christian's guide to the armour of God, Evangelical Press of Wales.

The Perseverance of the Saints

Progressive sanctification commences with and springs out of regeneration. Perseverance is allied to progressive sanctification. Perseverance is the engine by which the process of sanctification is constantly propelled forward. Without perseverance the thorough work of transformation of our natures to conform us to the likeness of Christ falters.

Perseverance as an essential quality of the Christian life is affirmed by Paul in Romans 5:3, 'Suffering produces perseverance; perseverance, character,' as well as James when he reminds us, 'The testing of your faith develops perseverance' (James 1:3). Again James says 'We consider blessed those who have persevered,' and holds up Job as a model of one who persevered in an exemplary manner (James 5:12). Peter, in outlining a way of certainty against falling requires of us that we make every effort to add perseverance to self-control, and to perseverance godliness (2 Peter 1:6).

The letter to the Hebrews is the principal source of teaching on this theme of perseverance. From first to last its style is one of admonition to persevere and avoid apostasy. Psalm 95:7-11 is cited in Hebrews 3:7-11, and 4:3,5 and 7. The writer reminds the Hebrews that they did stand their ground (10:32, they persevered, *hupomenō*). They are exhorted to persevere in the race (12:2), remembering that Christ endured appalling agony for us (12:3).

We should note our Lord's affirmation, 'Because of the increase of wickedness, the love of many will grow cold, but he who stands firm (endures) to the end will be saved,' (Matt 24:13). Perseverance is an integral part of the believer's spiritual equipment and character. It is the basic attitude of the righteous That this is so is seen from the parable of the sower, 'But the seed on good soil stands for those with a noble and good heart, who hear the word, retain it, and by perseverance produce a crop' (Luke 8:15, see also Romans 2:7).

❧ Chapter 22 ❧

Holiness and the
Problem of Backsliding

Ideally progressive sanctification is a process that proceeds from strength to strength, from spiritual infanthood to spiritual maturity. Alas, that is not always so. There are cases that remind us of the children's snakes and ladders game. Just as progress looks fine a player hits a snake and drops down the board to another level. Believers sometimes react badly to disappointments and decline in their spiritual lives. This subject becomes even more complex when we find the occasional situation of apostasy and have to conclude that the work of regeneration did not in fact take place in that person who gives up the faith.

Sadly most of us can remember friends who once maintained a consistent Christian profession. Gradually they fell away and now oppose what they once believed and even preached. I think of two pastors in particular. One was systematically destroyed through studying modernist theology. He fell away, divorced his wife, and now is fiercely opposed to the gospel. Another, a very successful pastor, became morally compromised, is now divorced from his wife, and at this time appears to be alienated from his former Christian friends. These cases are rare but when they occur there is much grief for those related to them and in the churches they served. Time tells the difference between those who are backsliders but come to be restored and those who backslide into apostasy.

Backsliding and apostasy – a biblical survey

The word backsliding is used several times in the Old Testament (Hebrew *meshubah* Jer 2:19; 8:5; 14:7, Hos 14:4 *shobab* Jer 3:14,22;31:22 and *sarar* Hos 4:16). The word backsliding does not occur in our English translations of the New Testament. In Luke 8:13 our Lord speaks of those who in times of temptation fall away *(aphistemi)*, Hebrews 2: 1 speaks of drifting away *(pararreō)*, and Peter warns against being carried away *(sunapagō)* by error and falling *(ekpiptō)* from a secure position (2 Peter 3:17). John concludes his first letter by speaking about those who commit sin from which there is no recovery and those who do not, as he writes, 'there is sin that does not lead to death' (1 John 5:17). James draws attention to those who wander *(planaō)* from the truth (James 5: 19). In the letters to the seven churches our Lord warns against losing our first love (Rev 2:1-7) and against lukewarmness (Rev 3:14-21). These are sober warnings to local churches and show that caution is needed to safeguard against decline in each church. Paul's warning of the Ephesian elders recorded in Acts 20 seems to foretell the Ephesian decline. Churches in whole regions can slip into decline. Hence Paul expressed sheer amazement *(thaumazō* – I am astonished – Gal 1:6), that the Galatians should so quickly abandon the gospel.

Generally speaking we regard a backslider as one who has run well and been consistent in Christian practice but who becomes lethargic, unenthusiastic, half-hearted, inconsistent and unfaithful in his profession, one who needs to repent spiritually and repair his life by recovering his devotional and practical Christian walk. Backsliding casts doubt on a person's standing. Will that one turn out to be true or not? Or will he so slide away as to become an apostate?

An apostate is one who abandons Christ altogether. Even though he has professed Christianity in word and deed he backslides and then falls away becoming an apostate for whom, according to the letter to the Hebrews, there is no hope of recovery (Heb 6:4; 10:26-31). To apostatise is to revolt against, to repudiate or renounce the faith.

The word in Greek is *apostasia* (2 Thess 2:3; 1 Tim 4:1-3).

The letter to the Hebrews implies throughout that Jewish believers were going backward, that is backsliding. We dare not reduce the force of the solemn warnings in the two climactic passages just referred to, namely, Hebrews 6:4-6 and 10:26-31. It is usual to concentrate on the first passage to the neglect of the second, but the two passages belong to each other. They teach that it is possible to go a long way into the Christian faith and yet not be born again. The second passage affirms that there is no judgment so severe as that which comes upon those who have abused such a privileged position. 'How much more severely do you think a man deserves to be punished who has trampled the Son of God under foot, who has treated as an unholy thing the blood of the covenant that sanctified him, and who has insulted the Spirit of grace?' (Heb 10:29). That is consistent with what our Lord said about Judas and what he declared about it being more bearable for Sodom than for those who trample on gospel privileges (Matt 10:15).

There is terrible danger in backsliding. True, those who have been truly born again will always be reclaimed as we see with Samson, David and Peter. But we are left wondering about Demas who forsook Paul, having loved this present world (2 Tim 4:10). By no means do all those who profess faith and then backslide recover. Some, having gone back, never recover. John's words are apposite here: 'Their going showed that none of them belonged to us' (1 John 2:19). There is also the awesome truth of God's sovereignty declared in John 15:2, 'He cuts off every branch in me that bears no fruit.'

John intimates that there are three trends toward apostasy: doctrinal, moral and social. Going back from Christ into apostasy can manifest itself in heterodoxy (rejection of the deity of Christ), living in immorality, or hatred of fellow believers (1 John 3:14,15). The signs of declension are evidenced in carelessness about worship, irreverence, frivolity, and the lack of love and esteem for God in worship.

General apostasy

It is important to distinguish between personal apostasy and general apostasy. In the New Testament two quite distinct general apostasies are referred to.

The first concerns the period leading up to the downfall of Jerusalem and the dispersion of the Jews. Jesus gives clear warnings about that in the Olivet discourse (Matt 24, Mark 13, Luke 21). In other places he warns of the testing conditions that would apply particularly at that time. For instance in Matthew 10:22 he says: 'All men will hate you because of me, but he who stands firm to the end will be saved.'

This passage should be compared with Matthew 24:11-13. The implications are very serious. Notice that it is a majority that grow cold and also that the increase of wickedness has an adverse effect on the believers. While there is uncertainty about the dating and background of the letter to the Hebrews it is not misplaced to associate the message of that letter with the tremendous upheaval surrounding the demise of Judaism, the aftermath of the fall of Jerusalem and the dispersion of the Jews.

The sternest warning in the New Testament concerns not a local or even national apostasy but one which is world-wide. This is the warning of 2 Thessalonians 2:11-12, which represents the purpose and heart of this epistle. We must note the background to this passage and the application that flows from it. This passage should be compared with the general warnings given by Paul to Timothy (1 Tim 4:1-5; 2 Tim 3:1-5 and 4:3).

The Reformers and Puritans interpreted 2 Thessalonians 2:1-12 as the great apostasy in the Christian Church dating from about 500 to the time of the Reformation and subsequently in an unrepentant Roman Catholic Church. In his commentary John Calvin interprets the passage as apocalyptic in style and not literal. Concerning *the man of sin,* he says 'Paul is not speaking of one individual, but of a kingdom that was to be seized by Satan for the purpose of setting up a seat of abomination in the midst of God's temple. This we see accomplished in popery.' Concerning the antichrist Calvin asserts, 'For quite certainly Paul meant that antichrist would seize the things which belong to God alone, his purpose being to exalt himself above every divine power, so that all religion and all worship of God should lie beneath his feet.' Calvin points out that the Pope claims complete authority. A threefold universal claim of authority is symbolised in his tiara.

This interpretation is also taken by John Owen and is the view stated in the *Westminster Confession of Faith* chapter 25 paragraph 6 (cf. the 1689 *London Baptist Confession* chapter 26 paragraph 4). No apostasy from apostolic Christianity can be compared to the papacy. For over a thousand years the gospel became more and more subverted and covered over with error. The Church became the monolithic, sacral persecutor of the faithful, driving them to death or into the wilderness as described in Revelation chapter 12.

William Hendriksen takes a different view of 2 Thessalonians 2:1-12. F F Bruce' s scholarly commentary in the WORD series helpfully discusses one of the most difficult expressions in the passage, namely, the restraining power, 'but the one who now holds it back will continue to do so till he is taken out of the way. And then the lawless one will be revealed.' The Imperial power of Rome acted as a shield of protection as well as being a source of persecution. The waning of the Imperial power paved the way for the ascendancy of the papacy.

Applications

Application 1. A time of apostasy brings great pressure to bear upon the faithful. We deduce from Christ's warnings that times of declension lower the temperature of love for God. He says, The love of most will grow cold (Matt 24:12). It is no small blessing when those around love the Lord passionately but it is wretched to live in a lukewarm fellowship. The prevalence of evil in itself forms a great discouragement and a major factor in many going back on the faith. The letter to the Hebrews mainly concerns the increasing pressures on Jewish believers who had stood firm and sacrificed their goods and reputations but were now coming under increasing pressure to go back on Christ.

Application 2. Persecution can have an adverse effect on the Church. It is sometimes thought that persecution advances the gospel and suggested that if only we had persecution in the West the Church might grow. This is questionable. Persecution of Christians does sometimes cause many to enquire about the truth of the Bible especially when they see Christians prepared to suffer pain and loss and yet remain joyful. When Christians maintain a consistent testimony in adversity that does commend the faith. But severe suppression and persecution of Christianity in many countries has been successful in stifling the truth. Many examples can be quoted. For instance prior to the Reformation the true Church was almost blotted out and in Spain the Inquisition extinguished the Protestant cause completely. There are some countries today (Saudi Arabia is an example) where conditions forbid any kind of public Christian expression. 1 Timothy 2:1-4 suggests that peaceable conditions are advantageous to the promotion of the Gospel.

Application 3. Christian leaders are of vital importance to withstand apostasy. The small number of outstanding Christian leaders in the history of the Church is quite amazing. Even in the New Testament so much rested on the reliability of the apostle Paul, especially when Peter was muddle-headed (Gal 2:11-21). In the fourth century there was a point when it seemed that it was Athanasius alone who stood in defence of the Faith. In 1522 at the City of Worms, Luther stood alone against the whole panoply of religious and secular power, the Emperor Charles V and the Papacy combined in authority to intimidate Luther. At the end of the nineteenth century Spurgeon as a leader among Baptists stood firm and clear against the majority who were willing to compromise with liberal theology. Dr Martyn Lloyd-Jones was an outstanding leader! How greatly we miss his stand for biblical truth today. And living in the same time span was Rehwinkel an extraordinary Lutheran leader who single-handed saved his great seminary and denomination (The Missouri Synod) from compromise. Let us pray for leaders who are excellent statesmen. In a time of declension it is easy to be separatist and isolationist and blow the trumpet from a lonely hill afar off. It is another thing to be involved on the battlefield with those who most need help. Leadership is crucial if the Church is to be kept from decline. Let us pray for men like Albert Mohler in his courageous efforts to reform Southern Seminary, Louisville, Kentucky, and all that it stands for in the context of the Southern Baptist Convention. Leaders of calibre are rare.

Provisions against backsliding

The central question, which we now consider, is: what provision is there in the Word of God to prevent Christians from backsliding which turns into apostasy.

There are basic axioms or principles that underlie this subject.

Axiom 1. Perseverance is the antidote to apostasy. The reality of apostasy means that we do all we can to ensure perseverance. Jesus said that those who endure to the end will be saved.

Axiom 2. Perseverance involves divine sovereignty and human responsibility as summarised in Philippians 2:12,13, 'Continue to work out your salvation with fear and trembling, for it is God who works in you to will and to act according to his good purpose'. God's purpose to save his elect is absolute but it lies with our responsibility to make our calling and election sure.

Axiom 3. Perseverance involves the primacy of the affections. Proverbs 4:23 says, 'Above all else, guard your heart, for it is the wellspring of life'. Our first parents fell first in their affections and then in their actions. Maintaining a daily devotional spiritual life is paramount.

The most relevant scriptures

While all Scripture is designed to keep the Christian strong in faith there are some parts specifically addressed to this issue. John 15 –

abide in me – is an example. Ephesians 6:10-20 – the whole armour of God is another.

The necessity of being kept is everywhere present as we are reminded in the doxology of Jude that there is only One 'who is able to keep you from falling' (verse 24). Two passages which stand out are 2 Peter 1:5-11 and Romans 8:28-39. Peter urges that the Christian should add to his faith a set of virtues and if he does, *he will never fall.* The word *epichorageō* (2 Peter 1:11) is expressive because it reminds us of a conductor of an orchestra who calls into play the various instruments all contributing to the harmony of the whole. Likewise the faithful practice of all these virtues together will guarantee your entrance into the kingdom, as the KJV expresses the matter: 'For so an entrance shall be ministered unto you abundantly into the everlasting kingdom of our Lord and Saviour Jesus Christ.'

Paul tells of the work of the Father. He has loved us from eternity. He has predestined us to be conformed to the image of his Son. He has called us and justified us and our glorification is certain (Rom 8:28-30). Emphasis is on the certainty of God's purpose. Even though all hell should conspire against God's elect they will be kept from falling. Paul is defiant: 'Who can separate us from the love of Christ?' A firm permanent hold on these truths is designed to keep believers from backsliding.

The letter to the Hebrews

The Hebrews epistle is the *locus classicus,* the central place of teaching on this theme. From first to last the style of Hebrews is admonition to avoid apostasy and to persevere. The genius of the Hebrews letter is to fortify against backsliding. The thrust of the message is to show how we are constantly in the present tense preserved through our union with an omnipotent divine intercessor who is presently active on our behalf. This active intercession is the principal theme of Hebrews. Note well Hebrews 8:1, 'The main point' *(kephalaion* means 'the sum of' or 'main point').

The principal reasons advanced in Hebrews as ways to avoid apostasy are as follows.

1. Live day by day in union with our great high priest

A constant and consistent prayer life, drawing near to God with a sincere heart in full assurance of faith is the essence of the Christian life.

2. Live in union day by day with other members of the church.

Beginning at chapter 10:22 we are told that prayer, meeting together and observing how we might spur each other on toward love and good deeds, are essential. The sure way to backsliding and then to apostasy is to devalue the means of grace. Hebrews 10:24,25 suggests that it is essential to meet together for mutual encouragement. In the same context of application the writer urges the importance of meeting together. We are members together in the body of Christ. Each member belongs to all the others (Rom 12:4,5; 1 Cor 12:13-27). The spiritual condition of a Christian is reflected by his relationship to the body (Eph 4: 15,16).

3. Live by faith and do not shrink back

The justified must live by faith (10:38). The salvation which is ours in Christ is stupendous. Nothing can compare with it. There is no other salvation (Acts 4: 12). This salvation is through union with the Triune God. It is just too great to forfeit. We have everything in Christ (1 Cor 1:30). We are heirs of God and co-heirs with Christ (Rom 8:17 and Heb 2:10-13). 'How shall we escape if we neglect so great salvation?' (Heb 2:3). To shrink back will result in destruction.

4. Live by viewing the examples of others who have run well

Hebrews 11 is the story of faith in action. Our hearts are moved by the example of others. Church history and biography occupy an important place in the teaching ministry of the Church. The history of the Reformation and the history of past revivals greatly encourage God's people. Stirring descriptions of the pioneer missionaries quicken desire to finish the missionary task.

5. We must live with the idea that hardship is normal

Hebrews 12:4-13 exhorts that we endure hardship as discipline. We must not be discouraged by hardship.

6. We must live with a diet of solid food

In times of declension it is misguided to water down doctrine. First century Jewish believers found it hard to cope with the taunt that Jesus of Nazareth could not possibly be God since he died a criminal's death. Note that Hebrews is utterly uncompromising on the theme of the divine nature of Jesus. It was hard for them to accept that Judaism was now valueless. Hebrews is uncompromisingly clear about that.

Conclusions

First, concerning general apostasy. If the Reformers and Puritans were correct in their interpretation of 2 Thessalonians 2:1-12 then we have seen the worst of the apostasy and should focus our attention on the open doors to fulfil the Great Commission. The future is as bright as the promises of God. Promises such as Psalm 110:1; Daniel 2:35; Micah 4:1-5; Malachi 1:11 and Habakkuk 2:14 are bright indeed and await fulfilment. Surely great progress and encouragement lies ahead for many countries coming into gospel truth for the first time. We must plead for a mighty harvest for the Prince of Peace.

Second, concerning personal apostasy. There is abiding responsibility to do all we can to discourage backsliding and to seek the restoration of the backslider. Jesus suggests if a shepherd has 100 sheep and loses one, he will leave the 99 and go out and seek the one that is lost. John declares at the end of his first letter that we are to pray about this issue (1 John 5: 16,17). James is emphatic: 'My brothers, if one of you should wander from the truth and someone should bring him back, remember this: Whoever turns a sinner from the error of his way will save him from death and cover over a multitude of sins' (James 5:19,20).

Recommended reading.

John Owen is the richest resource of theology in the English language. Time and time again he comprehends central themes with unexcelled depth and power. This is true on the nature and causes of apostasy from the gospel, being the title of the Banner of Truth 166 page paperback, which is a summary of volume seven of Owen's work on apostasy. The abridged work has been skilfully prepared by RJK Law.

The Qualities of the Resurrection Body

Robert L Dabney (1820-1898) was an outstanding American theologian who spent most of his life preparing men for the ministry. The following quotation comes from his lectures in Systematic Theology.

'The qualities of the resurrection bodies of the saints are described in 1 Corinthians 15:42-58, with as much particularity, probably, as we can comprehend. Whereas the body is buried in a state of dissolution, it is raised indissoluble, no longer liable to disorganisation by separation of particles, either because protected therefrom by the special power of God, or by the absence of assailing chemical forces. It is buried, disfigured and loathsome. It will be raised beautiful. Since it is a literal material body that is raised, it is by far the most natural to suppose that the glory predicated of it is literal, material beauty. As to its kind, see Matthew 13:43 and Philippians 3:21. Some may think that it is unworthy of God's redemption to suppose it conferring an advantage so trivial and sensuous as personal beauty. But is not this a remnant of that Gnostic or Neo-Platonic asceticism, which cast off the body itself as too worthless to be an object of redeeming power? We know that sanctified affections now always beautify and ennoble the countenance. See Exodus 34:29,30.

'And if God did not deem it too trivial for his attention to clothe the landscape with verdure, to cast every form of nature in lines of grace, to dye the skies with purest azure, and to paint the sun and stars with splendour, in order to gratify the eyes of his children here, we may assume that he will condescend to beautify even the bodies of his saints, in that world where all is made perfect. Next, the body is buried in weakness; it has just given the crowning evidence of feebleness, by yielding to death. It will be raised in immortal vigour, so as to perform its functions with perfect facility, and without fatigue.'

☙ Chapter 23 ❧

Holiness, Enoch and
the Second Coming

<hr>

It is appropriate that we look to the grand final event of this age, namely the Second Coming of Christ because this will be the consummation of our sanctification. The Second Coming of Christ to judgment has been proclaimed through all the centuries. We can go as far back as Enoch to find that this is true.

If we were to go down in a time machine to thousands of years ago we might make our way to an open-air meeting to hear .the preaching of one called Enoch. The subject of his preaching is the Coming of the Lord.

> 'See, the Lord is coming with thousands upon thousands of his holy ones to judge everyone, and to convict all the ungodly of all the ungodly acts they have done in the ungodly way, and of all the harsh words ungodly sinners have spoken against him' (Jude 14-15).

How does this preacher know this? He has no Bible, no Old Testament, no New Testament. Christ has not come to earth yet and here a preacher of righteousness is describing graphically his Second Coming!

Enoch was of the seventh generation from Adam. He was born when Adam was 622 years old. Since Adam lived 930 years this means that Adam and Enoch were contemporaries for 308 years.

Elijah and Enoch are the only two in history who have been translated physically out of this life into the next. Both battled to the extreme with the ungodliness that surrounded them, an ungodliness characterised and illustrated by the defiance of Lamech who was contemporary with Enoch and who defied God to his face:

> 'If Cain is avenged seven times,
> then Lamech seventy-seven times' (Gen 5:24).

We learn from the example of Enoch that when times are evil our focus must be on the Second Coming. The second Coming formed the substance of Enoch's preaching and walking with God characterised his life. 'Enoch walked with God; then he was no more, because God took him away' (Gen 4:24).[1]

Enoch was surrounded on all sides by ungodliness. We are too. Our response must be to walk with God as we are exhorted in Ephesians, 'Walk in love, as Christ loved us and gave himself up for us, a "fragrant" offering and sacrifice to God' (Eph 5:2 ESV). Walking, in Scripture, is used to convey the idea of constancy. Hence with regard to the old life we 'walked in trespasses and sins' (Eph 2:1 ESV) but now must walk in 'good works which God prepared beforehand' (Eph 2:10 ESV). To walk constantly with God pleases him. 'Enoch was taken up so that he should not see death, and he was not found, because God had taken him. Now before he was taken he was commended as having pleased God' (Heb 11:5 ESV).

Enoch had sons and daughters. He was a family man. 'He was no hermit or monk. He did not make the things of this world his life, not even his family. God was his life. This life with God could not end. To prove it God took him. He changed places but not company.'[2]

A six year old Dutch girl described Enoch like this, 'God and Enoch were great friends; God often came to visit Enoch. And then they talked together. One beautiful morning the Lord said: "My friend, what about a little walk?" And Enoch said, "All right, my Lord, I come." "See you again," he said to his wife and children, and closed the door. God and Enoch had much to speak about. So Enoch walked with God. They saw the birds, they saw the flowers, they saw the she-goats with their little ones, until all of a sudden Enoch was alarmed and said, "My Lord, we have walked too far! There's your house! How will I ever find my way back?" But the Lord said, "Well, Enoch, some time or other you are coming to stay with me; is that not so? So, why not now?" And Enoch was no more for God took him.'³

We return to that open air meeting and Enoch's preaching on the Second Coming. These are the salient points:

1. Christ's Second Coming will be personal
2. Christ's Second Coming will be glorious
3. Christ's Second Coming will bring judgment
4. Christ's Second Coming will be the consummation of all things

1. Christ's Second Coming will be personal

In Acts 1:11 Luke describes the ascension of our Lord. He was taken up before their very eyes, and a cloud hid him from their sight. They were looking intently up into the sky as he was going, when suddenly two men dressed in white stood beside them. 'Men of Galilee,' they said, 'why do you stand here looking into the sky? This same Jesus, who has been taken from you into heaven, will come back in the same way you have seen him go into heaven.'

This Jesus who had been with them and led them for three years was leaving them. Their focus was upon him personally. 'They were looking intently up into the sky' is the way the NIV translates the word gazing (Acts 1:10). Their whole focus was on him. Everything they hoped for and everything they knew of life and salvation centred in him. Their gaze focused on him as he ascended out of their sight.

Note that Jesus is the centre. This is very personal. This is a man who bore in his body the marks of intense suffering. He will return.

Every eye will see this same man. On that day he receded away out of sight. On his return he will come closer and closer and we will see that same man who was so loved by his disciples.

Paul assures the Thessalonians that no believers will be left out at the Second Coming. All those who have died in Christ will be raised first and all who are alive at his coming will join them. That day will be a day of glory for every one of the redeemed. They will have glorified bodies. Every one of them will be freed forever from the presence and power of sin. Christ's glory will shine in every one of them. But he himself will be the centre, and he will be seen as the centre of their glory. Every one of them will marvel at him. They will view him with glad astonishment and with grateful wonder.

> 'Look, he is coming with the clouds, and every eye will see him' (Rev 1:7).

Note the personal emphasis. Every eye will see him. Even 'those who pierced him' will see him. The soldiers who drove in the nails will see him. The soldier who pierced his side with a spear will see him. For all the ungodly Christ's Second Coming will be utterly distressing. It will be horrendous. 'All the peoples of the earth will mourn because of him.' There is nothing secret about his coming. He will be seen by every soul that has ever lived.

2. Christ's Second Coming will be glorious

There could hardly be a greater contrast between Christ's first coming and his second. In his first coming he was seen by few. His birth in a stable and his upbringing in a poor village was hidden to all but a handful of people. When he entered upon his ministry he became widely known. But then after only three years everything went wrong for him. He was betrayed, He was arrested, tried, condemned. When he was on his way to condemnation and death all his disciples forsook him and fled. He was alone. When he stood before Pontius Pilate there was nobody to stand with him. He was alone. There was no highly paid barrister to plead his cause.

His humiliation was abject in the extreme. He could hardly have suffered more than he did. But he humbled himself even to the death of a cross. He was treated like the worst criminal. His dead body was removed from where it had been impaled (how did they disengage his hands from the nails?). His mutilated body was buried in a tomb. When he comes again he will not be alone. He will be flanked on both sides with his angels, 'numbering thousands upon thousands, and ten thousand times ten thousand' (Rev 5:11). He will come with all his people, galleries upon galleries of them (1 Thess 4:15-17).

We will all be part of that Second Coming. We who have confessed him before men will have the privilege of coming with him then (Rom 10:9). When he was tried the soldiers mocked him. 'They stripped him and put a scarlet robe on him, and then twisted together a crown of thorns, and set it on his head. They put a staff in his right hand and knelt in front of him and mocked him. "Hail, king of the Jews!" they said. They spat on him, and took the staff and struck him on the head again and again' (Matt 27:28-30).

In his glorious advent he will come robed in majesty and in his right hand will be a sceptre of righteousness and power, a symbol of his authority to judge all mankind. He will come as the only Ruler, the King of kings and Lord of lords (1 Tim 6:15; Rev 17:14). From the lowest place on a cross he will be exalted to the highest place on a throne of majesty. At his name every knee will bow (Phil 2:6-11).

Twenty-eight times in the Revelation, Jesus is described as 'the Lamb'. This suggests that there will always radiate in his character and appearance the fact that he stood in our place as the sacrificial lamb who has taken away our sins.

3. Christ's Second Coming will bring Judgment

The Apostles' Creed summarises the principal events of history: 'The third day he rose from the dead, he ascended into Heaven, and sitteth on the right hand of God the Father Almighty; from thence he shall come to judge the quick and the dead.' Those who live in a flood of dissipation will have to account to him 'who is ready to judge the living and the dead' (1 Peter 4:5).

Enoch prophesied, 'See, the Lord is coming with thousands upon thousands to judge everyone.' The emphasis in Enoch's description is that ungodliness is the root of all unrighteousness (cf. Rom 1:18). He will 'convict all the ungodly of all the ungodly acts they have done in the ungodly way, and of all the harsh words ungodly sinners have spoken against him.' The striking and salient features of this judgment are:

(i) It will be just

It will be just because Christ will be the judge. 'When the Son of Man comes in his glory, and all the angels with him, he will sit on his throne in heavenly glory' (Matt 25:31). Terrible miscarriages of justice have taken place in this world. Bribery and corruption have despoiled courts. Witnesses have been intimidated by the Mafia. Sometimes judges who have sought to be upright have been assassinated. There will be none of that at this Great Assize. This judge possesses omniscience and this judge will judge rightly (Ps 75:2).

John Flavel, referring to James 5:1-7, points out that sometimes God intervenes in providence and punishes evil men of power. But this is rare.[4] It would seem that corrupt politicians who predominate in our world are men who use their power for their own ends and care nothing for the suffering of their people. There are many rich oppressors who hoard their wealth at the expense of the exploited poor whose cries reach the ears of the Lord Almighty. The answer to these horrors is the Second Coming. 'Do not take revenge, my friends, but leave room for God's wrath, for it is written, "It is mine to avenge: I will repay," says the Lord' (Rom 12:19). In similar vein Psalm 37:1 and 10, 'Do not fret because of evil men ... a little while, and the wicked will be no more' (see also Prov 24:19,20).

(ii) It will be universal

Jesus declared that all the nations will be gathered before him (Matt 25:32). In another place Jesus says that 'the men of Nineveh will stand up at the judgment' and condemn that generation of Jews who witnessed the life and miracles of Jesus because the Ninevites repented at the preaching of Jonah (Matt 12:39-41). Chapters in Isaiah, Jeremiah and Ezekiel are devoted to judgment on the nations surrounding Israel in those times. The city of Tyre, whose ships visited every harbour in the ancient world, will be judged as will the great empires of Egypt, Babylon and Assyria. Modern empires will be judged. Hitler and his Nazi cohorts will be judged as will the powers of Stalin and the Kremlin.

The prophecies concerning the nations that surrounded ancient Israel imply assessment and judgment. The Psalms imply that we will witness the Lord's assessment and judgment of all movements tribal, national and political throughout history. 'He will judge the world in righteousness and the peoples with equity' (Ps 98:9 cf. 96:10; 82:8).

(iii) It will be thorough

The judge 'will expose the motives of men's hearts' (1 Cor 4:5). Consciences will be opened 'in the day when God will judge men's secrets' (Rom 2:16). An account will be required for words, 'But I tell you that men will have to give account on the Day of Judgment for every careless word they have spoken' (Matt 12:36). 'God will bring every deed into judgment, including every hidden thing, whether it is good or evil' (Eccl 12:14). 'There is no dark place, no deep shadow, where evildoers can hide' (Job 34:22).

Some court cases take months to process and some can take over a year for a verdict. This is mostly due to the difficulty of accessing accurate and reliable evidence and unravelling both sides of a case. But God in his omniscience holds all the data available. Nevertheless processing billions of people and assessing nations and movements is a matter of colossal proportion. If history lasts 10,000 years how long by human reckoning will the great judgment take? One Puritan writer suggested 6,000 years! Realistically it will be more like 100,000 years. As creatures of time we can only understand details like this in terms of an extended period of time.

(iv) It will include the saints

Paul warns against judging each other since each one of us will give an account of himself to God (Rom 14:10-13). He assures us that 'we must all appear before the judgment seat of Christ, that each one may receive what is due to him for the things done while in the body, whether good or bad' (2 Cor 5:10; cf. 1 Cor 3:10-15). What factors will be taken into account at this judgment seat of Christ? Thomas Vincent suggests four.[5]

First, Christ will take an account of their graces. The vessels of the virgins will be looked into, what oil they have obtained; the hearts of the saints will be looked into, what graces they have obtained. Christ will then take notice what godly sorrow they have had for sin; their secret weeping and mourning will then be made manifest. He will then take notice what humility and especially what faith, love, hope, and spiritual joy they have had, and all their raised affections towards himself.

Second, Christ will take an account of the improvements of their talents of graces, gifts and opportunities of service, which he has entrusted to them (Matt 25: 19).

Third, Christ will take an account of their works of mercy (Matt 25:35-37). 'For I was hungry and you gave me something to eat ... I was sick and you visited me.' It will even astonish and confound the righteous to hear such language, and they will say, 'Lord, when did we see you hungry?'

Fourth, Christ will take an account of the afflictions which the righteous have endured; especially their suffering for his sake such as reproaches, losses, imprisonments, banishments and buffetings. If they have suffered death, with what honour will this be made mention of; with what great esteem will he receive and speak unto them which have come out of great tribulation! Then will they find that their momentary troubles have gained them an eternal weight of glory (see 2 Cor 4:17).

It is not plain to what extent our sins will be brought out at this judgment since they are sins that have been atoned for and blotted out. Also we are assured that the Lord will not hold against us sins of which we have repented. But an assessment there will be.

(v) It will be eternal

The great judgment terminates in eternal condemnation. 'Then they will go away to eternal punishment, but the righteous to eternal life' (Matt 25:46). For the lost this is the greatest conceivable calamity.

Jesus describes his Second Coming as a trap that comes upon all those who live on the face of the whole earth (Luke 21:34,35). John says that 'all the peoples of the earth will mourn because of him' (Rev 1:7). Those who have gambled their souls away will experience remorse which is indescribable. The word 'mourn' could be translated wail. They will be overcome with grief. 'They called to the mountains and the rocks, "Fall on us and hide us from the face of him who sits on the throne and from the wrath of the Lamb"' (Rev 6:16).

For this reason we dread the Second Coming. We fear for those we love dearly, relatives, neighbours, friends, workmates. One part of us longs for his appearing, the other seeks its delay for the sake of the lost. We accord with 2 Peter 3:9, 'He is patient with you, not wanting anyone to perish, but everyone to come to repentance.'

Two longings run beside each other. The first is the longing for justice to come to end the injustices and the corruptions of this world. That is the principal context of Enoch's prophecy. He was surrounded, as we are, by ungodly speeches, ungodly actions and ungodly atrocities. He looked forward to the end of the reign of sin. John Flavel declares that the trumpet sound of the last day will be a trumpet sound of terror to God's enemies but to his people it will be like the roaring of cannons when armies of friends approach a besieged city for the relief of those within it.[6]

4. Christ's Second Coming will be the Consummation of all things

Christ's Second Coming represents the consummation of all history. All the strands of world history have their culmination in Christ's return, which represents the *terminus ad quem* of his mediatorial reign. *Terminus ad quem* (end to which) means that the goal is reached for a course of action. *Terminus ad quem* also means a final limiting point of time. This is expressed perfectly in 1 Corinthians 15:24-26, 'Then the end will come, when he hands over the kingdom to God the Father after he has destroyed all dominion, authority and power. For he must reign until he has put all his enemies under his feet. The last enemy to be destroyed is death.'[7]

At the time of his resurrection Jesus declared that all authority had been given to him in heaven and on earth (Matt 28:18). This conferring upon him of all authority followed the ascension when he took his place at the Father's right hand, as it says in Psalm 110:1, 'The LORD says to my Lord, "Sit at my right hand until I make your enemies a footstool for your feet."' Christ reigns as Mediator and King until his return. The extent to which Christ will subdue his enemies before he returns to destroy the last and greatest enemy, death, we do not know. Paul intimates that evil will flourish (1 Tim 4:1-5; 2 Tim 3:1-5) but at the same time Christ will build his Church to the ends of the earth and the gates of hell will not prevail against it (Matt 16:18). For Christ to subdue the formidable powers and false religions that oppose the gospel is hard to imagine but we must go by the promises and not by our imagination. The text suggests that as time goes by our Lord progressively overthrows his opponents. Death holds out only because it is permitted by God to remain until Jesus comes back. Then it too will vanish.

Having achieved his purpose, the Son hands over the kingdom to the Father. 'Then the righteous will shine like the sun in the kingdom of their Father' (Matt 13:43). Everywhere in Scripture we are given to understand that Christ's kingdom is before his second advent and the Father's kingdom after that advent. This is a matter of order as B B Warfield asserts, 'Nothing suggested is in the remotest way inconsistent with the co-equal Deity of the Son with the Father and of his co-regency with him over the universe.'[8]

Jesus has taught us to relate to our Father by way of adoption (Matt 5-7) and in the new earth we will live in relationship to our Father who is over all. As expounded in chapter five we relate to our Lord Jesus Christ by way of union. He will always be our meritorious Head and our eternal security and we will always be close to him and under his leadership, as it says in Revelation 14:4, 'They follow the Lamb wherever he goes.'

Prior to the *terminus ad quem,* the handing over of the kingdom to the Father (1 Cor 15:24-28), there are three events of momentous magnitude and to each of these we look forward with longing (2 Tim 4:8).

(i) The resurrection of the body

Some more than others suffer in their bodies as physical death takes hold, described by Paul as 'wasting away'. This condition increases our longing (groaning) to be clothed with our heavenly dwelling (2 Cor 4:16-5:4). We groan inwardly as we wait eagerly for our adoption as sons, the redemption of our bodies (Rom 8:23).

(ii) The wedding day of the Church

We do not meet Christ in our diseased, decaying bodies. We do not meet him in wheelchairs or with hearing aids or horn-rimmed spectacles, but we meet him in glorious, perfected, resurrection bodies and minds. Shining in all the saints at the Second Coming will be a perfected work of holiness. Thus in Revelation 21:2 the redeemed are described as those who have been perfected and have been made beautiful in holiness.

(iii) The new earth and heavens

The meek will inherit the earth (Matt 5:5; Ps 37: 11). We will reign with Christ. We will probably be very surprised at the similarity of the new earth with the present world. 2 Peter 3 suggests that the renewal by fire seems so intense that the new creation will bear no resemblance to the old. We should note however that the Greek word *neos* means new in time and origin whereas the word *kainos* means new in nature or in quality. There will be a glorious renewal but the continuity with the present cosmos will be maintained. Also we should note that the passage in Romans 8 testifies to a liberation from corruption, not to something wholly different but liberation from the awful effects of the fall to perfection that was originally intended. Allied to this is the fact that we were created for the habitat of this world and the resurrection of our bodies will be related to that. Wonderful though our resurrection bodies will be there will be continuity with the habitat of this world.

Christ's return is the consummation of human history. All lines of history converge in the Second Corning. For all believers from the beginning of time to the end this is their wedding day. This is when, as the New Jerusalem, we unite to meet our Bridegroom (Rev 21:2). This is the day when we see our Saviour. This day heralds the new heavens and the new earth where we will reign and live with Christ forever!

Evidently the Lord revealed this to Enoch. That accounts for his fervent preaching of it and his eager anticipation of it, so eager as to seem imminent to him, though he lived thousands of years ago. How much more should we, who are indeed near that soon coming day, proclaim it with equal fervour!

Enoch's ministry of preaching repentance in the light of the Second

Coming of Christ is similar to that of the apostle Peter who describes the Second Coming of Christ in graphic terms. In his second letter (2 Peter 3) he describes the end of the world. Peter's call to repentance is similar to that of Enoch. Peter tells us why time is extended. It is because of God's patience: 'The Lord is not slow in keeping his promise, as some understand slowness. He is patient with you, not wanting anyone to perish, but everyone to come to repentance' (2 Peter 3:9).

In view of the soon coming great judgment Day Peter calls us to concentrate on personal holiness. 'What kind of people ought you to be? You ought to live holy and godly lives as you look forward to the day of God and speed its coming' (2 Peter 3:11,12). The apostle employs constraining language that is difficult to translate from Greek into English. He uses three words in the plural: *holiness, conduct* and *piety*.[9] In this way he urges that holiness pervade every part of our conduct and this includes our devotional practice (piety). All aspects of daily behaviour are to be holy. No sphere of our living lies outside this call to holiness. Not one of us would claim to be perfect. It is a matter of striving to be perfect and of growing in grace and knowledge of our Lord and Saviour Jesus Christ (2 Peter 3:18).

As we look forward to that coming great day when Jesus returns in glory we must live holy lives and so speed its coming. It is hard to imagine how we can possibly speed the coming of that Day but we can grasp speeding its coming if we read it in the context of Matthew 24:14, 'This gospel of the kingdom must be preached in the whole world as a testimony to all nations and then the end will come' (Matt 24:14).[10] The Great Commission (Matt 28:18-20) constrains us to do all we can to reach the ends of the earth with the saving gospel of Christ. When the gospel has pervaded all nations then the time will be ripe for the Lord's return.

---

1   *peripateō*, to walk, is lost in the NIV but regained in the English Standard Version. Like the New American Standard Bible, the ESV is a more literal translation.
2   Philip Eveson, *The Book of Origins, Genesis simply explained*, 592 pages, EP, 2001, page 145.
3   Cited by Prof Jannie du Preez. Article on Enoch. Banner of Truth magazine, double issue number 82-83: pages 5-45.
4   John Flavel, *The Fountain of Life, Works*, vol 1, page 527.
5   Thomas Vincent (1634-1678) *Christ's Sudden and Certain Appearance to*

Judgment. 300 pages hardback *Soli Deo Gloria,* 1996, p 45 ff. Thomas Vincent was a minister in London. He was one of the approximate 2000 ejected in 1662.

6   John Flavel, *ibid,* page 529.

7   Peter Naylor, 1 *Corinthians,* A Welwyn Student Commentary, EP, 1996, page 336. The reign of Christ between his two advents extends and increases according to Jonathan Edwards, *Works,* vol 2, page 287 ff., Banner of Truth edition, 'A time shall come wherein all heresies and false doctrines shall be exploded, and the Church of God shall not be rent with jarring opinions .. ' and, 'a time shall come wherein religion and true Christianity shall in every respect be *uppermost* in the world' (see Zech 14:9).

8   B B Warfield, *Biblical and Theological Studies,* P and R, 1952, page 487.

9   *hagiais anastrophais kai eusebeiais.*

10   In the context of the Olivet discourse some interpret (I believe correctly) that this is one of the signs signalling the destruction of Jerusalem and the termination of the Old Covenant order (Heb 8:13).

Justification	Sanctification
Is righteousness imputed.	Is righteousness imparted.
Is by the declaration of God the Father.	Is by the internal working of the Holy Spirit.
Is God's external work outside us and for us, like clothing.	Is God's internal work inside us.
Is the work of a Judge which is legal.	Is the work of a surgeon who gets inside to accomplish his work.
Is God reckoning sinners to be righteous.	Is God's working in us to make us holy in heart and behaviour.
Concerns guilt.	Concerns pollution.
Is legal or forensic which takes account of Christ's righteousness on our behalf.	Is the spiritual work enabling believers both to will and to do God's good pleasure.
Is complete and perfect and knows of no degrees.	Is never complete or perfect in this life.
Is the foundation of our acceptance before God.	Is a purifying work God does within us because he has accepted us.
Is a once-for-all act never to be repeated.	Is a work which prepares us for heaven.
Our good works have nothing whatsoever to do with it.	Good works are the evidence of saving faith.

❧ *Chapter 24* ❧
Holiness, An Historical Overview

H istorical Theology is a vital subject. It traces out the manner in which Christian doctrine has been contested and formulated. By the study of controversies in the past errors can be avoided in the present.

Here I will trace out the history of the doctrine of sanctification. As we have seen both justification and positional sanctification take place when a believer is united to Christ by faith. At the same time progressive sanctification is initiated.

Sanctification is inseparably joined to justification. Destroy justification and you demolish sanctification because if you reject the perfect righteousness imputed freely as a gift and rely instead on your law-keeping you cannot please God. 'All who rely on observing the law are under a curse, for it is written: "Cursed is everyone who does not continue to do everything written in the Book of the Law." Clearly no-one is justified before God by the law, because 'the righteous will live by faith' (Gal 3:10,11).

Again, as we have seen, this does not mean that good works are not essential. James affirms that Abraham's faith was reckoned to him as righteousness and then reminds us that Abraham's faith was a living vital trust that inspired good works, not a mere intellectual assent to truth, as Luther affirmed, 'To believe God means to trust him always and everywhere.'[1]

The first attack made on justification was to add Jewish rites such as circumcision to justification. In other words false teachers suggested that you can believe in Christ for salvation but it is essential to add works of the law in order to be saved. That heresy is firmly repudiated by the apostle Paul in Galatians.

Another way to destroy justification is by denying the reality of imputed righteousness. This took place gradually in the Roman Catholic Church culminating in the Council of Trent in which salvation by works righteousness was proclaimed as the way of salvation and justification by imputed righteousness of Christ was anathematised (cursed).

In this historical overview I will proceed as follows:

1. Sanctification perverted
2. The unique contribution of the English Puritans
3. The modern era and perfectionist teachings

1. Sanctification perverted

Toward the end of the fourth century the doctrine of baptism gradually changed from 'symbol' to 'performance'. By symbol is meant that converts were baptised to illustrate their union with Christ in his death, burial and resurrection. After emerging from the water it was often the practice to clothe converts with white clothing as a symbol of Christ's righteousness imputed to them. 'When they emerged from the font, the baptised were "robed in white, dressed in heavenly vesture," with the promise that if they did not soil the baptismal garment they would possess the kingdom of heaven'. 'They were robed in white. The baptised heard the singing of a hymn'.[2]

By 'performance' is meant that the Church claimed that baptism actually in itself as a rite confers multiple blessings upon the candidate. This idea led to the baptism of sick babies in order to save them in case they died. The rite itself rather than Christ became the guarantee of salvation. Gradually the Church took complete control of the ordinance and established the doctrine of baptismal regeneration and applied it to all infants without exception. Those infants not baptised were regarded as eternally lost while those baptised were born again receiving the remission of original sin. However Jesus teaches that the new birth is under the sovereign power of the Holy Spirit (John 3:8) and he employs the preaching of the Word of God to give new birth (1 Peter 1:23; James 1:18). The Holy Spirit is likened to the wind. He blows where he wills. He is not under the control of a priest claiming that regeneration takes place when he sprinkles water on a person and repeats the name of the Trinity.

Baptismal regeneration was designed to give the infants a start along the road of sanctification. 'Holy Baptism is the basis of the whole Christian life. . Through baptism we are freed from sin and reborn as sons of God' (Catechism of the Catholic Church).[3] The aim was to make progress by the practice of confessing sins and receiving remission for them at the confessional box, and also by regular attendance at Mass. Because sanctification in this life can never be perfect a place needed to be invented where the process could be completed. And so the doctrine of purgatory was established by Gregory I. This took place in 593 and was later proclaimed as official dogma by the Council of Florence in 1439.

If we stand back and view these developments we observe that the Roman Catholic Church claimed sole custodianship control of salvation. Right up until Vatican II, 1964, the doctrine of 'Extra Ecclesiam Nulla Salus' was held, which means only those in the Roman Catholic Church can be saved![4] That claim was logical since Rome claimed exclusive use of the keys of the kingdom of heaven which can only be reached through the fires of purgatory. Rome teaches that if anyone dies with mortal sin then that soul goes to hell without hope of salvation. Before death mortal sin must be confessed to a priest to obtain remission before death. Time spent in purgatory can be shortened by purchasing indulgences.

For about 1000 years before the great Reformation of the 16th century, the Western Church was increasingly dominated by the papacy. In 1517 Martin Luther sounded the alarm. A priest by the name of Johann Tetzel was the chief salesman hawking indulgences on authority of the Pope to free people from purgatory.

'Listen to the voices of your dear dead relatives and friends, beseeching you and saying, "Pity us, pity us. We are in dire torment from which you can redeem us for a pittance." Do you not wish to? Open your ears. Hear the father saying to his son, the mother to her daughter, "We bore you, brought you up, left you our fortunes, and you are so cruel and hard that now you are not willing for so little to set us free. Will you let us lie here in flames? Will you delay our promised glory?" Remember that you are able to release them for,

"As soon as the coin in the coffer rings,
The soul from purgatory springs."'

It was this wickedness in particular that stirred Martin Luther to write 95 statements exposing the corrupt practices of Rome. Luther nailed the 95 theses to the door of the Castle Church in Wittenberg. The Printing press had only recently been invented and developed. The 95 theses were translated from Latin into German immediately by the media of the day and rapidly sold over a wide area. In a very short time Luther was spoken of everywhere as the monk who had defied the Pope. The Reformation had begun.

The reason why all the 16th-century Reformers and 17th-century English Puritans believed that the papacy was antichrist (*anti* meaning in the place of) was that system took the place of Christ. The Pope claims to be the vicar of Christ. The New York Catechism says: 'The Pope takes the place of Jesus Christ on earth.' With regard to purgatory Luther said, 'If the Pope does have the power release anyone from purgatory, why in the name of love does he not abolish purgatory by letting everyone out? If for the sake of miserable money he released uncounted souls, why should he not for the sake of most holy love empty the place?'[5]

The courage of Luther requires explanation. We must spare a minute to see that the genesis of the Reformation lay in Luther's discovery of justification by faith alone, by grace alone and on the authority of Scripture alone. At that time Johannes von Staupitz was vicar- general of the German Augustinian monasteries. He wished to free himself from that responsibility. He prepared Luther to be his successor. Under his spiritual guidance Luther graduated through all levels of theological study up to and including his doctorate – and this within the shortened time frame possible. Five years of study were the minimum requirement.

All this took place in spite of the fact that Martin was in spiritual turmoil. He was tormented having no assurance of salvation. He tried everything including fasting and confession of all known sin. At any rate in 1513 he began lecturing on the Psalms. He went on to expound Romans and then Galatians and Hebrews. This intense study of the Scriptures was the means of his conversion. He wrestled with the meaning of the word 'righteousness' in Psalm 31 and followed that up by studying the New Testament equivalent in Romans 1:17. When he saw that God's righteousness is a free gift received by faith he was instantly liberated. He declared, 'Thereupon I felt myself to be reborn and to have gone through open doors into paradise.'

How can we explain the fact that justification by faith, a truth so clearly taught in the New Testament, could become obscure and then lost entirely by the majority? James Buchanan (1804-1870) in his book on justification draws attention to the fact that Augustine (354-430) conflated justification and sanctification instead of seeing them as entirely different entities.[6] Augustine while exemplary in opposing Pelagius and clear in maintaining the sovereignty of God in salvation, was not clear about justification. He knew little Greek and worked in Latin. The verb *justificare* in Latin means *to make righteous*. The Greek verb *dikaioō* means to declare righteous. Imputed righteousness and imparted righteousness are antithetical.

If our justification is to be based on the notion of self-merit we are lost indeed for all our self-righteousness is as filthy rags before God (Isa

64:6). If Christ's perfect righteousness is imputed to us we are justified indeed (Rom 8:33). '[God] reckons righteousness to them, not because he accounts them to have kept his law personally (which would be a false judgment), but because he accounts them to be united to one who kept it representatively (and that is a true judgment).'[7] Writing to the Philippians Paul renounced works righteousness. 'What is more, I consider everything a loss compared to the surpassing greatness of knowing Christ Jesus my Lord, for whose sake I have lost all things. I consider them rubbish, that I may gain Christ and be found in him, not having a righteousness of my own that comes from the law, but that which is through faith in Christ—the righteousness that comes from God and is by faith' (Phil 3:8-9).

James Buchanan maintains that there is a supply of testimonies, 'extending from Apostolic times down to Bernard of Clairvaux (1090-1153), the last of the Fathers, abundantly sufficient to prove that the doctrine of justification by grace alone had some faithful witnesses in every succeeding age of the Church'.[8] He asserts that 'Faber adduces quotations from sixteen of the Fathers who wrote before the middle of the fifth century, and refers to twelve more as having been adduced by Archbishop Ussher, making together twenty-eight Fathers, and who in every century down to the twelfth furnishes one or more witnesses to the truth'.[9] Buchanan provides sample quotations from the writings of Cyprian, Athanasius, Basil, Ambrose, Jerome and Chrysostom. It would be more convincing if actual treatises on the subject of justification could be located in lieu of Buchanan's very brief quotations from the patristic writings.

The 16th-century reformation constituted a massive return to the biblical doctrine of imputed righteousness. The Roman Catholic Church responded to this by calling the Council of Trent.

Over the centuries Ecumenical Councils have proved essential in clarifying doctrine and maintaining unity. There were eight such councils from 325 to 880. Of those the Council of Chalcedon was the most decisive and useful. Chalcedon provided wonderful clarity on the nature of the Person of Christ. Between 1123 and 1517 there were eighteen Councils convened and just three between 1545 and 1962.

Of all Councils ever convened none has been more damaging and disastrous than the Council of Trent. The Council of Trent (*Latin*: Concilium Tridentinum) was the 16th-century *Ecumenical Council* of the *Roman Catholic Church*. It is considered to be one of the Church's most important councils. It convened in Trent (then capital of the *Prince-Bishopric of Trent*, inside the *Holy Roman Empire*, now in modern *Italy*) between December 13, 1545, and December 4, 1563 in twenty-five sessions for three periods. Council fathers met for the first through eighth sessions in Trent (1545–1547), and for the ninth through eleventh sessions in Bologna (1547) during the pontificate of *Pope Paul III*. Under *Pope Julius III* the Council met in Trent (1551–1552) for the twelfth through sixteenth sessions. Under *Pope Pius IV* the seventeenth through twenty-fifth sessions took place in Trent (1559–1563).

The Council issued condemnations on what it defined as Protestant heresies and defined Church teachings in the areas of Scripture and Tradition, Original Sin, Justification, Sacraments, the Eucharist in Holy Mass and the Veneration of Saints. It issued numerous reform decrees. By specifying Catholic doctrine on *salvation*, the *sacraments*, and the *Biblical canon*, the Council was answering Protestant disputes.

Instead of making *sola scriptura* the basis of its study the thirty-seven appointed theologians devoted their energies to the task of agreement on what the Roman Church had maintained in the medieval period on the subject of justification. Anathemas were compiled rejecting the biblical doctrine of justification by faith alone. In architectural and engineering terms Trent constructed the medieval fabric of salvation by works in steel girders and then set the whole framework in concrete. To remove or change such a structure is well-nigh impossible. All subsequent attempts to bridge the gulf between salvation by works and salvation by God's imputed righteousness have proved futile. Imputed righteousness can never be the same as infused righteousness.

The denial of the perfect righteousness of Christ imputed by God the Father to the believer had a disastrous effect on the doctrine of assurance of salvation. Trent Canon 8 explicitly rejects any suggestion that the believer may know with certainty that he is among the predestined, or that he will persevere to the end, apart from special revelation. The matter was discussed over the period 15-26 October 1546. Of thirty-seven theologians who expressed their views twenty were in favour of the possibility of assurance, fifteen against, and two undecided. The seven Dominicans were against assurance but the Dominican bishop Ambrogio Catharino was outspoken in favour of the possibility of assurance. The Franciscans present were deeply divided. The language of the Bible from beginning to end is the language of assurance. Romans 8:16 is typical, 'The Spirit himself testifies with our spirit that we are God's children.' The psalms and hymns we sing reflect assurance. 'Happy are those beyond all measure blessed, who know their guilt is gone, their faults forgiven'[10] and:

> Jesus, Thy blood and righteousness,
> My beauty are, my glorious dress;
> Midst flaming worlds, in these arrayed,
> With joy shall I lift up my head. (Christian Hymns 545)

Before proceeding to consider the unique contribution of the English Puritans it is necessary to recall that early the idea developed that to be truly holy one needed to be a monk or a nun. Monasticism developed in Egypt in the fourth century and spread from the East to the West where it became widespread. Basil the Great (330-379) held that 'the monk is the perfect Christian; the ascetic life consists not in the specific practices of self-denial but in the sanctification of the whole personality.'[11] The proliferation of monastic orders can be appreciated by the size of the different monastic orders in 1901: Christian Brothers 20,457; Fransciscans 16,458; Jesuits 15,073; Capuchins 9,464; Marists 6,000; Benedictines 4,350; Carmelites 2,000; Augustinians 1,858. In spite of the decline since the 1960s of those coming forward for the priesthood and for monastic status the statistics for the monastic orders in 2010 are about twenty percent up on what they were in 1901.

Holiness is not going to progress where there is no regeneration. The depravity of the heart will not change by flight from the world or even by rigorous disciplines as is illustrated in the experience of Martin Luther who endeavoured to obtain salvation by observing all the requirements of the Church including confession of all known sin without success.

The moral state of the monasteries has never been easy to assess.

Charles Chiniquy, a Roman Catholic leader in Canada, was converted and became a Protestant. Several thousand followed him out of the Roman Catholic Church into evangelical Christianity. Before his conversion he described the high esteem he had for Roman Catholic Bishop Vandeveld but was distressed by a visit of this respected man only a year later. The bishop had decided to abandon his diocese and explained to Chiniquy, 'I cannot bear any longer the corruption of my priests. There are only five honest priests in this diocese, so I asked the Pope as a favour to transfer me to another place.'[12]

2. The unique contribution of the English Puritans

William Cunningham's two volumes on Historical Theology reflect the emphases of the Continental Reformers. After detailed treatment of justification by faith Cunningham omits sanctification entirely and proceeds to baptism and the Lord's Table. It is surprising that a scholar of such calibre should miss the body of writings on sanctification by the English Puritans who are unrivalled for their balance of doctrine, experience and practical application: mind, hearts and hands. Francis Turretin (1623-1687) is appreciated for his doctrinal lucidity. In his 2,100 page work he devotes only about ten pages to sanctification and concentrates on the question: *Is sanctification so perfect in this life that believers can fulfil the law absolutely? We deny this against the Romanists and Socinians.* Turretin then proceeds to persuasively refute the idea that believers can be perfect in this life.[13] He cites 1 John 1:8, 'If we claim to be without sin, we deceive ourselves and the truth is not in us' and James 3:2, 'We all stumble in many ways' and 1 Kings 8:46, 'There is no one who does not sin.' Turretin also argues that the wretched man of Romans chapter seven represents Paul and all regenerate souls who have an inward battle which is also described in Galatians chapter five: 'For the sinful nature desires what is contrary to the Spirit, and the Spirit what is contrary to the sinful nature. They are in conflict with each other, so that you do not do what you want' (5:17). Turretin refutes the invention of 'a new and third state between the state of nature (in which man is yet unrenewed) and the state of grace (in which he is now renewed)' as though the wretched man of Romans 7 is a man half-way between being regenerate and being unregenerate.

William Perkins was the most popular author of his day followed by his disciple William Ames.

The English Puritans were just as concerned as the Continental Reformers for justification by faith alone and by grace alone, but they developed the doctrine of progressive sanctification in much more detail. Foremost in their minds was the subject of practical holiness of life. In other words the doctrine of sanctification was paramount. The Puritans made personal holiness of life a matter of scrupulous study and careful application to daily life. Maurice Roberts suggests that the doctrine of sanctification 'was the distinct and special contribution which God ordained that the Puritans should make to the advancement of the gospel in all time to come – there is no doubt that the Puritans regarded godliness and saintliness as the *summum bonum* of the entire Christian life – there must scarcely be a sermon, a treatise, a pamphlet, a diary, a history or a biography from their pens which was not in one way or another aimed at fostering the spiritual life.'[14] The expression *summum bonum*, the highest good, describes well the Puritan view of holy living. For them the highest good was the glory of God. Everything in our thinking, conversation and way of life is to have the glory of God in view.

Two central issues fill the horizons of sanctification. The first is the rôle of conscience and the second the place of the moral law.

'All Puritan theologians from William Perkins on were agreed in conceiving of conscience as a rational faculty, a power of moral self–knowledge and judgement, dealing with questions of right and wrong, duty and desert, and dealing with them authoritatively, as God's voice.'[15] William Fenner (1600-1640), an excellent Puritan pastor who turned many to righteousness, wrote a treatise on the subject of conscience. In it he speaks for all the Puritan divines. His method was to open up Romans 2:15: 'Which show the work of the law written in their hearts, their consciences also bearing them witness, and their thoughts in the meanwhile accusing or else excusing one another.'

Fenner proceeds as follows:

1. That there is in every man a conscience. [Their consciences bearing them witness] Every one of them had a conscience bearing them witness.
2. That the light which conscience is directed to work by is knowledge [written in their hearts].
3. That the bond that binds a man's conscience is God's law [which show the effect of the law written in their hearts].
4. That the office and duty of conscience is to bear witness either with ourselves or against ourselves, accusing or excusing ourselves or our actions [bearing them witness and their thoughts accusing or excusing one another].

William Ames (1576-1633) was converted under the stirring preaching of William Perkins at Cambridge University. Soon Ames evidenced leadership abilities. His forceful preaching drew persecution and he was expelled from Cambridge. He moved to the Netherlands where he remained in exile for the rest of his life. His books were written in Latin for the international community of scholars and translated into Dutch and English. His work *Conscience, with the Power and Cases Thereof*, 293 pages, was printed in Latin in 1630 and in English in 1639 going into nearly twenty editions in less than thirty years.

To the Puritans the moral law was basic in the cultivation of holy living. To the Puritan mind the Decalogue was the framework provided by God by which the believer's life is to be fitted and conformed. About one third of the Westminster Larger Catechism is devoted to the Ten Commandments, 60 questions out of the 196.

> *Question* 99. What rules are to be observed for the right understanding of the Ten Commandments?

> *Answer.* For the right understanding of the Ten Commandments these rules are to be observed. 1. That the law is perfect, and bindeth every one to full conformity in the whole man unto the righteousness thereof, and unto entire obedience for ever; so as to require the utmost perfection of every duty, and to forbid the least degree of every sin.

Does God demand what is impossible? Yes. No person has ever fulfilled God's laws except Christ who kept the law perfectly.

John Flavel goes to the very heart of the subject of holiness in his work titled A Saint Indeed which is an exposition of Proverbs 4:23. 'Keep thy heart with all diligence, for out of it are the issues of life.'

He begins by asserting that 'the heart of man is the worst part before it be regenerate, and the best afterwards: it is the seat of principles, and the fountain of actions. The eye of God is, and the eye of the Christian ought to be, principally fixed upon it.'[16]

Flavel divides the text very simply:

1. The exhortation, *Keep thy heart with all diligence.*
2. The reason, *For out of it are the issues of life.*

'Keeping the heart is understood to mean the diligent and constant use and improvement of all holy means and duties, to preserve the soul from sin, and maintain its sweet and free communion with God.'

Some Puritan writings are written in a style which will not appeal to readers today. For example Lewis Bayley wrote a 363 page book on holiness, *The Practice of Piety: Directing a Christian Walk, that he may Please God.* It was translated into most European languages.

By 1792 it had reached an astonishing 71 editions. Walter Marshall's *Gospel Mystery of Sanctification* republished by Evangelical Press in 1981 lacks the colour and vivacity we find in Thomas Watson's *A Body of Divinity* which is one of the most popular books published by the Banner of Truth .

The most readable English Puritan by far on the subject of holiness is the scintillating Thomas Brooks. His is a 446 page work to which he gave two titles, *The Crown and Glory of Christianity*, and *The Beauty of Holiness*. This makes up volume four of the six volume set of The Complete Works of Thomas Brooks.[17]

Through his writings John Owen (1616-1683) continues to influence Evangelicals today. His *The Mortification of Sin* is a classic and is available as an abridged and easy to read paperback. Richard Baxter wrote as extensively as Owen did. Baxter's first book *The Saint's Everlasting Rest* was an instant success. His work *A Call to the Unconverted* was a best seller. It is an exposition of Ezekiel 33:11, 'Say to them, "As surely as I live, declares the Sovereign LORD, I take no pleasure in the death of the wicked, but rather that they turn from their ways and live. Turn! Turn from your evil ways! Why will you die, O house of Israel?"' Rendered into modern English by John Blanchard this work has been republished with the title An *Invitation to Live*. Baxter's book *The Reformed Pastor* is one of the best ever written. It continues to serve the Church as a paperback published by the Banner of Truth.

Baxter's *A Christian Directory* is the most extensive practical exposition of sanctification that has ever been written. It has been republished by Soli Deo Gloria. Its value is increased by an introduction by J I Packer.

The apex of Puritan theology is reflected in the Westminster Confession of Faith. The doctrine and practice of sanctification is expressed in the three paragraphs of chapter 13. The Congregationalists in their Savoy Confession improved this a little as did the Baptists in their Second London Confession of 1677/1689.

The Comprehensive Nature of Sanctification

To the English Puritans doctrine (teaching – *didaskalos*) consists of correct theology which is processed through the mind into holy living. This is illustrated well in Paul's letter to Titus. He speaks of 'the knowledge of the truth that leads to godliness' (1:1). He proceeds to describe the qualifications for elders. In these we soon see that holiness includes life in the home as well as exemplary behaviour in public:

> 'An elder must be blameless, the husband of but one wife, a man whose children believe and are not open to the charge of being wild and disobedient. Since an overseer is entrusted with God's work, he must be blameless—not overbearing, not quick-tempered, not given to drunkenness, not violent, not pursuing dishonest gain. Rather he must be hospitable, one who loves what is good, who is self-controlled, upright, holy and disciplined. He must hold firmly to the trustworthy message as it has been taught, so that he can encourage others by sound doctrine and refute those who oppose it' (1:6-9).

Titus is exhorted to apply sound teaching to various groupings in the assembly: older men (2:1), older women (2:3), young men (2:6). Slaves are addressed. Holiness in the lives of Christian slaves was obviously for the glory of God but also designed to win the owners, 'Teach slaves to be subject to their masters in everything, to try to please them, not to talk back to them, and not to steal from them, but to show that they can be fully trusted, so that in every way they will make the teaching about God our Saviour attractive' (2:9-10).

Sanctification then is comprehensive. It applies to all behaviour and is to be seen in all kinds of environment; the home, school, work-place and public assemblies.

3. The modern era and perfectionist teachings

This subject is described in the chapter 6. Here I will describe it in a little more detail.

The first major nonconformist deviation from the Puritan doctrine of positional and progressive sanctification came through the perfectionist teaching of John Wesley. Perfectionist teaching separates justification from sanctification into two experiences. The believer is first justified by faith and later in a second experience receives sanctification. The nature of sanctification is diminished from the totality of life to the believer's present battle with sin. Contrast this with positional sanctification.

I quote a long paragraph from B B Warfield whose grasp of the issues is brilliant. Of Wesley Warfield wrote:

'It was John Wesley who infected the modern Protestant world with this notion of "entire instantaneous sanctification." In saying this we are not bringing a railing accusation against him. There was no element of his teaching which afforded him himself greater satisfaction. There is no element of it which is more lauded by his followers, or upon their own possession of which they more felicitate themselves. "The current orthodoxy," they say, "limited the salvation of Christ." It had limited it "in the degree of its attainability as well as in the persons by whom it is attainable". It was the achievement of Wesley to lift these limitations and to make it clear not only that the salvation of Christ is attainable by all but that it is completely attainable by all. "Knowing exactly what I say, and taking the full responsibility of it, I repeat," John McClintock solemnly asseverates in describing the result in the church which Wesley founded, "we are the only church in history, from the apostles' time until now, that has put forward as its very elemental thought . . . the holiness of the human soul, heart, mind and will." Nothing less than a new epoch in the history of the Church has thus, in the view of Wesley's followers, been introduced. "Historically," writes Olin A Curtis, "Wesley had almost the same epochal relation to the doctrinal emphasis upon holiness that Luther had to the doctrinal emphasis upon justification by faith, or that Athanasius had to the doctrinal emphasis upon the Deity of our Lord." We are merely recognizing, therefore, what is eagerly proclaimed by his followers, when we attribute to Wesley's impulse the wide prevalence in our modern Protestantism of what has come to be known as "holiness teaching". The fact is, however, in any event too plain to be overlooked. As wave after wave of the "holiness movement" has broken over us during the past century, each has brought, no doubt, something distinctive of itself. But a common fundamental character has informed them all, and this common fundamental character has been communicated to them by the Wesleyan doctrine. The essential elements of that doctrine repeat themselves in all these movements, and form their characteristic features. In all of them alike justification and sanctification are divided from one another as two separate gifts of God. In all of them alike sanctification is represented as obtained, just like justification, by an act of simple faith, but not by the same act of faith by which justification is obtained, but by a new and separate act of faith, exercised for this specific purpose. In all of them alike the sanctification which comes on this act of faith, comes immediately on believing, and all at once, and in all of them alike this sanctification, thus received, is complete sanctification. In all of them alike, however, it is added that this complete sanctification does not bring freedom from all sin; but only, say, freedom from sinning; or only freedom from conscious sinning; or from the commission of "known sins". And in all of them alike this sanctification is not a stable condition into which we enter once for all by faith, but a momentary attainment, which must be maintained moment by moment, and which may readily be lost and often is lost, but may also be repeatedly instantaneously recovered.'[18]

Charles Finney (1792-1875) followed Wesley's perfectionist teaching. Finney denied the biblical doctrine of the fall of man into sin and rejected the doctrine of the bondage of the sinner's will. Indeed Finney placed the free will of man above the sovereign power of God. He taught that some men are too sinful to be saved. Moderately sinful souls can be saved but very sinful souls are beyond the possibility of salvation.[19] As in salvation so in perfect sanctification the will of man is everything. It is the will of man that determines salvation and it is the will of man that determines the leap to perfection. This is known as Pelagian doctrine. Denial of original sin permeates Finney's theology. Born in Connecticut in 1792 Finney practised law before entering the Christian ministry. He was suddenly converted in 1821. After his conversion he experienced what he describes as the baptism of the Spirit. He felt immediately the call to the Christian ministry and was licensed to preach in 1824. That was a time of extensive powerful revivals when sinners were being converted in droves. Unlike present day England or France where it is as hard to get unbelievers to enter a church as it is to get a wild zebra to enter a horse carriage, people flocked to hear the gospel and were amenable to hearing preaching.

As a preacher Finney possessed unusual gifts. He made the most of the revival period (1824-1832). His manner was dramatic and very direct to the conscience. He called for immediate decision. He believed regeneration to consist of an act of the will. He called upon his hearers to make themselves new hearts and pressed hard for immediate surrender to God. He called for and pressed for repenting sinners to come forward to the anxious seat.

In 1835 Finney became Professor of Theology of the newly formed Oberlin College in North Ohio, a school which he made famous. His work in two volumes, *Lectures on Systematic Theology,* sold in thousands. Perfectionist teaching flourishes in Arminian ground and thrives even more vigorously in Pelagian soil. Finney made perfectionism a trademark of Oberlin.

Finney's Pelagian theology was the basis for a morphology which turned Jonathan Edwards' theology of revival into 'Revivalism', the concept that revival follows paying the price of passionate expenditure of time in prayer and use of the means of grace. As J I Packer observes, 'The finding has not been commensurate with the seeking.'[20]

There was no shortage of disciples who took on and developed Finney's perfectionist teaching. Asa Mahan is the best known of these. He was the leading teacher at a well-known theological seminary called Oberlin. Warfield describes his energy: 'From this time to the end of his life, a half a century later, he knew nothing but the twin doctrines he acquired in this moving religious experience: the doctrines of Christian Perfection and the Baptism of the Spirit; and he gave himself to their exposition and propagation with an unwearied constancy which his readers may be tempted sometimes to think wearisome persistency. He infected his colleagues with these doctrines; but they never took the place in their theology which they did in his. In the succeeding adjustments it became thus his function to emphasize the new doctrines to the utmost.'[21]

Perfectionist teaching spread through America and entered the British Isles. The prevalence of perfectionist teaching motivated the famous Bishop J C Ryle to publish his best known book which bears the simple title *Holiness*.

The first-born of wealthy parents J C Ryle was educated at Eton and then at Oxford University where he was captain of the cricket team. Large and powerful in stature he rowed for Oxford which is regarded as a great honour. Equally gifted in academic abilities he was esteemed as a distinguished classicist. While studying at Oxford he was converted in a service even though he arrived late!

Ryle's ministerial life can be divided into two parts. Firstly he served for 39 years as a vicar in country parishes. Secondly for twenty years he was bishop of Liverpool.

J C Ryle exemplified holy living. Tragically he lost his first wife after only two years of marriage and his second wife was ill for most of the ten years they were together. He predeceased his third wife. In one night in 1841 his father, a banker, lost everything in hopeless bankruptcy. Ryle confessed that the humiliation of that event cast shadows over him for the rest of his life.

J C Ryle was a prolific author. He avoided complex words and expressions and wrote with a wonderfully simple, clear, direct style. Technical details were relegated to footnotes. Today his commentaries on the four Gospels (seven volumes in all) are loved in Africa where English is a second language for millions of indigenous people.

Ryle's book *Holiness* began life in 1877. It was expanded in 1879 to consist of twenty sermons with an average of fifteen pages each.

Perfectionist teaching was embraced by a number of denominations and flew under several titles such as 'The Higher Life Movement', The Fellowship Movement', 'The Victorious Life' and 'The Keswick Movement'.

In 1955 in a fifteen page review article in *The Evangelical Quarterly* J I Packer exposed the fallacies of Keswick teaching. This sent theological tremors up and down British Evangelicalism. J I Packer was born in 1926. He earned his PhD at Oxford in 1954 with the subject of 'The Redemption and Restoration of Man in the thought of Richard Baxter'. In 1949 together with O R Johnston, J I Packer was a prime mover in the establishment of the two-day annual Puritan Conference now called the Westminster Conference. In the 1960s and 1970s Puritanism emerged strongly among nonconformists largely through the ministry of Dr Martyn Lloyd-Jones, the Banner of Truth publishing industry, and the writings of J I Packer.[22] In 1979 J I Packer re-located to the other side of the world to take up a professorship at Regent College, Vancouver, Canada.

A prolific author Jim Packer has two books which crystallise his teaching on holiness. There is a twenty-five page chapter in his book *Keep in Step with the Spirit*,[23] and a comprehensive study of holiness in his book *A Passion for Holiness*.[24]

J I Packer provides the contours of his exposition on holiness as follows:

1. The nature of holiness is transformation through consecration.
2. The context of holiness is justification through Jesus Christ.
3. The root of holiness is co-crucifixion and co-resurrection with Jesus Christ.

4. The agent of holiness is the Holy Spirit.
5. The experience of holiness is one of conflict. (Mortification of sin is subsumed here).
6. The rule of holiness is God's revealed law. The heart of holiness is the spirit of love.

What of the future?

J Ligon Duncan III describes a Reformed resurgence taking place transdenominationally today which is young and vast in Australia, North America, Britain and other parts of the world.[25] Of course this movement is not perfect and we would not agree about all the facets it contains precisely because it is transdenominational. Duncan describes Reformed preachers of the past such as C H Spurgeon and Martyn Lloyd-Jones who continue to exercise a powerful influence through their writings. He describes the ministries of John MacArthur, John Piper and Albert Mohler who is the president of the largest seminary in the USA. In his Book *Young, Restless, Reformed* Collin Hanson[26] describes this reformed resurgence and the ministries of Mark Dever, C J Mahaney, Wayne Grudem and R C Sproul. This theological renewal will certainly advance the Reformed doctrine of sanctification in lieu of perfectionist teaching. To what extent the unique contribution of the English Puritans will be discovered has yet to be seen. Of this we can be sure – the future is as bright as the promises of God. The Reformed doctrine of sanctification when applied to public worship will transform it and bring it back from man-centredness to God-centredness. 'My name will be great among the nations, from the rising to the setting of the sun. In every place incense and pure offerings will be brought to my name, because my name will be great among the nations, says the LORD Almighty' (Mal 1:11).

---

1   Martin Luther, *Romans*, Zondervan, 1954, page 66.
2   Everett Ferguson, *Baptism in the Early Church*, Eerdmans, 2009' page 650. This massive 951 page historically objective study makes easy reading and is user-friendly. It covers the first five centuries. With the same title, *Baptism in the Early Church*, Hendrick Stander and Johannes Louw of the Dutch Reformed Church of South Africa describe baptismal practice in

the first three centuries. Reformation Today Trust, 1994, 192 pages. In the introduction Jim Renihan draws attention to the fact that this book is not written to win an argument but rather that readers may consider the evidence for themselves.

3   Geoffrey Chapman, 1994, page 276.
4   Francis A Sullivan, *Salvation Outside the Church?* Geoffrey Chapman, 1992.
5   Roland Bainton, *Here I Stand,* A Lion paperback, 1983, page 81.
6   Alister McGrath provides a detailed exposition of Augustine's teaching in his treatise *Justitia Dei – A History of the Christian Doctrine of Justification,* Second Edition, Cambridge University Press, 1998.
7   *J I Packer* Justification. in *Evangelical Dictionary of Theology,* ed. Walter A. Elwell , Grand Rapids, MI: Baker, 1984, page 596.
8   James Buchanan, *The Doctrine of Justification,* Banner of Truth, 1961, page 22,
9   ibid page 93.
10 As rendered in number 32 PRAISE!
11 *The New Schaff-Hertzog Encyclopaedia,* vol 7, pages 464-467.
12 Frederick Hodgson, *Salvation for Chiniquy and French Canadians,* Reformation Today, Issue 234.
13 Francis Turretin, *Institutes of Elenctic Theology,* vol. 2, page 693.
14 Maurice Roberts, *Aspects of Sanctification,* Westminster Conference, 1981, page1.
15 J I Packer, *Among God's Giants,* The Puritan conscience, Kingsway, 199, page142.
16 John Flavel, A Saint Indeed, Works, vol 5, page 423.
17 Thomas Brooks, *Works,* James Nichol, Edinburgh, 1867.
18 B B Warfield, *Perfectionism,* P and R, 158, page 350.
19 *Ibid,* page 61.
20 *The New Dictionary of Theology,* IVP, 1988
21 *Ibid* B B Warfield, page 66.
22 J I Packer's in-depth studies in Puritanism are found in a volume titled *Among God's Giants,* Kingsway, 444 pages, 1991.
23 IVP, 300 pages, 1984.
24 Crossway, 1992, 276 pages.
25 *The Resurgence of Calvinism in America* by J Ligon Duncan III in *Calvin for Today* edited by Joel R Beeke, 278 pages hardback, Reformation Heritage Books, 2009.
26 Collin Hanson, *Young, Restless, Reformed.* The sub-title is *A journalist's journey with the new Calvinists,* Crossway, 160 pages, paperback, 2008.
27 *Ibid,* page 163.

Available books on justification.

When the Banner of Truth reprinted James Buchanan 19th-century work in 1961 gross general neglect of the doctrine prevailed in evangelical circles. There was a drought as far as readable books were concerned. John Owen is the most thorough of all exegetes on the subject of justification (Works volume five). But we can hardly give that 400 page treatise away as a tract. At least three outstanding books have been published recently. In 1992 D A Carson edited a 300 page symposium of studies for scholars on justification published by Paternoster and Baker Book House. In 2001 *The God who Justifies* by James R White (374 pages) was published by Bethany House, USA. In 1996 Day One published Philip Eveson's very readable 200 page work with the title *The Great Exchange*. Included in his book is an exposure of N T Wright's denial of imputed righteousness. When Paul and Silas answered the cry, 'What must I do to be saved?' the answer was immediate: 'Believe on the Lord Jesus Christ and you will be saved' (Acts 16:33). According to N T Wright the answer should have been, 'Let's have study sessions to find out how you can become a member of the covenant community.' The manner in which Tom Wright deletes righteousness imputed together with the disastrous consequences of such a deletion is explained well by Philip Eveson in his book *Justification by Faith Alone*.[27] Likewise John Piper describes what is at stake in his *The Future of Justification – A Response to N T Wright*, Crossway, 238 pages, 2007.

Index to
Names and Subjects

on original sin   179, 181
marriage
  marriage with unbelievers   243
  union with Christ and   70-2
Marshall, Walter, *Gospel Mystery of Sanctification*   337
materialism, the great temptation   247-8
McClintock, John, and Wesleyan perfectionism   87, 339
meditation   275-6
Melchizedek, peace and   53-4
Miriam, song of   29
Modernist theologians, the Bible not enough   216
Mohlala, Jimmy   268
Mohler, Albert   303, 344
monasteries   261-2, 332-3
monasticism   332
Moo, Douglas, interpretation of Romans seven   169
Moody, D L   242
moral law
  eternal, transcending time   190-1, 192
  the giving of   217
  and God's holy character   37, 38, 189-90
  and the gospel   193
  a guide for Christian living   193-5
  holiness and   187-95
  human conscience and   192-3, 334-6
  mortification of sin and   130, 169
  the power of the law   167-8
  the preaching of   177-9
  in Puritan theology   174, 335-6
  Sermon on the Mount and   51
  unique and separate   188-9
  Wilhelmus à Brakel and   186
  see also ceremonial law, civil law
moral relativism   22

Morley, Richard, *The Enemy Within*   122
Mormons   95, 216, 236, 284
Morris, Leon   169
Moses, by faith resisted the world   248-51
Murray, Iain
  on Charles Finney   88
  Lloyd-Jones Messenger of Grace   96
Murray, John   80, 169, 224
  Definitive Sanctification   81-2

Nadab and Abihu, God's dealing with   27, 28
Nettles, Tom   116
new birth *see* regeneration
New Covenant Theology   174
New Testament
  redeemed and regenerate   118
  Tyndale's   214-15
Nicodemus
  Jesus and   106-8, 118-19
  and regenerational water   111-12
Noah, his sin   28
North, Brownlow   234-5
Nygren, Anders   169

Oberlin College (Ohio)   87, 341-2
Old Testament, redeemed and regenerate   118
original sin
  Council of Trent   331
  denied by Arminians   184*n*
  denied by decisionists   116
  denied by Finney   88, 340
  expounded by Puritans   179-81
  see also sin
orphans and widows   52, 262-5
Owen, John
  apostasy and the papacy   301, 307
  chastisements and self-examination   206

Index to
Scripture References